INDY

USS Independence CVA-62

"FREEDOM'S FLAGSHIP"

"DON'T TREAD ON ME"

The Navy's only Forward Deployed Aircraft Carrier

By

James A. Gunn

Library of Congress Control Number: 2003091030

Printed in the USA by
MORRIS PUBLISHING

E. J. "Buddy" Gunn

This book is dedicated to E. J. "Buddy" Gunn.

On a bookcase across from my desk is a photograph in black and white of a blonde-headed young man taken in 1944. He is about 15, not tall, but well set up, with a symmetrical face, and a dimple can be seen on his left cheek dancing around an impish smile. He was always smiling, always joking. Six years older, he regularly took care of me. When I was in the third grade, a bully fifth grader decided to make life miserable for me. One day the blonde young man with the impish smile came to the school grounds doing a bit of misery making on his own; I had no more trouble at school.

He bought me a $5 bike when I was seven, he taught me to drive when I was ten, he bought me a $40, 1936 Ford when I was 14, and paid the 50¢ for the driving license. He loaned me money when I needed it, and got me my first job. He came and spent a weekend with me in the Marine Barracks at Camp Pendleton, California when I came back from Korea, a tired, lonely 20 year-old. We never fought. Not once. Not even as children. He never criticized me.

He was the joker, the clown of the family, who quit school at 15 to go to work to help out. He was the one who was brought home by the local sheriff two hours after Dad told him not to drive the old car downtown. Where did the sheriff find him? Downtown!

He was Dad's favorite, but, I did not mind. In a sense, they were both fathers to me. I was the serious one, the bookish one; he was the happy one, the cut-up. Dad never spanked me once in my life.

I once asked him "why?"

"Hell!" he replied, "I was to busy beatin' on your brother!"

He is my brother. My brother "Bud." "Buddy" Gunn. "E. J." Gunn. Now he is older and tired: he seldom leaves his home, he does not always recognize old friends, but he still has that impish grin, that blonde hair, that dancing dimple. If I had a choice—If someone tells me someday here, or in a place far away—if someone says:

"Hey! It is now time for you to pick a brother!"

I would pick him.

"As slow our ship her foamy track
Against the wind was cleaving,
Her trembling pennant still looked back
To that dear isle 'twas leaving.
So loath we part from all we love,
From all the links that bind us;
So turn our hearts, as on we rove,
To those we left behind us."

Thomas Moore

“Indy”

Introduction

"With its twelve nuclear aircraft-carrier battle groups,
The United States stands alone in the world and in history."
U.S. Naval History

It looks like a damn spaceship.

Feet planted firmly, head thrown back, I stood directly in front of the colossal gray slab of steel towering above me, blocking the sky. *It's right out of a science fiction movie. A Star Treck space voyager*. But this was the real thing; this vessel was not imagination, which made all the more impressive, it is much more. It is not a movie model, not a figment of some writer's imagination brought to life by the magic of the movie and television screen, but the *real thing. A* real big bastard of a ship! What held my attention so intensely and what I was staring open-mouthed, goggled-eyed at, was one of the most complex pieces of machinery ever built—consisting of over one hundred million individual pieces—one of the largest ships afloat: a United States Navy nuclear aircraft carrier

The popular, long running television series *Star Treck* started right after the real *USS Enterprise-65* was introduced to the world. The famous *Enterprise* of television was an imaginary warship that can do fabulous, wondrous things; the real Enterprise is just as amazing. In 1961, the *Enterprise* was the sole craft in its class, the first Nuclear-powered aircraft carrier. Commissioned in November of that year, the *Enterprise* cost $500 million and was the largest warship ever built. It displaced 90,000 tons and was based on the design of the Kitty Hawk Class carriers, which are non-nuclear. From its keel to its highest point, the Enterprise is 25 stories high; it has a flight deck of 1,040 feet and is 257 feet wide.

Analogous to the bow and arrow of Cro-Magnon used against the Neanderthals; the grooved rifle barrel of the colonists against the British in colonial days; the nuclear aircraft carrier would revolutionize the way wars were fought in the future. The *USS Enterprise CVN-65* was the first of its kind, a new, controversial hybrid that, in the next three decades to come would give birth to a new kind of warship, the *super carrier*. The *Enterprise CVN-65* was the first of its breed. It was only the beginning.

The birth of the age of the nuclear carrier was not without its labor pains. Construction of the *USS Enterprise* was criticized forcefully by its opponents in Congress: it was nuclear with all the suspicion that went along with building a ship that would carry massive radioactive reactors along the sea paths of the world. *It was also very, very expensive!* At a projected cost of 451 Millions,[1] it was twice the price of a conventional warship. However, more forward-looking members of the Navy and Congress understood the advantage of this type of warship for the future: its longevity and range. The *Enterprise* would be able to travel 238,000 miles averaging 586 miles per day at an average speed of 24 miles-per-hour *without stopping for refueling!* Modern day carriers of the Nimitz class can far out perform this traveling a staggering *900,000 miles without refueling.* However, at the time, over forty years ago, the performance of the *Enterprise* was truly radical.[2]

Today, though, I was not looking at the *Enterprise* class of carriers. I was standing before the Nimitz Class[3] *USS Carl Vinson* (CVN 70); as different from the *Enterprise* of the sixties as a 1929 Model-A Ford automobile is from a new 1999 Baritz Cadillac.

Clothed in an ominous coat of light gray pain, that did not completely hide the seasoned scrapes and dents in the massive steel bow plates, the *USS Carl Vinsion CVN-70 towered* above me as I stood hick-dumb, mute and naively wide-eyed on the wide concrete dock at Alameda Naval Station across the bay from San Francisco, California. Like most civilians, I had no idea of what a nuclear carrier was *really* like. I did some piddling research prior to driving to the bay area from Sacramento—mostly information from the Internet. Called the *Golden Eagle* by its crew, the *USS Carl Vinson's* statistics are impressive. The height from keel to mast top is 244 feet—as tall as a 25-story building! And the edge of the flight deck is some seventy feet above the surface of the sea. The flat, massive keel is twelve stories *below* the surface of the water line, and, when it powered under the Golden Gate Bridge a few days later, the ship had to depart at high tide to keep from drag-

---

[1] The USS Harry Truman, longer than five blocks of Manhatten, launched in 1999, cost close to *five billions.*

[2] Commissioned 1961. Displacement: 90,970 tons. Length: 1,101 feet. Speed: 30+ knots. Armaments: 3 20 MM Phalanx 3-barrel guns and Air Wing. Crew: 3,319 Navy, 2,625 Air Wing, 72 Marines.

[3] Nimitz Class: USS Nimitz (CVN 68), USS Dwight D. Eisenhower (CVN 69), USS Carl Vinson (CVN 70), USS Theodore Roosevelt (CVN 71), USS Abraham Lincoln (CVN 72), USS George Washington (CVN 73), USS John Stennis (CVN 74), USS Harry S. Truman (CVN 75).

ging the bottom of the channel in order to pass out of the bay into the swells of the open sea. I watched with apprehension that day as the top of the mast glide serenely a few feet below the marvelous Golden Gate bridge thinking: *"This is one big sucker!"*

Earlier in the year, in August, I happened to read a travel article in the Sacramento Bee about PACE (Pacific Academic College Education), an article written by a retired teacher chronicling his experiences in teaching a six-week college course aboard a Navy ship during Desert Storm. The narrative was absorbing and at the end of it the author listed the address of the sponsoring college.

"Umm . . ." I thought. *"What about me?"*

I was interested.

I wrote an inquiry.

Just maybe!

So, I wrote to the address in the newspaper—to Central Texas College in Killeen, a city in the great state of Texas. Surprisingly, in just a few days—very efficient—I received a letter about the program. Being curious about a college in central Texas administrating a Navy educational program on the seas, I phoned the number listed to ask for an application and was connected to a well-informed lady who said that she would send me the requirements and forms needed. She explained that the college did administer the program—she gave me some background on PACE. She informed me that if I worked for PACE, I would be working with their extension office in San Diego—that office administers the programs on all the navy ships in the Pacific area.

As I was about to hang up the telephone, a question came to mind: I asked her if she ever had a call for someone to teach anthropology on the navy ships. She replied that, "No! . . . They had never before hired an anthropologist to go to sea." *Oh Well!* I thought. It had been worth a try. She then added, "However, you are probably qualified to teach the Basic English and math courses, so you should go ahead and fill out the application."

So, when the packet of papers duly arrived by mail a week later, I did work on the long, detailed application notwithstanding a real lack of enthusiasm—it sounded too grand an adventure—sailing with the modern navy at my age. But the seed of interest began to germinate little roots, and kept growing. I investigated the Internet and found a plethora of information on our military—such explicit information as to bring of charges of treason if the time line was 1944 instead of 1995. There is a tremendous amount of information about our modern navy: names of ships, where they are on station, names of the crews,[4] how they can be reached on web pages, characteristics of weapons systems and so on. I began to read. I began to learn about the navy

The application required original transcripts sent from colleges attended—which irritated me—until I drove over to Sacramento City Community College (when I attended it was Sacramento Junior College—but that is no longer politically correct—the "Junior" part.) I enjoyed revisiting the campus and halls I walked so many years ago as a twenty-year old ex-Marine living on my $110 per month G. I. Bill. I remembered long forgotten faces, pretty female countenances. We sat our backs against trees and lay among books and binders on the green lawns talking and flirting. Girls wore dresses, skirts, resplendent sweaters—well filled out; they were bright, colorful flowers gliding against a background of verdant ivy-covered buildings across the quad.

Today it's different. The bright clothes were absent; one had to scrutinize to tell the boy dress from the girl dress—there didn't seem to be much difference. It reminded me of Mao's China—there every body wearing unisex trousers and shirts; here scruffy jeans and $50 Adidas. *And ear rings!* The only men I ever saw wearing earrings when I was a teenager were a bunch of gypsies and maybe Zorro. Not only did the ears support rings of metal and plastic: guys and gals had chunks of metal everywhere. Noses, eyebrows, navels . . . *tongues*! Also—I thought "I'm probably putting my brogan in my mouth" at the time—the general populace—student body—seemed fatter! I even went to the trunks in the attic at home digging out some old college photograph albums; today's college students are *fatter*! *A lot fatter!* Lordy! Lordy! What happened to physical fitness and stylish dress and chic clothing—or is this the "chic" clothing of the day? If it is, these kids don't know what they are missing! (I think that my folks said the same thing to me about the fifty's as they longed for the twenties'.)

I wondered at the courses I had taken as I read the microfilmed reproduced transcripts—classes forgotten for so many years. One amusing incident: when I informed the registrar clerk what I wanted and gave her the year—1953—she had to go to the basement, rum-

[4] After September 11, 2001, crew information became much more difficult to obtain.

maging through the old files to find my records—I was such a dinosaur, I wasn't in the computer!

From the Community College—still City Junior College to me—I drove to Sacramento State University ("Sacramento State" in the "old" days) to order my Upper Division and Graduate transcripts. Paying the ten bucks, I took them home to pour over the results of hours, days, weeks, and years of study and dreams. Finally, I filled out all the forms, added the transcripts, bundled it up a big manila envelope, and mailed it away to Central Texas College in Killeen, Good Old Texas.

Eight days later a letter arrived from Central Texas College down in the ol' pan handle—the flat lands—Yippee tie-yi-yo! Git alon' Littl' Doggie . . . stating that I was *qualified* for the PACE program. My documents would be forwarded to the San Diego office. *Qualified!* Big deal! I knew what *qualified* meant. I ran track for many years. Qualified means you get to enter—it does not mean you won anything. Wastin' postage. Probably don't like anthropologists. Bureaucrats. Probably suffer from a bad case of the *congested files.*

On September 8, 1995, I received a telephone call from "Barbara" from the Naval Air Station at Alameda—I was never to meet Barbara face-to-face although I talked to her many times. I was a bit confused at first to be hearing from Alameda until Barbara explained that personnel in San Diego had sent my papers to her for the PACE Program. I didn't know that our navy based carriers at Alameda—in fact, I knew nothing about where our carriers were based, or how many we had, or what they really did in peacetime. Barbara further explained that when she contacted me for an opening it would be most likely to teach Basic English or math—no anthropology had ever been taught as far as she knew. Oh Well! Same old story. I was just getting bureaucratic procedure. I began to lose the small amount of enthusiasm I still possessed. Enough of this foolishness waiting for these people. I needed stability; I needed intellectual stimulation in my life. I went back to watching Oprah.

However, the call did come. I went aboard the *Carl Vinson* for a couple of months off the coast of Mexico. I sailed on the *USS John Young* in the Persian Gulf and across the Indian Ocean; I was on the *USS Peleliu* from San Diego to Thailand, and the *USS Abraham Lincoln* in Seattle where I played a role from the movie *Titanic* breaking the rules by standing with arms spread on the bow one dark, foggy night sixty miles off the coast of Oregon. I was also fortunate enough to sail on the *USS Independence*—Freedom's Flagship.

It looks like a space ship.

A modern carrier has over 100 million individual parts.

Chapter 1

USS INDEPENDENCE CV 62

"True strength is to go where we want,
Whenever we want,
At the speed we want."
Military quote of the day.

***

USS INDEPEDENCE CV-62
Welcome to the home of
FREEDOM'S FLAGSHIP
The Navy's only Forward Deployed
Aircraft Carrier

***

The big plywood sign, startling white, stretched across the middle third of an old weather-beaten, World War II clap-board warehouse, nestled against a cliff face just across the pier from where the aircraft carrier *Independence* was docked.

Lettered in blue was this dictum:

MILESTONES OF THE "INDY"
Oldest carrier in the Navy
Price Fighter Award
340,000 Arrested Landings
1995 Ogden Award Winner

The *USS Independence CV-62* did not look as big or as long as the nuclear powered *USS Carl Vinson CVN-70* and, I discovered later, it was not. The difference, however, is modest. In length, the *Vinson* is 22 feet longer and in height 15 feet taller. The *Independence's* flight deck measures 4.1 acres compared to the *Vinson*'s 4.5 acres. I believe the real reason the *Indy* seemed smaller as I first gazed on it was the forest of gigantic derricks, cranes, and hills crowding the ship in the cozy Japanese harbor.

Shivering in the coldness of the morning, I stood on the concrete wharf in Yokosuka, Japan, home base of the *USS Independence*, about 36 miles north of Tokyo, head back, hands thrust into my jacket pockets staring up at the gray carrier, my first view of the honored warship—the oldest carrier in the United States Navy Fleet. Neither the carrier nor the day seemed to be putting out a welcoming mat; the carrier sat there, its stern toward me, silent, motionless, the overcast sky a ribbed pattern of gray—rain seemed in the offering. I shivered in the cold morning air. What day was it anyway? My sluggish thoughts tried to juggle the calendar and the International Date Line. My mine raced like a 1947 Nash running on low octane regular. It was February 13, had to be . . . and I was tired. Bone tired. The flight across the vastness of the Pacific Ocean was long, the diminutive seat of tourist class—after a few hours—a torture rack. However, it was a good tiredness; my body was drained but the old brain was still on track albeit, the track may be a tad dusty and with not a few potholes; sometimes it misfired, got out of timing easily like a 1936 Ford, but mostly it worked. I had been having a pretty good time lately, and another adventure was beckoning. I am interested in adventure. Laurence Sterne once wrote, "A large volume of adventure may be grasped within this little span of life, by him who interests his heart in everything."[1] In the first part of my years most of the adventure my heart had been interested in was supplied by the dozens of National Geographic magazines in the school library as I grew up, went into the military, and taught and raised a family. Now, like many sexy senior citizens, I did not have to keep the nose to the grindstone, had few responsibilities, and had some free time to roam about.

Sometimes, a new life does begin after forty. At least, partially new. Prior to reaching the fortieth year, I traveled to Korea (the Korean War—eight months and ten days—all expenses paid by the U.S. Government—traveling Marine Infantry class, a lot of walking), Mexico (one week), Canada (three days vacation), Japan (one day on the way to Korea), and Panama (sailboat for two weeks). After forty, I stopped counting at 68 countries. After forty, I rode several aircraft carriers across the Pacific, a destroyer from seven miles off Iraq across the

[1] Lawrence Sterne. (1713-1768) English author. A Sentimental Journey, 1768.

Indian Ocean to Perth, Australia. After forty, I caravaned across the Sahara—when you are on an animal that stands six feet at the shoulder, and weighs in at over a ton, and spits a lot, you know that you are not in Kansas—and traveled around the world thrice—once at the United States Navy's expense, twice at mine—it is a lot cheaper to go at the Navy's expense and you eat better. After forty, I rode down the mightiest of rivers, the Amazon on a ninety-foot wooden boat (the Amazon has more volume than the next ten largest rivers in the world combined), and did the same on the longest river in the world, the north flowing Nile. I have not been down the Mississippi yet, but plan on it.

However, after a close family life for many years versus an adventurous life, there are always tradeoffs. There is loneliness. You miss the family, the little kids, your own things, and your own house. Also, keep in mind: an adventurer is not a tourist. I wish to make that very clear. I am a traveler, sometimes a novice adventurer. Once I was a tourist—never again!

A modern-day tourist supposedly travels for pleasure. In the Middle Ages, people were tourists because of their religion, whereas now they are tourists because tourism *is* their religion. Many people travel to have a vacation, to spend money on lodging, food, transportation and then gripe about it . . . not being like home. "Dog-dang hit Emmy Lou! These here Eye-tal-iuns doen even unnerstand American!" In addition, the problem with American tourists to other lands is that they have little time—two weeks perhaps—two weeks to fill their experiences with pseudo-events. They have come to expect exotic and more intimacy than the world naturally offers, more than they find at home. They have been told that they can have a lifetime of adventure in fourteen days—two of those days coming and going—and all the thrills of their life without any risk. Well . . . they cannot.

Risks for a traveler are there no doubt. I have been chained to a ring in the wall at the San Francisco International airport because I forgot I had a loaded derringer in my camera bag. (That one cost me $1,500 bucks!). I have been locked up for two hours in a hot little room in Cambodia—no pages left in my passport for a stamp—by a Mao-faced customs officer who expressed all the warmth of an unflushed toilet. I have been stranded in the middle of the night in the middle of nowhere in Turkey—the train didn't show up—and read where fifteen tourist were machined-gunned on the steps of a hotel—I had left the same hotel three days previously—and I have slept with a bandanna over my nose all night in Costa Rica—the overflowing, non-flushing toilet was by the head of my cot. There are all kinds of risks. On more than one occasion I have fallen in with female travelers winding up at a different destination than planned—*but I do not want to go down that road!* Now the terrorist bomber boys are about. (Terrorists do not concern me much when traveling; it is much more dangerous driving on the Sacramento freeway) Yes; there *are* all kinds of risks, however, if common sense is used, it is no more dangerous than taking a vacation in Los Angeles. Believe me! I have been *there*! In traveling, the worst risk is intestinal, intestinal as in bacteria, amoebas, and other unfriendly little tiny critters. Remember your high school science: the most dreadful attackers of humans cannot be seen with the naked eye.

No matter how careful one is, one will eventually get sick. Count on it. Plan on it. You will eventually—if you travel extensively—be on your knees praying to the White Throne, that is, if you are in a tourist type hotel, otherwise you might be kneeling over a foul, encrusted brown-rimmed hole in the floor. However, when the wee microbes do their little Mexican Hat dance in your stomach, do not despair. You will recover—eventually—well . . . usually. Amebic dysentery can knock you off, or at least do some serious damage to your 27 feet of intestines. I know that it is not much succor when you are doing the two-step shuffle to the bathroom, but remember, when you have Montezuma's revenge; the folks from other countries often get Roosevelt's revenge here. Different microbes for different folks.

Because of my background, adventures, and risks, I find that Thorton Wilder's description of "Adventure" is appropriate. He states:

"The test of an adventure is that when you're in the middle of it, you say to yourself, 'Oh, now I've got myself into an awful mess; I wish I were sitting quietly at home.' And the sign that something is wrong with you is when you sit at quietly at home wishing you were out having lots of adventures."[2]

Whatever! Stay at home and wish, go and complain. A fellow high school buddy of mine who married in his senior year of high school, and has been married to the same lady for over forty years, *and* who has not been out of the West, once said to me, "Why do you want to go *there*?"

---

[2] Thorton Wilder. (1897-1975), U.S. Novelist. The Matchmaker, act 4.

"Well . . . that's obvious" I answered, "Because I have not been there and—like the guy who kissed the cow—it seemed the thing to do at the time!"

The best reasons to go somewhere is simple—you go because it is there—because you want to! Why did you climb that mountain? *Because it was there—because I wanted to!* Why did you kiss that cow! *It seemed the thing to do at the time!* Why did you let her buy you all those drinks? *It seemed . . .* Oh! Well, sometimes you do things for different reasons. However, if humans did not do those *"Why did you want to go there?"* things, then we would probably still be up in the trees with the rest of our relatives wearing lots more hair and never doing the horizontal mambo in the missionary position.

Another best reason for "going off somewhere" is expressed by Voltaire in *Candide:*

"If we do not find anything pleasant,
At least we shall find something new."

That is good enough for me. Like the gal answered when asked, "Why do you want to trade your old husband for one you have never met? You don't know what you're gonna git!"

The gal answered, "Well! I know what I *got!"*

Earlier this month, on the fourth, I was up at what most would consider the ungodly hour of 0400, reading the Sacramento Bee newspaper—nothing new going on in Sacramento—as usual—then I showered, shaved, and dug my good dark gray suit out of the closet. I grabbed an overnight bag and by 0600 was in my ten year-old El Dorado Baritz—old, but classy, warm leather, smells good—headed for the airport a dozen or so miles northwest, out highway 5 among lovely, verdant rice fields and ugly new track homes toward Woodland. The good ol' U.S. Navy had a prepaid ticket for me at the Southwest Airline counter—$181round trip—Sacramento to San Diego to Sacramento.

Cynthia, a very lovely, lithe young lady, from the San Diego offices of Central Texas College, phoned me a few days prior asking if I would be interested in a little jaunt from Japan via Guam to Australia—all expenses paid plus salary. *Does a bear crap in the woods? Does Elvis wear blue-suede shoes? Does Slick Willie like playing his own version of cross-word puzzles?* . . . I stuttered for an answer. The brain was workin', but no messages were getting to the voice box. Laughing at my childish enthusiasm, Cynthia suggested that I come down to San Diego for an orientation. Happy for a free round-trip to that bright, sunny city—it was a dismal rainy day in Sacramento—I replied as fast as an old maid gossip's tongue, "I'm on my way! Cyn-thee-ah!"

Gate 28 was not difficult to find. Sacramento International is not that large. (Sacramento International! Hah! "International" implies worldly or cosmopolitan. Although Sacramento *is* the state capitol of perhaps the richest state in the country, the only planes that land here are shuttles form Los Angeles and San Francisco. Oh Yeah! United—the worst airline in the country—also drops in occasionally—literally. The local rice surrounded landing patch should not be called "International." I think Rice-Patty Strip would be a more apt moniker.) Gate 28 was the same gate I left from last month, when I wandered down to Costa Rica via El Salvador to visit my friend Jim Mayo. El Salvador. Now there is a place you can leave off your vacation list. Every pizza parlor, every service station, bank, department store, and whorehouse has a uniformed guy standing by the door packing an automatic rifle. I spent a month there one week; take it off your list.

At the gate check-in counter reigned a flaming, redheaded female—about 5' 5", attractive—I noticed her earlier downstairs working at the ticket counter as I was headed to the coffee shop (Airport coffee: $1.79 a paper cup! As Cliff says on *Cheers*, "What's up with that?"

The redhead was arranging papers as I came up to the counter humming a cheerful morning rendition of *Suicide is Dangerous*; last night I watched a rerun of Mash.

She remarked, "You certainly are happy for so early in the morning."

Long eye lashes, nice complexion. I glanced at her bust. Hmmm! *All guys do it! Don't get on my case!*

Pasting a Sean Connery smile on my smacker, I explained I *was* a morning person, going on a journey, a free flight, and "Didn't have to go to work either" all in one sentence. A regular blabber mouth, but an all-around fellow.

"Well . . . I won a trip to Malaysia" she said. She had a nice smile. She wanted to talk to me; people usually don't . . . well . . . not beautiful women anyway.

We prattled a bit about traveling among other things, then she became busy as other customers came up, butting in, interrupting a serious discussion just because they wanted to go visit their nana some place. I sauntered around a spell, checking my fly with the little finger of the left hand—a trick I learned reading Woman's Day Magazine. (The writer wrote that it was not cool to try to approach a lady with your shorts poking out of the fly of your trousers) I found a discarded newspaper and keeping a keen eye in the gate-lady's direction, I wandered back finally sitting near the entrance to the boarding gate. I had a clear view of her profile. She dealt adroitly with sleepy-headed, rumpled, paper-cup holding coffee drinkers fumbling with their tickets. One Yuppie type, a chap with his little beeper hooked to his belt and his little cell phone attached to his ear, holding his little lap-top in one hand, tried to flirt with her while jabbering into the phone at the same time. *What a clod!* Trying to pick up a lady obviously out of his class. Some people! *Probably married. Looks like a chauvinist pig! Probably never read Woman's Day.*

I thought of asking for a telephone number. *Boy, I hadn't done that kind of stuff in a long-long time.* I decided no; she was too young. But she *had* let me know that she was divorced for four years . . . Hmmm . . . I decided to go talk to her as she became less busy with the Los Angeles yuppie check-in herd. Checking my fly again with the little finger of my right hand—without looking down—and a quick glance in the glass of a cigarette machine—I'd learned that from an old Dick Van Dyke television episode and—sucking in the ol' paunch—just need to drop a couple pounds—I ambled over using my Gary Grant saunter.

She looked up, smiled, and said, "You know, I find you very attractive and interesting."

Just like that!

Outta the blue!

Damn!

". . . uh! . . . " I was glad she said attractive first; no one in the last ten years had commented on my kisser except to annotate on the number of wrinkles playing across my forehead like the ridges on a $1.98 tin washboard. When I shaved in the mornings, *I* saw a combination of Burt Reynolds/Sean Connery/John Derek . . . the resemblance was quiet clear to me . . . but others are not as astute as I am. Evidently. Clods!

"I don't usually do this but . . . " she continued while I was still " . . . 'Uhing . . . "

She wrote on a piece of paper. Handing it to me, she said, "Here is my number, if you'd like to call." *Cute little wrinkles at the corner of the eyes.*

I felt my face becoming warmer. *Was I flushing?*

"Well! . . . Every few weeks I . . .uh . . . have dinner and drinks with . . . uh . . . three married couples, friends of mine for many years." Nobody was around—listening. She smiled, but kept making notes.

"I'll be gone for a few weeks. Why don't I drop you a line from the ship? And I can call you from San Diego!"

My theory is that women feel more comfortable on first dates in groups—I do! Besides I wouldn't have to carry the conversation and maybe I could get my friends to brag a bit about the ol' fellow!

We parted with smiles and a waving of the fingers.

God! Was I out of practice!

Filing down the incline to the plane's entrance I mused, *"I should wear a suit more often."*

Ha! The old boy isn't counted out yet.

If I were taller, I probably would see Clint in the mirror when I shave tomorrow. *Cowboy boots add a couple of inches!*

Flying! . . . The only way to travel!

And the food is good.

I know! I know! Airline food is terrible!

Well . . . hang around my place and eat what I eat. I promise you that you want turn up your nose at the airline's victuals. Baloney sandwiches on white bread, with a big slice of red onion, is what Mom used to make for us kids as Dad drove a series of dilapidated old Model A Ford jalopies and Plymouth cars from town to hamlet—cotton camp to another camp—up and down the Great Sacramento Valley following the crops—cotton, grapes, lemons, and oranges. With a frosty coke, drunk out of the bottle, no straw—straws are for sissies—a slice of baloney on white bread is hard to beat for a feast. Slide in a slice of sweet red onion or a big white slice of a Vidalia and a slather of French's Classic Yellow mustard . . . Um! . . . Um! . . . makes my mouth water just to think of it. I still have it for breakfast once in awhile if there is no cold pizza left in the icebox.

My folks used to work in the agricultural belts of the San Joaquin Valley and San Berdu—San Bernardino—and the lemon and orange groves of Santa Paula, Ventura, and Oxnard. Back and forth, up and down southern California all through the forties—Sacramento to Fresno to Los Angeles to San Diego and all the little side towns along the way: Merced, Tulare, Firebaugh, Mendota, Fresno and many, many more—picking the cotton (three-cents a pound), oranges and lemons, and cutting grapes. (I hear people on television say, " . . . pick grapes. You do not pick grapes when you are earning a living at it; you cut the stem with a hooked knife.) In those days highway 99 down the Central Valley was not a freeway, but a three-lane thoroughfare with a passing lane—called in those days a "suicide" lane. When passing a vehicle you chanced meeting another car head-on, coming the other way, passing also and one of you had to get back into the driving lane or a head on collision was likely—hence, "suicide" lane.

One of our old Fords had a "suicide door" in that it opened with the hinges at your elbow with the door latch up near the steering wheel, hinges to the rear. The door swung back toward the rear of the car when opened. Why was it called a "suicide door"? I don't know unless you opened it doing sixty, then all kinds of uninteresting possibilities opened up. We would ride along the hot highways, watery mirages glimmering on the black top in the distance, and someone would mention that it was hot. Then they would get a surprised look from the rest of us. Someone would invariably say, "Wow! We didn't know that! It's hot! Whataya know!" Or, " I thought this was rain pourin' down my forehead! Hot! Coulda fooled me!"

Dad would then say, "Well . . . we got four-forty air!"

And although everybody knew the answer, someone would always say, "What's that?"

He would rejoin, "Open four windows an' go forty miles an hour!" We laughed at the tired old joke every time. Why? I dunno. It seemed the thing to do at the time. You know . . . "Like the guy who kissed . . ."

Today I was not in an old Ford, but a sleek aeroplane soaring the some odd 500 miles down the great valley, doing in an hour and fifteen minutes what it used to take us a couple of days in the forties—top 1929 Model A Ford speed of 47 miles per hour—with my dog Curly in the back.

I enjoyed leaving rain-dreary Sacramento behind for the sunny blue skies and warm balmy air of San Diego. San Diego is a beautiful city with its green hills and big, blue harbor. San Francisco and San Diego are two of the best anchorages in the world, both in the same Golden State of California. I have been fortunate in that I have sailed out of and into both harbors standing on the bows of the flight deck of two nuclear carriers: the *USS Carl Vinson* and the *USS Abraham Lincoln.* From the flight deck of those two moving mountains, the big harbor and the city are laid out like a colorful, giant monopoly board. I have also sailed out of San Francisco Bay in Russ Gant's self-built sailboat drinking Walgreen Drugstore gin with he and Bill Solenberger—it is not the same. Once, as I lay with head hanging over the side of Russ's boat like a soon-to-be-plucked chicken, puking my sea-sick guts out, my two best friends stuck a glass of warm gin under my nose saying, "Here, Ol' Buddy—this'll help." *Aagggh!*

The taxi driver in San Diego was Indian, an Indian from India, not an Indian from America. American Indians were named after India Indians, but are not India Indians. Not even remotely. Even India people are not Indians, well . . . not the Hollywood red-Indian type. (Indians are not really red either.) Early exploring Europeans were always going around naming places that the locals had already named. American Indians, it is generally agreed, by the people who study such things, came from ancestors who entered the Americas from Asia by way of the Bering Strait around 40,000 years ago. The term *Indian* has always been a misnomer for the earliest inhabitants. Many people now prefer *Native American*—which is what Columbus should have named the indigents or, maybe, he could have *asked* them their name—but he had more serious problems at the time than worry about names—namely trying to keep the King and Queen of Spain from loping off his head for lying about real estate. In addition, *Native American* avoids the stereotype of *Bloodthirsty Indian, Wild Indian*, or *cowboys and Indians.* I like American Native Indians, but I do not like their acorn soup; if I want to chow down on something that tastes like boiled sawdust I'll chew on a piece of timber or I'll pass and look for a baloney sandwich. Some uppity people call baloney 'bo-log-na". You go ask for a bo-log-na sandwich from my Mom and she would have you in washing your mouth out with Tide or maybe grinding up some acorns for soup.

However, there is always a problem when dealing with the Human Condition I was teaching an Indian studies class at Solano Community College when a student, an elected leader of a local Indian association, once reprimanded me for calling her a *Native American.* She wanted to be called an Indian. She continues to use *Indian* as a term of pride and respect, as in: "*It was about this time I began to see myself as an Indian.*" Therefore, it cannot be assumed that *Indian* is necessarily out of date. So, what do you call the Amerindian—another term that has problems—when you are addressing them. Well . . . I am an anthropologist. Take the scientific approach. Do what an expert does: play it by ear, improvise, or guess. From experience in the classroom, I have learned that it does not matter how correct you attempt to be as an instructor; someone is going to complain anyway. As Ricky Nelson sings in *I Went to a Garden Party*, " . . . ♫You can't please 'em all, so ya gotta please yourself ♫♪."

The Indian taxi driver (from India) had a little difficulty finding the offices of Central Texas College. When he did, I was pleasantly surprised for the offices were in a building about a hundred and fifty feet diagonally across the street from the entrance to the Marine Corps Recruit Depot (MCRD), where Marines go to boot camp on the west coast. I matriculated through this particular College of Hurts and Degradation—The University of MCRD—in 1954, with high school buddies Bill Lesher and Otis Hunt. We graduated with the degree of PVT—Private First Class. I visit this former part of life about every eight years. MCRD has a fascinating military museum, a very good library, and a lot of bewildered young soon-to-be-Marines.

A feeling of nostalgia flows through me whenever I see this place where torturing young hayseeds and punks out of their sloppy civilian ways is a fine art. Where Mommy's little boy is molded into one of the elite: a *United States Marine*.

*"Private Gunn you are a feather merchant! Private Gunn you will **never** make it! Private Gunn! I try to play ball with you and you jam the bat up my ass! Private Gunn . . .!*

The voice of Sgt. Reese, our D.I. (Drill instructor) is still back there, in the rear of my brain, just waiting for me to foul up—again! Shaved heads. Stiff boots. Starched dungarees buttoned to the Adams apple.

"GET THE LEAD OUT!" D. I's shout a lot. *"WHEN I TELL YA' TA FALL OUT, ALL AH WANNA SEE IS ASSHOLES AND ELBOWS!"*

At the end of ten weeks of intense training, lack of sleep, and much torment, I loved him like Charley Manson loves his warden.

The college administration offices of CTC are in a two-story, wooden building, built along the southern California Spanish style; an outside balcony runs clear around the second level. Following arrows up splintered wooden stairways and around corners, I hiked upstairs to look for room 221. Ahead, in the bright sunlight, two ladies were leaning on the wooden railing taking a smoking break, arms akimbo, their butts butting the black balustrade. My shoes reverberated on the plywood deck as I came within voice distance—in my new suit, carrying my raincoat Frank Sinatra style. The taller female said looking up:

"Are you Mr. Gunn?"

She must be psychic! Giving her an affirmative nod, I rested my arms on the railing, directing my best Clint Eastwood squint at the barracks across the street. I replied, "Ahhh . . . Yeah! . . . I spent some time with the Devil Dogs over there," pointing with my chin.

"Oh, you were a Marine?" (I always capitalize "Marine" when it means a United States Marine . . . it is not grammatically correct . . . but it should be.)

Steely eyed, I again nodded as if to say: "I know there's a heaven, Lady, for I've spent my time in hell." Us leather necks don't jaw around much. We are action guys. If I had had a chaw, I'd a spit, nailing a fly to the tarmac twelve feet below.

She introduced herself as Dr. Sherry Bates. She was to be my boss.

Well! . . . Okay. Too skinny anyway. Besides, she smokes . . . like a chimney . . . sign of weakness. Most would not believe it, but I am slightly chauvinistic—but I do not smoke. Stinks!

Orientation was like all orientations: too much information and too many forms in too short a time from too many people.

As mundane after mundane paper accumulated in the manila folder before me and my eyes were beginning to glaze *and* my bladder was whispering *"Rain Drops keep Fallin' on my Head"*, Sherry . . . uh . . . Dr. Bates told her boss that "I was a quick-study" and that we could deal with a lot of the paper work later. I liked her for that, although I was not quite sure what "quick study" meant. I looked it up later to find it is *"one who is able to understand and deal with something easily and successfully."* That was nice of her. I figured all along that I was pretty smart: nice to have it confirmed. Maybe all nicotine addicts are not so bad!

At first contact with the college on this assignment, I was informed that I would be teaching one cultural and one physical anthropology class. Now it turns out that there will be *three* cultural and one physical. At $1,080 per class for six weeks, plus travel, plus expenses . . . I could live with that. In addition, I have to ride around the ocean on a big ship and pretend that I was a lieutenant commander.

I was to be ready to leave next Tuesday for Japan.

Iciban number one!

Maria, one of the young ladies working in administration handling travel arrangements, drove me to the Comfort Inn near historic Old San Diego. I would spend the night, then fly back to Sacramento next day. I could have flown back that afternoon but . . . one of our senators, of the Great White Way in Washington, just took all his relatives to study beach sand and pineapples in Hawaii on the tax payer's back, so I thought I would let them put me up for the night.

San Diego is a city full of memories for me. Sitting by the Inn's pool, not more than sixty yards from highway I-5, I remembered that just last year I drove the lane nearest the fence surrounding the motel in my old Pace Arrow motor home on my way from Arizona, back to Sacramento. A quarter mile or so on the other side of I-5, I could see the Marine Corps Boot Camp and make out one of the buildings where in Bill Lesher, Odis Hunt, and myself were vaccinated and issued equipment way back there in the early fifty's. I was 18, they both 19. Almost half a century ago. *Whow!* Where did the fifty years go? Now my friend Bill is 65, and has been ill for awhile. To me though, seeing the scene below, he is still the slim young Marine with a grinning smile and tousled black hair. High school president, captain of the football team when he was a senior and I a junior. A leader of men. He was Best Man at my wedding. Odis, an All-American swimmer while at Sacramento City College, is now an executive at Aero Jet Corporation. El Dorado High turned out some good boys.

In the evening, I strolled historic Old San Diego, about ten blocks from the motel, and walked right by the old Indian cemetery that Judy and I visited when we debarked from a Mexico cruise some years ago. Felt strange; a bit lonely to be back here now. Window shopped, the best kind of shopping, and sipped a tangy-cold Margarita at the same table where Judy and I sat; it was more enjoyable when she was with me. After eight years of courting, someone mentioned what did I think of getting married. I said it sounded all right, but who would have us? I should not have said that. Dumb! But it seemed the thing to do at the time.

The plane lifted easily out of Lindbergh Field the next day, dipped its right wing turning toward the north, leaving San Diego, reaching for the clouds over the twisting highway called the Grapevine threading its way through the Coast Range. The beach shimmered between the dark blue ocean and the rectangular patches of the city. As we headed out over the ocean, I saw a large wake—at first I thought it was a carrier—but as it caught the sun, I could see it was a submarine. A long black hull pushing the foaming water ahead of it . . .on the surface, a nuclear submarine going about its stealthy business. Two football fields long. Long and ominous looking: dangerous.

On February 11, I was ready to leave the capitol of the Golden State again. Awake since three-thirty, I was packed by seven, dressed in my Indiana Jones Raiders of the Lost Ark outfit. I went next door to say good-byes to my daughter, her husband Gary, and my granddaughters Brittney and Katy. ("Good-bye" is a contraction of the 16th century phrase "God be with ye!") The blue shuttle van was on time, sitting in the driveway, an efficient way to get to the Sacramento International Airport AKA the Rice Paddy Strip. I was early—usually am, and an efficient female clerk got me on the 9:30 flight rather than wait for my scheduled 11:30. I had a few extra minutes, so I dashed to the Southwest counter for a chat with Vickie, the cute lady who had given me her telephone number. The day before she and I had lunch at the Rusty Duck and she gave me a little kiss goodbye in the parking lot of the restaurant standing by her new Land Rover. Today I got a big hug right there in the terminal. Ah! If Adar Bray and Dave Dun could see me now! We taught in the same department for some years. They had suggested that by retiring early, I was losing some cash. I was here kissing an attractive woman of good breeding while embarking on a paid adventure. They were working. Go Figure!

For a long half-hour, I was trapped in the unpretentious Sacramento-San Francisco shuttle waiting area. It was packed. All seats were taken and the television was blaring, reverberating off the tile floor and concrete walls like hailstones off a galvanized tin-roofed Georgia outhouse. One of those inane Ricky Lake clones talk show host was seriously interviewing a barely literate, young female teenager—a child really, painted with overdone make-up and to-tight clothing that caused her baby fat to bulge like a spicy Jimmy Dean sausage. This child-mother was insisting that *her* pre-school daughter would be raised in the church, would no doubt become an astrophysics person, but for now the tyke—made up like a hooker—was participating in a beauty pageant. *Yuck!* Four women on the show than got into a screaming argument—two for, two against—about beauty pageants for girls under nine. It was one of those "discussions" where everyone discussed—loudly—but no one listened. I think all of them should have been home cleaning house, in a nut house, or going to school.

Finally, the flight was called. Everyone made way outside for a short walk across the tarmac to the shuttle plane. Cigar-shaped, with two props humming, the silver bird quickly lifted off, turning right over the Port of Sacramento, lining up for the 20-25 minutes flight to San Francisco, the City by the Sea.

Below the neat, squared paddies of rice, sugar beets, corn, and orchards of peaches, apples, and olives presented a patch work of the color green: verdant shades of green, emerald-green, lime-green, yellow-green, olive-green, blue-green—a mixed-salad of greens interspersed with chrome flashes of flooded rice paddies, rivers—the American and the Sacramento—and sloughs.

I sat across the aisle from a Japanese couple who could communicate only by yelling at each other. Must be the result of living in a crowded country. Notice the Thai's do the same, talking loud. And some Americans. Chinese as well. Mexicans, surprisingly, are fairly quiet travelers. Scientific fact. Probably 'cause they eat a lot of frijoles—saving their wind for other things.

San Francisco was wrapped in a filmy gauze; fog blanketed the city as the plane droned past it southwest for a 20-minute holding pattern, landing about 11:10. We stepped off the plane in a different climatic zone than the one we left a few minutes ago in the Sacramento Valley. A chilly fog-laden wind chilled the bones used to an eighty-degree morning less than an hour earlier. The safari from Gate 88 to Gate 58 took awhile, however an abandoned luggage cart—they charge $3 for the things—I found along the way helped. Helped that is until I arrived at the security gate: No Carts Allowed.

For some reason, my large sample-type brief case, filled with books and desk accessories, attracted the interest of the rotund female black lady guard, she giving it a thorough going over inside and out ostensibly disappointed not to find something lethal. I am inspected seemingly more than others who stream right on by. *Must be the beard, unsmiling demeanor, and beady eyes.* Out of boredom, I have taken to glancing furtively away when one of the security guards eyes meets mine. I am inspected a lot, more than most. Pure prejudice.

I found the gate with an hour to spare before takeoff, captured a window table at a kiosk: coffee $1.49 Help-Yourself. So I did—help myself, that is . . . half a cup. I always carry a folding cup in case of emergencies. (In Japan—at the airport—coffee is $3 a cup! Coca-Cola in an ice-cold bottle in Katmandu, Nepal is 17¢. In Thailand 23¢. In Japan in a paper cup, it is $3.75.) Near the coffee pot a small luncheon listed at $5.50 and a cinnamon roll $1.75. So, I rummaged in my bag pulling out one of the Nature Valley granola bars my daughter had packed away for me. It went well with the free coffee.

An older Japanese couple—obviously married to each other for decades and a young Japanese female, in her late teens, sitting it the next table, oblivious of me—burst out every few minutes, the old couple vitriolically chastising the young female. Airing their dirty kimonos in public. There were many passengers of oriental ancestry in the waiting area: Japanese, Malaysians, Chinese, and a few Thai's. Understandable. This was the departure wing for the Far East to countries such as Japan, Japan, Korea, Vietnam, Malaysia, Cambodia, and Thailand. When peoples go to the Near East—Turkey, Lebanon, Iraq, Iran—they usually fly from the East coast of the United States, as do those going to the Middle East to Saudi Arabia and East Africa. What we living in California on the West Coast do not readily understand is that the Far East is really the nearest east to us and the Near East is really the farthest east to us. As for the Middle East, who cares; no one wants to go there anyway.

The electronic departure board flashed the flight was leaving on time at 1:40. I made one last phone call to Teresa, my daughter, saying I would telephone or write when settled in on the ship. The 747 lifted off an hour late—mechanical troubles—that's okay with me about leaving late if something has to be fixed. Going down in Arctic waters because of a broken valve is not something I look forward to happen. The departure time would put me into Tokyo around six P.M. Japanese time, shortening me on time to catch the Navy bus.

I talked to the female flight attendant about the hundred or so vacant seats. She said she too was surprised that there were so many empty seats; that it was unusual. She lays over for 25 hours in the States, then returns to Japan, working three days on, and five off. She says she is always pestered by jet lag, a phenomenon of the modern day. Columbus and the pioneers had no trouble with jet or time lag: they just lagged. Before high-speed jet travel, there was no such phenomenon as jet lag. Columbus did not know about it; people travel in the forties and fifties didn't worry about it. Only when passenger planes began to out race the sun did the problem crop up. Personally, as opposed to some travelers, I do not experience much of the effects of jet lag traveling west. Coming back however, is a different pot of tortillas and beans. It now takes me a solid week to adjust to the disruption of bodily rhythms caused by high-speed travel across several time zones; the clock and part my brain would say it is noon, but the old body and the other part of the brain would say you're out of half of your mind dumkoft—go back to bed. If you are wondering what high-altitude jet travel can do to your body, go to a website compiled by Diana Fairchild, a flight attendant grounded by chemical sensitivity to jet cabin conditions. Her site lays out cases against jetliner air quality, dehydration, oxygen, airline food, insecticides, airborne diseases, jet lag, and seating. You may want to read her book *Jet Smart.* According to Ms. Fairchild it is safer to swim across the Pacific than take a 747, however, here I think she may be exaggerating just a tad. .

I ate a dinner of airplane food—gourmet cuisine—followed by a banana, a couple of granola bars, peanuts, and orange juice while seven miles above a chain of rugged volcanic islands of southwest Alaskan waters curving out from the Alaska Peninsula right where the Bering Sea meets the Pacific Ocean: the frigid Aleutian Islands. Eskimos down there probably chowing down on some seal blubber pizza—Pizza Shack is everywhere. I have been across the 6,000 plus miles of the Pacific to Japan several times. The first time in 1954 was on a troop ship named the *Marine Phoenix* taking 12 days; this trip will take 11 hours. To while away a some time, I read a brief description of the USS Independence.

Independence
CVA 62-CV 62

"Built by New York Navy. Laid down 1 July 1955, launched 6 June 1958, commissioned 10 June 1958. Redesignated as a multimission carrier (CV-62) 28 February 1973, after being modified to operate ASW aircraft. SLEP qt Philadelphia Navy Yard 4/1985 to mid-1988.
Replaced *Midway* as forward-deployed carrier in Japan, 1991. Island was extensively enlarged during SLEP and other modernization. Replaced by the *Kitty Hawk* 7/1998 and decommissioned to reserve 30 September 1998."

10:23. Some where over the Pacific.
Only five Caucasian passengers on this plane.
Been flying about 8-9 hours.
12:15: Light snack.
No sleep yet.
5:21 Japanese time. We are an hour late. Most go through customs. Find Navy country and catch bus.
Will be close.

Chapter 2

"Never give in, except to
Honor and good sense."
Military quote of the day.

The hefty 747's tires set down on the runway of Tokyo's Narita International Airport as lightly as the meringue sits on my Aunt Eller's deep dish lemon pie. I am no stranger to Narita having been here several times on my way to Thailand, but it has always been at night and then only to change planes or to clear the plane for an hour while maintenance crews clean the Jumbo Boeing 747 of trash accumulated by the 400 plus passengers after a nine to twelve hour flight—usually from smoggy Los Angeles. (Los Angeles is called "the City of Angels." If so, there must be many with tarnished wings.) I have not seen the metropolis of Japan—the world's largest city by light of day. At night, there are just miles of multicolored flashing neon; it made one think of an immense carnival.

I remembered reading that when Narita airport was under construction there were violent protests by farmers and students delaying the May 1978 opening by two months. It does smother a big chunk of rice paddies. Although it is Tokyo's international airfield, it is a good, long trek to the city proper located at the head of Tokyo Bay. As a teenager, I was raised in a town of 6,685 souls in the California foothills of the Sierra Mountains—Gold Rush Country. To Christmas shop, my family would go to Sacramento, a big city—to us—of 350,000 population. We would gawk and stare, amazed that people could live so crowded! Greater Tokyo is a bit larger than Sacramento: down-town Tokyo has approximately 12,000,000 people, however, with its urban area of the Izu Islands and Yokohama, Greater Tokyo forms the world's most populous metropolitan area in 2000 of over 30,000,000.

Although inhabited for many centuries,Tokyo has become one of the world's most modern cities peculiarly through catastrophes: in 1923 an earthquake and fire destroyed half the city, and heavy Allied fire-bombing in World War II devastated nearly all of Tokyo, including all of its industrial base. After the war, the U.S. helped Japan rebuild as well as assuming the expense of its defense, and ironically, since the entire industrial base was new, its industrial complex is one of the most modern and up to date in the world.

My flight landed an hour late.

Apprehension crowded my thoughts brought on by being late. I have a schedule to meet and the directions given to me at the college orientation were a bit perplexing. I was to explore through the swarming international airport, find a counter somewhere near the main entrance—my orientation director didn't know exactly where—and his offhanded "*I couldn't miss it*" did little to bolster my confidence. *Couldn't miss it!* Ha! That's the same thing they told me about traveling on the underground in Paris; I became disoriented everytime I ventured down there. With my sense of direction, I could miss a lady of accommodating virtue in a whorehouse.

I had exactly *sixty minutes* to navigate all the hallways, find customs, wait for four pieces of luggage to trundle down the chute, then find the meeting point, *and* I didn't speak any Japanese except a phrase taught me by a Marine Corporal and, the only time I ever used it, I was pushed out the door by a Japanese female who said that she did not do that kind of thing, that it was against the law. Under her breath, I think she breathed "*anymore,*" but I was not entirely sure.

On the plane, I talked to a young American guy traveling the same route as I. A couple of other times, once in Tangiers, once in Turkey, I have hooked on behind someone such as he, pretending I was an old fuddy-duddy who needed directional orientation—at least I *think* that I was pretending—but it was his first trip to Japan and he said that " he didn't know nothin' from no-how!"

The Japanese reputation of efficiency was well evident; ten minutes after landing all the passengers were off the plane and in the exceptionally clean, brightly lit terminal, a cavern well-nigh devoid of people. In fact, they are a bit too officious for me, too robotic. All-important directional signs in the terminal building are in English as well as Japanese, so no trouble in that regard. Robert, the American I met on the plane, and I watched each other's bags while rounding up the stray ones—that took half-an-hour. The luggage carts were free and plentiful. Luggage carts are furnished free also in Thailand and, come to think of it, in every other airport terminal I have been in except those in the U.S. As I noticed earlier, the ones in San Francisco are *three bucks*! Grabbing one, we stacked our bags aboard and headed for the dreaded immigration stations.

That was easy!

A trim, neatly dressed customs gentleman, square cut, about five feet two inches short, black hair of course, beamed two gold incisors at me as he smilingly began looking at my barbarian whiskered face, peering over the top edge of my beat-up, wrinkled, water-sweat-stained passport, barely glancing at my travel orders, and, with what I think was a symbolic karate chop, motioned me into the land of the Rising Sun. (We have gold in our molars, the Japanese in front. Why? I do not know. Anthropologists are not dentists.)

Now to find the Navy counter. Forty-five minutes of my hour was left. Amazing! Fifteen minutes from plane to street. I had sweated an hour of apprehension, worry, and energy, but made it from the plane to the exit area in a quarter of an hour.

Once, in Egypt, it had taken two hours to accomplish the same type of debarking. The Japanese are a tad more organized than the Egyptians—somewhere around 98% more organized. The Japanese supply modern automobiles to the world while Egyptians bounce around on a few camels. Both cultures build nice temples, though. Americans do neither, but everybody watches our soap operas. Manhandling the luggage cart, I made way through passageways under construction, around temporary plywood barriers, winding up in the main entrance terminal. (Why is every airport in the world under construction?) The main terminal was cavernous: restaurants, kiosk, tax-free shops, moveable tramways, stairwells, escalators, and people, people, people. *Lots of people.* Not many at Arrival, but lots at Departure—more people going than coming.

I was to look for a Navy information booth lettered "Navy Personnel Bus." I looked. Nope! No where in sight.

"Do Maid Goto all to hell!"[1]

Here fifteen minutes and I am speaking Japanese like a native.

Where am I going to find a small-lettered sign in this half-mile long chamber?

"Pardon me."

"Huh?" I am not at my most eloquent voice-wise when tapped on the shoulder in a strange airport, especially in Japan, *especially* when the melodious voice is in soft, feminine voice, speaking English.

---

[1] Thank you.

I looked over my right shoulder to see a white-haired American lady dressed in a stylish, well-cut dark-blue suit with white piping on the jacket and skirt. She smiled, little dimples dancing at the corners of her mouth, asking, "Was that flight 837 from San Francisco that just came in?" "Uh . . . duh . . . Oh yes . . . I said eloquently, and in return, catching hold of my half-wit that was remaining, before she finished thanking me, I asked her if she knew where I might find the airport information booth.

Pointing to my front, about ten feet away, she indicated the booth as she walked away.

"Do Madi Goto all to hell!"[2]

Again!

She must have thought I was a dope! *I was a dope!* If the sign had been an elephant it could have peed on me, or stepped on me, or whatever elephants do to ejits. (Mom used to call my brother and me "ejits!" We thought that was how the word was pronounced and spelled until we went to school and learned differently. When, smugly, we told her it was "idiots," she said, "I know that. I save that term for humans, not ejits like you!") That is about how I felt anyway after crossing the Pacific. Stepped on. Or sat on. Shoe-horned into one of those made-for-ten-year olds airline seats, strapped in for sixteen or so hours give or take, and then torment myself through customs. No wonder they offer you free booze on those flights. You need it!

Yeah! I don't drink anymore. Don't drink any less, either. Wife says to husband, who has just walked in, "What do you mean comin' home half-drunk?" He says, "I ran out of money!"

Quit that!

Concentrate!

Hands covering giggling mouths, two kimono-clad, very cute Japanese girls in the information booth welcomed me with short bows of their heads. One was clad in a red kimono with a big white chrysanthemum printed on it; the other wore a white kimono with a red chrysanthemum printed on it.

I asked, "Could you please tell me where the American Navy bus booth is located?" I flung my arm out indicating the dozen's of booth selling everything from silver digital cameras to gray-black pickled octopi and other strange-looking, non-discernible food.

---

2 Thank you, again!

Giggling even harder, both pointed to another booth next to theirs—about six feet away. Wheeling the cart about I headed that way thinking that they probably thought I was a dope also. *Well!*

In plain view so that a blind person could have read it was a two by four foot sign printed in black, block letters: YOKOSUKA NAVAL BASE BUS.

Well . . . perhaps I was looking too hard.

At least I found the booth on time.

With three minutes to spare.

I knew I would make it! Never doubted it.

I really hope there is no such thing as reincarnation; I might have to go through all this again.

The Navy bus was scheduled to leave Narita at 7:30 PM for the long drive to Yokosuka[3] on southern Honshu Island located in Tokyo Bay. On the plane, I perused a handout the administration at Central Texas College gave me about my destination. Yokosuka's sheltered harbor is headquarters for a large fleet of Japanese whaling ships: in addition, the harbor shelters submarines, Japanese, and American warships, yachts, floating barges and has extensive shipyards. The deep harbor accommodates the twelve-story hull of the *USS Independence* and is the permanent base for this non-nuclear carrier; the only United States carrier based in a foreign country.[4]

Done up in my heavy, rumpled raincoat, belt buckle playing volleyball against my crotch, I tottered over to three guys standing in front of the naval bus booth while trying to control two pieces of luggage, the kind with cranky little plastic wheels, each loaded down with another bag on top, (I had to leave the airport luggage cart upstairs). I puffed and huffed, stumbling up to them. The three young men—short hair cuts, inexpensive Western civilian clothing, plain black shoes—obvious military guys, were waiting at the unmanned (unperson?) cubicle. They also, I learned, were going to the *Independence*. They were wearing civvies, but their clean-shaven face and "side wall" haircuts labeled them military as well as their dress. In the old days—1954—when I was a gyrene, a Marine wearing civilian clothing usually wore his Class-A military dress shoes, polished to a gleaming midnight-black

[3] Yokosuka dates from 1865 when a shipyard was established. It now has several auto assembly plants and a population of about 500,000.

[4] Called "Forward-deployed".

when he on liberty. The military shoes and the sidewall haircuts said to the merciless merchants of the towns near military bases "Here is another lonesome kid that can be overcharged!" They did it too! Especially at Oceanside, California near the entrance to the sprawling Camp Pendleton Marine Base.

"Hi fellas. Do you know where the bus is goin'?"

"The next one goes to the *Independence*" the closest one said. He was tall, sandy-haired, wearing a Hawaiian shirt and baggy knee-length shorts about four sizes too large.

"Well! What a ya know! I made!" I said, steadying my pile of luggage. The damn stuff kept trying to fall over.

"Yo goin' ta the *Indy*?" another asked.

"Yeah". I said. "I'm an instructor."

They knew all about PACE instructors; a couple of them had taken classes. After I talked about the classes—everybody is interested when I mention anthropology—and where I come from. They showed me how to sign the bus list. There was a beat-up fiber clipboard hanging from a post on the right side of the booth and my name had to be on it, said a small sign posted near it, or no seat matey! Well, I sure wanted a seat so I signed big and bold. Just as I finished writing my name, a gray-bearded civilian guy, about sixty and looking untidily pregnant, came shuffling up, ignoring us all to go behind the counter.

I let my bags fall over and walked over to the counter—still being ignored—and asked loud enough for a deaf person to hear if I signed correctly and, upon looking at the clipboard, he discovered my name written twice, once by me and once by someone else in another column. With a sigh of having to put up with the "ejits" of the world who could not sign a simple form, he whipped out his handy White Out Stick and went to work. Someone had telephoned ahead and given him my name; someone was on the ball. Efficient. Expedient. Unusual.

So, after all the rushing and the anxiety, I still had a forty-five minute wait while Mr. White Out fumbled around with a bunch of papers, picked his nose, farted, and made a call while generally still ignoring us, the reason for him being there in the first place. I was too tired from the long flight, apprehension, and the stress of doing ordinary things in a foreign country to bait the old guy—who actually is younger than I. This guy didn't even have delusions of adequacy. I was stressed out from the flight. Whom ever said: *"Worry is rust upon the blade*"[5] knew what the hell he was talking about. At this time of night, after my trip, my blade was not only rusty; it was pretty well nicked and dented and could have used a re-chroming.

Chris, one of the sailors going to the *Independence,* said that he would watch my bags while I searched for a cup of java. I called it *Java* rather then coffee—I wanted them to think that I was pretty "salty." Salty comes from "Old Salt!" Originally a seasoned sailor who had crossed many oceans, hence the term "Old Salt!" Salty in the Marine Corps means a seasoned Marine. In the Marines, a new recruit is issued stiff, new fatigues of a dark green color, as ugly as the steel metal military desks of the same ghastly hue—Government Issue. A Marine that has been the "crotch" or Marines a long time wears fatigues or dungarees that have become faded from harsh washing. New recruits in boot camp scrub salt into the unyielding cloth of the stiff, new fatigues with a firm brush, along with lots of harsh soap and hot water, until the cloth is soft and faded to a pale green—almost bluish-green. This does not make him an old salt, but he looks like one. Kinda.

I found a hole in the wall, a minuscule restaurant, and a Styrofoam cup of tepid, watery coffee . . . Well, watery-caramel-colored-flavored water anyway. Only does the USA make good coffee. Other countries rarely do. Usually you can say, "Well, at least it's HOT!" Here you could say, "Well, at least it's TEPID!" This place was strictly Japanese, however, the music playing while I sat and sipped was *Rawhide* by Frankie Laine, followed by *Harbor Lights,* a song I had not heard since high school, and *Love Me Tender* by the king! Go figure! The Japanese *are* an enigma. Listening to the King sang *Love me Tender* reminded me of the time I asked Miss Mentally-Challenged Coed if she had ever seen the film *"The King and* I." She said "Yeah! It was some film about Elvis." Miss M.C. Coed was not too knowledgeable about movies, but I sure did like the way that she did homework!

It was cold in Japan.

"Cold!" It was really cold! Leaving Sacramento the weather was mildly warm, San Francisco was colder and foggy. But here it was *cold-cold!* As frigid as a fifty-seven year old Baptist spinster in South Texas during a howling blizzard. Taking me in tow, the three sailors helped with my bags as I followed them across the huge darkened, almost empty parking lot to where four or five busses of various colors

---

[5] Henry Ward Beecher

were parked, doors tightly closed. I was surprised at how chilly it was. Despite my old, much-traveled, salty safari jacket, gloves, and Alan Ladd rain coat, I was shivering, along with the rest—we looked like a group of Quaker-Shakers on the way to camp meetin'—and we would gladly have settled into the bus to wait, but no luck. It was locked up tighter than a South Texas 4-H virg . . . well . . . anyway . . . it wasn't open.

After fifteen icy minutes crawled by the civilian driver showed. There was no animosity displayed toward him; everybody's animosity was too stiff to unbend and show to anyone. Twelve men and one lone female stored our luggage and assorted paraphernalia into the compartments underneath the bus, then stiffly climbed aboard, thankful for the apparent warmth inside. There was no heater going, but it *seemed* considerably warmer out of the damp night air.

The bus's engine was cranky, so it bucked, coughed, and spitted out of the airport parking area turning toward the city proper. We began descending down a hillside allowing a view of Tokyo City: a glittering carpet of twinkling lights lay spread out, whites, golds, blues, greens: a Las Vegas kaleidoscope multiplied a dozen . . . no, a hundred times. The broad expanse of multicolored lights reached to the horizon and beyond. The faraway sky glowed, reflecting unseen illumination below, light from the environs of the city I could not see even from the elevated freeway. The handout from Central Texas College stated that Tokyo International Airport is on the southern rim of Tokyo Bay. In a straight-line north, across the wide bay, is Tokyo's new American import: Disneyland. Inland, beyond these two reference points, in a boomerang shape, lies the greater Tokyo Metropolitan area. Therefore, I was not even seeing the main part of the city, yet there were millions of sparkling jewels below of every color and brilliance. The urban and suburban populations of Tokyo, the 30,000,000 peoples in the city proper, is a staggering 14,100 persons per square mile. Truely packed like little sardines. The country as a whole, has a population density of 850 persons per square mile as compared to the United States population density of 29.5 persons per square mile. Awesome. Not for me. Too many people.

This was to be another trip where I did not see much of the city of Tokyo, Japan. As soon as the bus loaded up and the heater took the chill out of the air, people began to adjust seats and luggage to sleeping positions, some stretching full out on the hard black vinyl seats. Did they know something that I didn't? I found out. It took a long hour and an another *longer* forty-five minutes to reach the base. I thought it was only going to be a ride of under forty or so miles. The handout from the college offices read 58 kilometers that I calculated was about 36 miles; someone did not get the "skinny" straight!

Awake many hours, I kept nodding off—a metal window sill does not make a good pillow—as the bus rolled along a wide freeway, through many tunnels, stopping at five tollbooths. Everytime we came to a tollbooth I would think, *"This is it! We're at the base."* Only it wasn't. I hate tollbooths. I put them right up there alongside value-added tax, pay toilets, and pet rats—men or rodents. I mean, already in California we pay a gasoline tax for roads, then some bureaucrat invented tollbooths. Hate 'em. If I could find the bureaucrat that invented toll roads, I'd have 'em shot dead, then I'd pick 'em up and shoot 'em again.

What I saw of the roadway reflected in lights along side the freeway was immaculate; there were no graffiti, no trash, and *nada* billboards blighting the landscape—a custom that we could use at home.

Just after 10 PM, the bus's brakes squealed like a slaughterhouse pig bringing the bus to a shuddering stop; a sign over a street said that we were at the main gate of the Yokosuka Naval Base. A Military Policeman carrying a clipboard boarded the bus; he was a Marine, his belt buckle glowing like a jewel, as did his gleaming black combat boots with tucked in trouser legs. He wore starched, board-stiff dungarees with a knife-edge crease—only Marines make work clothes (fatigues or dungarees) look like a Class-A uniform—the stiff brim of his cover (cap) was so low over his eyes they were non-existent. How do they get those canvas caps so rigid and smart looking? Simple. You wash it in hot water with lots of Purex to give it that salty look, starch the hell out of it, then stretch it over a saucepan to dry. A gentleman killer, a leather-neck, "Gung-Ho" and *"I know there must be a heaven because I've been to hell!"* Well. . . you get the idea. I used to be a Marine as I will tell you multitudinous times. *"Once a Marine, always a Marine . . ."*

Many people, even Marines, are confused about the term "Marine." They generally know the term refers to water or the ocean, but not in what context. As stated, Marines are a part of the U.S. Navy: since 1775, the Marines and the Marine mission have been associated with the sea and amphibious military operations. The word "marine" itself comes from the Latin *marinus*, meaning "related to the sea." The "amphibious" comes from the Greek *amphibon* literally meaning, "living a double life." On all Marine caps and uniforms is a globe and anchor emblem with an eagle perched on top; it may be metal or cloth. The globe and anchor embodies the tradition of worldwide service and sea traditions as in the beginning stanzas of the *Marine Corps Hymn:*

"From the Halls of Montezuma
To the shores of Tripoli;
We fight our country's battles
In the air, on land, and sea."

The eagle with its spread wings, the symbol of American itself, holds in its beak a streamer upon which is inscribed in the famous motto of the United States Marines: "Semper Fidelelis," which in Latin means "always faithful."

Hang around any Marine—male or female—any time, any place, and you will eventually hear the saying, *"Gung Ho!"* usually quite loudly. (I used to shout GUNG HO! at Mom's house when she would ask me to do something and she would reply, "The toilet's down the hall." Mom was very basic—but she was no ejit.) Adopted from the Chinese guerrilla fighters during World War II, "Gung" means *work*, "Ho" means i*n harmony*. As used by the Marines, Gung Ho means "Work together" and is used as a battle cry. Now, since so many Marines have worked into the civilian population, the motto has become a slang term meaning: "Yes Sir! Eager, enthusiastic, zealous as in "He did more than his share of work, he was *Gung Ho*." Alternatively, "This Marine was Gung Ho!" Or "He drank 17 beers, he was *Gung Ho*!" Or the Captain says, "Run up that hill and kill a bunch of those bad guys!" and the troops answer, "Gung HO! Sir!" and take off all except . . . perhaps, moi, who might rejoin, "Well Sir! . . . Why don't we talk it over with those guys first! Sir, your honor! Maybe we could work out a deal, give 'em a couple hamburgers an' a Chevy—it don't have to be a new one . . . an' . . . talk it over, you know. I mean, it does not seem the thing to do at this time—running up a hill with a one-eyed, 30-caliber machine gun spittin' 30-caliber chunks of lead at you. Could cause *all* kinds of problems with your love life."

As soon as the Marine MP stepped inside the bus facing the driver, he came to full attention, did a smart left face, snapped a crisp salute to the sleep-drugged passengers—just in case there happened to be an officer aboard—then proceeded to examine our I.D's. Rather than a cursory glance, which is normal, he took a full twenty minutes to do the bus; he did his job the way it was supposed to be done. Someone in charge had impressed on him his duty. When finished (he did not even give me a curious glance when he examined my shelf of papers—this guy had control) he went to the front of the bus, turned, snapped another crisp salute and we were inside the base gate.

Finally!

The Yokosuka Naval base was socked in for the night. Clutching my Alan Ladd raincoat about me, I stepped out into a cold night devoid of visible human life, my breath vaporizing in the chill. Lampposts formed a line of frothy pearls in the night sea fog; rooftops gleamed white; hoarfrost was forming in the frigid wet air. After a two-minute ride into the base area the bus driver had dropped his human cargo in front of a wooden building—much like the old barracks of W.W.II—with a sign on the porch proclaiming Enlisted Men's Transit Barracks. Enlisted men's quarters was copacetic with me. I let out a sigh. I was tired. And I wasn't proud—I had been awake and traveling for over 20 hours, many of them in a cramped airliner seat (you know what that is like) and almost halfway around the world—I was really beat. It was going to feel good to hit a hot shower and then a rack . . .

"What?"

The skinny, blonde Petty Officer third-class clerk looked at my travel orders again. "I'm sorry Suh!" he said, handing my wrinkled travel orders. "This is the enlisted transit barracks. Yo have ta go ta the BOQ."

"But" . . . I stood there as if I'd been goosed by a nun . . . I . . . I don't know where the BOQ is . . . I just got here. I'm supposed to go to the *U. S Independence*, but it's to late an' . . . " *Don't whine! Why not?*

The tow-headed clerk shook his head. He looked about fourteen, small as a tenth-grader. *Chief Petty Officer third class. Southern accent. Georgia or ol' Miss . . .*

"Yo can take a taxi to the "*Indy*" Suh! I can call yo one if yo wan'."

I know. I'll appeal to his disdain for officers; no enlisted man likes officers. It's against their nature.

'Well . . . What was yo name?'

I looked again to read his name tag over the left pocket of his white jumper—single stripe under a spread-wing eagle. *Thompson!*

"Well . . . Thompson. What do yo know 'bout that? My maw was named Thompson . . . " (My mother's surname was Clark.) "I was a

Corporal in the Marine Corps. Now I'm just a civilian" I *doen like no stinkin'* officer! "So how's about puttin' me up 'ere?"

My southern accent was headin' south faster than a Maine hobo in late October with Jack Frost playing the Latin version of *Jingle Bells* nipping at his heels. Letting my voice slip into the vernacular did no good; this guy knew his job. Damn swab jockeys . . . why'd they have to be so disciplined—that's a Marine's job. Why couldn't they be dumb? Like the army. I looked out the window. Just as I thought: still dark, *still cold. COLD* out there!

"Sir! Here guys sleep two ta four inna room. No civil-yens allowed no how. I can call yo a cab."

I nodded.

He called.

Crappola! I did not know where *no* BOQ was, and I did not know where *no Independence* was *neither no how;* I only knew where I was, and where I was, I was cold and *tired*! But I *did* know what was going to happen if a bearded Indiana Jones look-alike character showed up at the brow of the *USS Independence* going on 11:30 o'clock at night. It would be like it was on the *Carl Vinson*; a good two hours or more to find a place to sleep. I would be waiting around—*in the cold*—until someone decided I wasn't a spy nor a weirdo—well . . . a spy, then the ESO[6] would have to be found—probably rousted out of his rack, up and down stairwells with four pieces of luggage, try to find an empty cabin—thanks . . . but no thanks!

There we were: Four pieces of uncooperative baggage and me. I felt like a plagued rat at a pet show. Standing on a wooden porch in the Land of the Rising Sun, in the dead cold middle of night in winter, with an inhospitable wind blowing up my ass, the moon a shining skull eerie in the fog, the leaf-less trees a line of scarecrows, waiting while a southerner made a phone call. I could feel the cold prickling my scalp and ears; probably hoar frost forming on top of my head right now. And, of course, what happens when you get cold? You have to pee, that's what! That old thought that I have had plenty of times before came back to haunt: *"What the hell am I doing here?"* A shiver played hopscotch up and down the xylophone vertebrae on my backbone and I was beginning to shake like a cat shitting peach pits—a fond old Marine Corps saying—when a yellow cab . . . yes! A yellow cab . . . just like those in New York except this was a Honda, pulled up. Well . . .

---

[6] Educational Service Officer

maybe they have Honda cabs in New York! I dunno. Never been to New York City proper. I was happy to know it was for me when the little cabby said, "You wan' go Beeoookue?"

"You betcha!" I started throwing luggage into the back seat. "How much to go to the BOQ?" *Oh Boy! The cab was warm!*

"Five dolla!"

"You got it."

I threw my gear in the back seat, climbed into the front passenger seat. *Where's the heater's blast?*

"Let's go."

The driver drove one-half block, turned left, drove three blocks, turned right, and drove one-half block stopping in front of a brightly-lit concrete building with a wooden porch. The driver jumped out. I waited figuring he was picking up another fare. I sat there, *just a-suckin' up the heat like a terrapin turtle on a pitch-pine log in a Louisiana bayou!*

"Beeoookue here" he said, opening the back door and grabbing luggage the same size as he was.

Damn! *Damn!* I coulda walked it. That blasted clerk . . . No. What the hell . . . he had been right. All that luggage. It was worth the five bucks. I was going to get a warm bed! *Maybe!*

I slipped the driver a fiver. No tip. The book says no tipping. Had not entered my mind anyway. Four blocks for five bucks. Twelve blocks is a mile. One-third a mile $5, one mile $15. 10 miles $150. Wow! Counts up. *No problem! I'm freezing my butt off.*

No problem checking into the BOQ. $12 for a suite with kitchen. Free coffee. A microwave oven in the kitchen with microwave popcorn in a basket atop it. Big color television. VCR. 100 first run movies obtainable at the front desk: no charge. Sitting room, bedroom, toilet articles (plastic razor, tooth paste, tooth brush, shaving cream, shampoo, soap, ironing board, hair dryer . . . $12. *Not bad.* Outside the gates, in a Japanese hotel, the room would run an easy $150 *dolla! I do not how many yen.*

I locked the door, dumped the luggage in a corner, shook my clothes off fast as a two-dollar failed-member of the sisterhood, climbed into a sweat pants and a cotton pull over, pulled on a stocking cap and jumped into bed. Reached over to the nightstand for my gloves, put them on. The bed was *cold* . . . then it wasn't so cold . . . then it . . . became . . . warrmmm . . .*Gung Ho!*

Chapter 3

"This officer should go far,
And the sooner he starts the better."
Officer's fitness report

I slept poorly. Dozed off right away—then awoke every couple of hours. Peculiar . . . because I was cold, tired, and bedraggled when I turned in. Maybe too tired. *Naw! Probably the animal/hunter/warrior instinct; just the man-animal protecting his* . . . Gave up my day/night dreaming around 0500, crawled out of the bed, a bed not a rack—this wasn't a rack—a rack is a military bunk, usually stacked two high, consisting of a thin cotton mattress resting on a wire base held to a steel frame by little springs around the perimeter. The steel frame, railings, and headboard were just the things to hit one's head and elbows when tossing around. This was not a rack, but a big, old soft bed; how do they expect anyone, especially an ex-Marine, to sleep all smothered down in a soft bed. Made my back hurt. *—Course anything I sleep on lately makes my back hurt. Forget that.* I stumbled into the bathroom, splashed cold water on my face, shivering looked in the mirror. My eyes looked like disgusting brown plankton mired in gray quicksand. Old brown eyes. *"Beautiful, beautiful brown eyes, I'll never love blue eyes again."* Remember that song from the forties. *Old Blue eyes—Frank Sinatra.* Why do people think of weird things when looking in the mirror? *Wish I had blue eyes.* Why? *I dunno.*

Bathroom lights are merciless. Like those in department store dressing rooms. I do not go into those changing rooms anymore—not because I might chance upon a pervert—it is just that I cannot look at myself in those mirrors. Having been such a good-looking dude in high school, I expect to see John Derrick in the reflection, but what I get is Lou Costello! I pushed at the bags under my eyes; it must have been the wind last night or maybe from being awake so long, maybe the cold. I do not know. I felt lousy. I am beginning to think that the sole purpose in my life is simply to serve as a warning to others.

The rooms were cold. The surface of my skin was cold; I didn't feel cold inside, but I wasn't warm enough to sleep comfortably—that probably was the problem . . . then my teeth started chattering like castanets played by a female Patagonian Seventh-Day-Adventist doing the Flamenco at a pineapple convention. I was as frigid as a frog in a winter pond. While the coffee was perking—real coffee, not those instant crystal things— I took advantage of my college education and vast experience by figuring out that if this was a dwelling the builders may have anticipated it may get cold in the winter and just may have installed a heating thing . . . machine? . . . unit? So I searched and found the thermostat on the wall fooling around with it. Something clicked, then a clank, a fan started up and, before you could say the *sick sixth sheik's sick sixth sheep* half-a-dozen times the room warmed a degree or so.

A fossilized, misshapen doughnut was sought out amid the tattered remains of an old restaurant napkin in a side pocket of my camera bag and, fortified with hot caffeine and this stale patisserie, life began to have a flicker of interest; not much mind you, but I was beginning to feel less like a sick oyster at low tide. It was still dark and cold as government charity outside: nothing seemed to be going on—no Marines running, taking their early morning ritual of torturing the ol' bod into shape while shouting cadence and little Boy Scout ditties to keep in step:

"Model A Ford
And a tank full of gas
Mouth full of pussy
And a hand full of Ass!"

The Marines always did like refined music and a good song.

Peered out a window.

Nope.

Nobody about.

Dark.

All the pogey-bait[1] sailors still in their racks even as late as 0600. *Burning daylight* as Dad used to say when he was trying to get my brother and me up to go to work at the lumber mill. Well . . . it was not daylight yet in the Land of the Rising Sun, but there was a red lobster

[1] Candy bar.

glow in the eastern sky. These guys were going to sleep the day away. They needed Dad to sing his little wake-up song he warbled for me, my brother-in-law Ted, a couple of cousins, and my brother Bud each dark, mountain morning, getting us up for a substantial breakfast and a day at the lumber mill.

"Come on boys, hit the rock,
It ain't daylight, but it's four-o'clock;
I know you're tired, and sleepy too,
I don't want you, but the Big Boss do!"

He only sang the ditty once; you didn't get up, next was a teaspoon of water in the ear. He was not actually sadistic; he just wasn't going to fool around with a bunch of lummoxes' who'd laid out the night before chasing girls and drinking two-point beer. Hell! . . . he'd go to bed at eight. We'd come in boisterously at two, gnashing gears and revving those 1950 Ford V-Eight's, stomping across the porch like a herd of wildebeests . . . an' he'd come in at six singing that song with a big grin on his face. I loved him. Maybe he was sadistic. When my kids were in grammar school, I would do the same to them. I suffered. Why shouldn't they? Why should they get off?

I dug some dirty clothing crushed into one of my bags: a shirt, socks, and underwear and took them to the free washer and dryer across the hall from my room. Bought fifty cents worth of washing powder from a wall dispenser throwing the whole lot into the machine: brown, white, blue. What the hell! I'm not married. Anyone comments on the strange combination of colors, I just tell 'em that the laundry did it.

Just inside the door to my room was a notebook sheet size plastic covered notice:

*****

Commander Fleet Activities, Yokosuka
Naval Base, Japan
Welcome Aboard
**

The Land of the Rising Sun
**

Yokoso Yokosuka **to Yokosuka)**

Welcome to the fleet activities, Yokosuka, (BQ). The Yokosuka BQ is one of the finest in the navy. It was built and furnished for the sole purpose of providing the best living accommodations and services to you, ensuring that your stay in Japan is a pleasant and enjoyable one.

*****

Yeah! Thanks.

At 06:30, outside was growing light and inside, my stomach that is, it was already light—as in "empty light"—and, taking precedence over every other part of the ol' body, cold or no cold, it led me downstairs. They say his dick leads a guy through life; that may be true, but only after he has eaten and scratched for awhile. The yeoman behind the counter directed me to the Officer's Club just a two-block walk away, a stroll in the fresh air across brown, frost-tipped grass.

"Yeah! It was open this early."

All bundled up, I stepped out on the porch into the dawn-night cold, my frozen breath pointing the way. A torpid-dark sludge of clouds seeps across the moon, itself a clumsy oyster in a sea of brilliant diamonds. Gawking, I took in the whitewashed buildings in parade file, the neatly manicured grounds leading to darkened, emerald-green mountains: a Japanese watercolor and only I was about to enjoy it. As my boots crunched on the protesting grass, I began to think I might live. It was going to be a beautiful morning. I began to feel fresh and alive . . . and hungry!

The Officers Club's coffeepot was smoking, and the colorfully designed menu offered brown waffles stacked in syrupy piles mounded with golden globs of butter . . . *umm-um!* The picture looked so damn good; I almost ate the menu! Prices: Tenderloin of beef with two eggs, coffee, hash browns: $3.50. Creamed beef on toast: $1.95. Boy! Are they polite. In the Navy it is "creamed" or "chipped" beef on toast. In the Marines, this expeditious dish is christened with the label of "Shit on a Shingle." Not a military man alive has not heard of this rib-sticking gourmet treat: hard, thin, dry toast from yesterday, roofed with a dirty-white milk gravy and blackened-tattered hamburger meat liberally sprinkled with black pepper; makes my mouth water just to think of it.

Feasting on a lovely breakfast of Eggs Benedict, toast, jam, juice and coffee—delicious—for $3.25, I was taken aback to read on the bill "No tipping allowed." *No Tipping! Boy! In Old Sacramento the restaurant owners would hang the manager of this place to one of the old-*

fashioned street lights! Tip: To Insure Prompt Service. *Tips!* I wrote a little book once called *A Journey to Egypt.*[2] Not a very good book—rather amateurish—but it was a first attempt. The cover does have a beautiful photograph that I took of four feluccas sailing on the Nile. On page 29 of the little book, there is a faultfinding minor paragraph on tipping and service charges:

". . . service charge of 12 percent. Let us talk about 'service charge's.' Service charges are endemic in many countries outside the USA. I never knew what to make of a service charge. I mean 'Are they charging you for waiting on you, for the service?' Isn't that what restaurant employees are supposed to do? You go in, purchase a meal for a price. Then the food is brought to you. They bring the food to you; they wait on you; they service you. That is why you go there in the first place; you do not want to wait on yourself. I think that a service charge is just another way to transfer more money from the customer's pocket to someone else's without really providing anything in return.

"In some countries, there is a 15% service charge, then a government 10% tax! Then a tip! And then there is the value-added tax! 'What's up with that?' as Cliff on Cheers might say. In Mexico, people call this insidious practice, 'El Rip-Off.' In southern Mexico they call it, 'El Rip-Off, You aalll!'

"This insidious practice is spreading like army ants in California, creeping in on little pernicious feet. I had occasion to take a high class person of the female persuasion, along with a buddy and his 'Latest in a Series' to a local restaurant in Sacramento that had on the menu a 20% gratuity charge right up front! In other words, the customers are informed—in writing—that they are going to be charged an extra 20% to eat here. Now, to me, a gratuity is a favor or a gift, usually in the form of money, and it is given—notice the term—given in return for service. The key word here is GIVEN! I get service, I like it. I decide to give a gratuity. The customers in this restaurant are charged before they eat.

"Upon beholding this preamble on a ersatz-leather menu the size of a beach towel, I inquired of 'Service Person'—they do not have waiters anymore—I asked the Service Person, 'What does this mean?'

"Speaking through lips hindered by rings of steel—I don't believe the kid could blink because of the weight of the metal in his eyebrows and he definitely was going to have Ubangi earlobes because of the weight they were carrying around—he replied, ' . . . that since tips were often unequal among the 'service personnel', the establishment (restaurant) decided to charge the tip up front and distribute it later to the service personnel!

"He ended with a chicken-shit smile, having explained to the old geezer the facts of life.

---

[2] *Journey To Egypt.* James A. Gunn. Morris Publishing 1999. Pg. 29

"Well . . .!' I said, in my best Ronald Reagan drawl. 'What if I may not want to give a tip? I mean what if the service is bad? I might want to experience the service . . . you know . . . see if it's worth 20%.' I ended with a county grin to let him know I was a good-ol' boy.

"'It is a gratuity Sir! If you want, you can give a tip.' A tinge, just a nuance of irritation shadowed the statement that had nothing to do with the question.

"'No it isn't' I pointed to the menu. 'See. It says upfront. I believe that is a charge. A gratuity comes after . . . '

"I do not want to bore you with the ensuing details. Being an anthropologist and budding writer, I sometimes am stuck on details such as the real meaning of words and the artificial fallacious reasoning of society.

"The Big Service Person—whom I will call the manager—was brought into the conversation with me and metal mouth, the Service Person whom I will call The Waiter. After a brief interchange, very mannerly on both sides, our foursome was allowed—much to the consternation of The Latest in a Series—to depart the eatery without a service charge (We did drink some water and nibbled on a few breadsticks). I was happy to leave. My buddy didn't care. He's known me for forty years."

However, his companion of the evening took umbrage saying, "That's how they make up for their poor salaries!"

"I replied to her that if we had spent, say $120 for wine and dinner and 20% of that a $24 service charge, then a tip, which customers usually leave even though there is a service charge, of . . . say . . . 20% (that's what Oprah suggests) another $24 . . . we would be shelling out $48 in addition to the price of the food AND tax. Now I do not believe the waiters or, even if you want to call them Service Persons, is going to get that extra moola. "Let the restaurant owner pay a decent salary, give em a raise, put the raise in the price of the meal, then let the customer decide if the service is worth a tip—but don't con me out of dinero I do not feel justified in spending" I told her. It was a charge, I tried to empress on her dim-witted-little-mind. I do not want to be charged to eat; I only want to be charged for what I eat!

Ms. the Latest in a Series said she was embarrassed. I noticed she did not offer to pay however."

The last time I was embarrassed was when Nixon was elected president.

No. That is not entirely true.

I feel embarrassed everytime I watch Oprah.

The Officer's club was well laid out, a place for a band and a sunken dance floor that doubled for evening dinning. All the tables were covered with spotlessly white cloths; a vase of silk flowers decorated the center. Japanese civilian ladies short, dumpy and smiling, did the serving with gracious friendliness.

Mr. Stomach, now comfortably content with Mr. E. Benedict, stopped making a nuisance of itself to the rest of the body, leaving it free to stroll around and enjoy the warming invigorating air and farm-fresh morning smells. Hoarfrost still tipped the winter-brown grass, but the early sun was friendly, melting the nip out of the air. The gate the bus entered the navel base last night is named the Womble Gate—I could not find the meaning of 'Womble'—and is one block from the BOQ. That sixty-year old bus driver passed right by it last night. Only one block! Had I mentioned to the driver what I was looking for last evening, he may have dropped me at the BOQ. Live and learn.

Using a "welcome" map that was included in the toilet articles from my room, I walked north on Nimitz Boulevard, the main thoroughfare running the length of the base. With the help of a young female M. P., I took a right turn on Howard Street down to Truman Bay to berth 12. There she/it was: the largest ship in the harbor, the *United States Ship Independence Carrier Vehicle number 62*. When I first saw the gray, box-like carrier, I was not terribly impressed. Later, I was impressed by the people I would eventually meet on her such as Chaplain Derek Ross who would teach a chapter on religion in one of my anthropology classes; I would meet Chief Boatswain Bob Yoder who would become a good friend, and Eric Klinker, a young man, wise beyond his years. He and I would drive the Outback of Australia together. On the *USS Abraham Lincoln*, I made no friends, here, many.

The original *Independence,* was a flat-bottomed steamboat that appeared in American history on the Missouri River before the Civil War, around 1819, taking settlers' west as well as handling timber, grain, fur, and coal. The present-day *USS Independence* (CV-62) was commissioned in January 1959 at the New York Naval Shipyard. With a length of 1,070 feet (more than three football fields), a flight deck 4.1 acres, and a height from keel to mast of 229 feet, she compares favorably in size with the new nuclear carriers of today and could easily transport, on the flight and hanger decks, half a hundred or more of the original 1819 *Independence*. The *Indy,* as the crew calls her, is conventionally powered: that means she burns oil for fuel instead of uranium. She has four main engines supplying heat to eight boilers producing steam to turn four 21-foot propellers at a speed of 30+ knots. That is like moving my hometown of Placerville—population 4,800 when I was in highschool—over forty miles per hour. Not only is the *Indy* large enough to move the people, it could load on their furniture and cars. The first time I saw the *USS Abraham Lincoln* was at

Alameda Naval Station in San Francisco Bay as she was loading the 3,500 ship's crew's automobiles, motorhomes, ski boats other assorted vehicles onto the flight deck and the hanger deck preparatory to taking them to Everett, Washington the *Lincoln's* new home port.

Checking onto the *Indy* was accomplished with dispatch. I was right when I decided not attempt to check in late last night. The duty officer—a slim, lieutenant wearing winter blues—said he was ashore; he was permanent personnel and lived in housing off the base. No one else was expecting me, the duty officer would had to telephone him—if the phone worked—then find a place for me . . . I'm glad I stayed ashore. He looked at my orders, giving me a temporary pass, later the ESO would order an eliminated card with a photograph of my mug on it to dangle from the left shirt pocket and, when I was officially signed aboard, handed me a printed welcome by the Captain:

From the Commanding Officer
USS Independence

On behalf of the more than 5,000 Sailors and Marines serving on the INDEPENDENCE, the U.S. navy's oldest active-duty ship, "Welcome Aboard Freedoms Flagship!" USS INDEPENDENCE (CV 62) is the United States navy's only forward deployed aircraft carrier and flagship for Commander, Carrier Group FIVE/Battle Force SEVENTH Fleet in Yokosuka, Japan.

A mobile airfield that's able to travel more than 500 miles (800 kilometers) a day, INDEPENDENCE is a completely self-contained city with aircraft repair centers, electric and steam power plants, medical and dental facilities and even a radio and television station. More than 70 aircraft of Carrier Air Wing FIVE provide INDEPENDENCE with awesome striking power and tactical flexibility, making her one of the most powerful weapons systems in the world today.

What we hope you remember most after your visit is that it takes well trained people with exceptional skills to bring this mass of steel to life. Young, dedicated, hardworking Sailors and Marines are Indy's lifeblood. They have volunteered to serve their country, and are proud of the role they play in the United States navy and Marine Corps.

Captain Tom S. Fellin
Commanding Officer

USS Independence (CV 62)

***

The duty officer summoned the Educational Service Officer right away. Remembering my battle getting luggage aboard the *Vinson*, I wisely left my bags at the BOQ figuring since the ship wasn't sailing for a couple of days, I might find an easier way of laboriously lugging luggage.

LTJG Rey Salvador Corpus, the ESO promptly appeared. Not a tall man, about 5'6", dark-hair, with a pleasing manner, Lt. Corpus took me in hand to the officer's mess to acquaint me with the schedule of the day, then to settle in. Since the ESO could not secure me a bunk right away, I decided to stay ashore one more night at the comfortable BOQ, sightsee a bit, and watch a few movies. It was fortunate I had used the ol' noggin the previous night in not trying to come aboard; no one would have been available who knew what to do with me.

As I was leaving the gangplank (brow) I stopped to watch a 10-story crane, painted blue, with a man in a little yellow control booth about 25 stories up, swinging the boom around. The operator up in his little tower was dancing that Godzilla crane around like a sixth grader playing with an Erector set. The refrigerator-size yellow hook of the crane was connected to four steel cables by tough webbing slung under the belly of a AV-Harrier airplane. The Harrier dangling about twenty feet off the ground resembled a Mattel toy model. I watched fascinated as the crane swung the warplane around—the plane's wheels were in the down position—and lowered it onto a flatbed tractor-trailer. Just to the rear of berth 12, where the *Indy* was docked, a short two-lane road lead into a tunnel cut into the hillside at the junction of Howard and Isherwood Streets. After the jet was unleased from the crane to the truck, and lashed down by three dockmen scurrying around, the semi-flatbed, spewing thick, black smoke from its twin stacks, crawled into the tunnel. I attempted to peer into the tunnel but was hampered by fearsome looking MP's from crossing the ribboned-off boundaries set strung across the roadway diverting traffic. I could see fifty or so yards into the blackness but could see no light inside. I assumed it was a regular thoroughfare to the other side of the mountain. The topography of what land area I saw so far was steep with little flat land in sight. Later, looking at a map, I saw that the base is honeycombed with miles of traffic tunnels. I suspected, and later my conjecture was confirmed, that these tunnels, impervious to shellfire and bombs, were originally dug during World War II and used to hide and transport ammunition, weapons, and troops. This particular tunnel went through one hill, came out the other side, then dived into another hill. On the other side of this small mountain, was located the naval maintenance shops at the edge of Tokyo Bay. This whole area must have been an important military site during World War II.

The AV-8 Harrier II is a vertical lift attack warplane used primary by the Marine Corps for close support of amphibious operations. It has a Pegasus vectored-thrust turbofan that can lift the plane straight up. They are terribly, terrifically noisy: on the *USS Peleliu* some months later, one lifting off made glassware dance three levels down drowning out conversation. The harrier first saw service for the navy in 1984 and is still a valuable tool today.

I was delighted to be aboard a ship such as the *Indy*. When I was a junior high school teacher, I used to stand on the ramp enjoying the sunshine while noisy students passed from classes, wishing that I were somewhere adventurous, on the Amazon River, trekking, or sailing at sea. However, like many husbands, wives—parents, I had obligations—a family to raise—limited funds, a home, and family to care for and who cared for me. Now, all that was past. I now *did* have the adventure; I have been on the Amazon in a wooden boat; I have been trekking and rode elephants in the Highlands of Northern Thailand; and I've sailed the seas in a sailboat as well as the biggest, most expensive warships in the world; and, moderately, have fraternized with not a few comely females. A full family life or a full adventurous life. Unfortunately, one does not seem to be able to have both. As Herodotus said: " . . . human happiness never remains long in the same place."[3]

Although the *Independence* was to depart Yokosuka within three days, not much was going on—to my surprise. Hardly anyone was aboard and, knowing I was going to be aboard for sometime, I left the ship for a look-see around the docks.

Across forty yards of oil-rainbow-streaked sea, at berth 11, a black ominous form lay low in the water—a submarine. I knew that it was not nuclear despite the absence of markings; it was too small and, besides, the Japanese do not allow nuclear vessels within its sea limits. I always find submarines foreboding looking. This one had no visible markings, no name, no numbers designation who it belonged to,

---

[3] Herodotus. The Histories. Oxford University Press, 1998. Book One, pg. 5

what type it was, or where it was from. A long, ebony metal shark, it was motionless in the blackened water as if in ambush, waiting for something, some expected prey, the conning tower dorsal fin ready to split the sea in its search for victims. There was no movement, no people about this silent killer. Surface ships seem to be alive, the foam in their teeth, winds in their sails, dashing across sun-silver seas, fighting gales with courage or gliding across calm, gentle swells with serenity. However, they are not really one with the sea, but rather always in contest with the mighty oceans: fighting, adjusting, dying. As Joseph Conrad writes in The Sea and Sailors:[4]

"The sea—this truth must be confessed—has no generosity. No display of manly qualities—courage, hardihood, endurance, faithfulness—has ever been known to touch its irresponsible consciousness of power. The ocean has the conscienceless temper of a savage autocrat spoiled by much adulation. He cannot brook the slightest appearance of defiance, and has remained the irreconcilable enemy of ships and men ever since ships and men had the unheard-of audacity to go afloat together in the face of his frown. From that day he has gone on swallowing up fleets and men without his resentment being glutted by the number of victims—by so many wrecked ships and wrecked lies. Today, as ever, he is ready to beguile and betray, to smash and to drown the incorrigible optimism of man . . . If not always in the hot mood to smash, he is always stealthily ready for a drowning. The most amazing wonder of the deep is its unfathomable cruelty."

Submarines, however, belong to the watery element: when the sea roars and rages like a wild beast in its terrible anger, the submersible seeks safety inside the womb of the seas, down to Davy Jones's deadly locker where it is dark, cold, silent . . . here, like a black shark, the submarine lurks, stealthily silent, waiting to kill. Reminded me of the fearsome African crocodiles lying submerged in muddy shore water up to their eye orbs, waiting for the luckless deer or wildebeest—or woman or young child—to take a sip. Then a swift terrible lunge. A slow choking death follows. Same with the killer submarine. Silent. Ominous. Dangerous.

On the other side of the submarine, a Japanese frigate was being serviced by men dressed head to toe in red suits looking much like ski togs. A frigate is slightly larger than a destroyer—a warship of 4,000 to 9,000 tons water displacement. They are used primarily for escort duty for protection of shipping (POS) missions, as Anti-Submarine Warfare

---

[4] *The Mirror of the Sea* by Joseph Conrad

(ASW) combatants for amphibious expeditionary forces, underway supply ships, and merchant convoys. They are high-speed and very maneuverable. This frigate was flying the flag of the Rising Sun with its round red ball and rays shooting out. The flag is still distasteful to me; I had seen that flag as a child in a dozen war movies in the forties, always surrounded by a bunch of Banzai, eye-glass wearing, blood-crazed Japanese soldiers bent on doing in Errol Flynn or John Garfield or sticking a bayonet into hapless Chinese women and babies. Of course, it *was* the movies and the United States had a pretty good propaganda machine at the time—it sure worked on me.[5]

Howard Street, where I was gawking around, ended at dry-dock number one. The dry-dock was empty of water allowing a view of its sides and bottom that were paved with cut stones in a stepped "V" shape. Resting on a wheeled, low-lying steel platform was a small Japanese gunboat—about a forty-footer—draped over with blue plastic tarps, undergoing bottom painting. When the workmen finished with the boat, the sea would be pumped into the dry-dock and the gunboat floated out pulled by lines attached to a mechanical mule—a small, usually electric tractor or locomotive used for hauling over short distances. An ingenious method for working on boats, but hardly new: the Phoenicians used the same methods, as did the Egyptians transporting huge monoliths by barge on the Nile.[6] These were powered by electricity, the Phoenicians and Egyptians used muscle power.

A dry-dock uses pumps to displace water to fill or empty the cavity of a dry-dock. In London, England, the wet-dock is used extensively. A wet-dock does not use pumps to fill and empty the dock. There, where the height of the tide is more than 3 meters, the vessel is brought into dock at high tide, put on a trolley or blocked up, and when the high tide recedes the boat is left high and dry and bottom work can begin. A gate, mechanical or hydraulic, is used to keep the ocean at bay until repairs or remodeling are completed. The combined length of quays[7] and piers in London—one of the world's great sea-faring nations—amounts to approximately 50 miles.

Just outside the Howard Street dry-docks, across part of Truman Bay, about three hundred yards away, a long, gray slender shape slid

[5] The Mirror of the Sea by Joseph Conrad

[6] See "Journey to Egypt" by James A. Gunn, Morris Pub. 1999.

[7] Quay: A structure parallel to the shoreline.

into view, its keen, knife-edge bow slicing the blue-gray water like a farmer's plow turning back gray sod. It was an American frigate. I wasn't able to make out neither bow numbers nor the name. Not a soul was in sight aboard her,[8] and no lights, no windows—it was a colorless ghost ship: projecting a semblance of lifelessness, it was enigmatic, dangerous.

I gawked on down Howard Street that I knew—from my little BOQ map—circled back toward the main gate and my quarters. Parked along the way was a white van about six feet long; it looked like a child's toy—great for getting around town. The Japanese are the world's leader in producing small cars: small cars, small people, large gasoline prices.

Glancing away from the bay toward the skyline of downtown Yokosuka, my eye was caught by a totally out-of-place object; there, standing about six stories high, gleaning white, her book clutched in one arm, the other holding aloft a flaming torch, was the Statue of Liberty! An exact smaller copy. Later, I asked around; no one knew why it was there. I would discover another, albeit considerably shorter, in Guam. I never did find out what the story was on either one.

Suddenly it popped into my thinking: it was February 14, Valentines Day. Hard not to realize it for in store window after store window there were reminders just like at home: big red hearts, Valentine bunnies for your sweetie, gaily wrapped boxes of candy. What the heck was going on? This is *Japan*! I discovered later, after talking to a couple of guys who lived in Japan full time with Japanese wives, that the Japanese, ever the astute business people, have absorbed many American customs and at Christmas time stores resounded with *Jingle Bells, Silent Night* and *Rudolph the Red-Nosed Reindeer!* Later that night I heard a Japanese female singer passionately blasting out *I Saw Mommy Kissing Santa C'ause* with all her might omitting all the L's and a few other consonants. It was certainly a different rendition, but enjoyable.

To celebrate Saint Valentine's Day—that has come to represent the union of love and lovers—I stopped in at a fast food place on the waterfront. Actually, I probably would have stopped whether it had been Valentine's Day or not. This antiseptically place was run by a tall skinny Japanese guy about 22 and two younger looking females. The only difference between a similar place at home was the oversized de-

[8] Americans give the female gender to their ships; Russians the male gender. Strange!

pictions of cups of coffee and other drinks here were spelled out in Japanese characters. (Collectors take note: I have seen Coca-Cola bottles labeled in over thirty languages. I started to collect them once upon a time, got to two bottles, one in Arabic and one in French, before I gave it up: too heavy to carry around. Besides, I reduced my collection by 50% one night when, desert thirsty and the only other liquid in the disreputable room I was in came tepid and rusty dribbles from the tap, I drank the French Coke—I never did drink the Arabic one. I was afraid of the water and Arab sanitary practices. I gave it to Gary, my son-in-law). The young man behind the counter took my photo and let me take his, but when I attempted to use the camera on the two girls, they ducked down behind the counter squealing and giggling, covering their mouths with cupped hands.

After sipping an icy coke—it tasted amazingly the same as the French and Americans ones—*how do they do that?* —I sauntered along the Nimitz Boulevard to the main gate and the BOQ, but, not yet ready to go in, I nodded to the smartly dressed Marine at the gate and turning right crossed the boulevard to a small shopping area. It was a typical small town with a four or five block commercial core that seems to grow around the entrance to most military bases. I've seen the same junky stores at Oceanside, California, Bremerton, Washington and a half-dozen other military municipalities around the world: lots of small one-person shops selling belt buckles and caps, all kinds of military gear and China-junk souvenirs. Prices were high, higher than at home on *everything*. Not having purchased anything, I stopped at a hole-in-the-wall restaurant for a not large bowl of rice and a Coke: price $7.20 US. Worth about $2.50 at home. What a difference from when I was in Sasebo, Japan in 1954; the same plate of rice would have cost less than fifty cents. The dollar then, just at the end of the Korean Conflict, traded at 365 yen; today it trades at 120 yen to the dollar. I wondered what a full dinner and a night on the town would set a sailor back? There is an old Jewish saying: *"What is the proper time to eat? If rich, when you will; if poor when you afford it."* Well . . . I was not poor, but I *can* eat on the base and after that exorbitant dine out encounter, I decided to chow down on the base in the future. Seven bucks for a handful of rice in a country that grows the stuff like a south Texas town grows sagebrush. Gimme a break! *AT least there was no gratuity or value-added tax!*

Both stomach and mind disappointed with the civilian commercial offerings of the place; any commercial center holds little interest for me, I decided to get back to the base. A small, somewhat run down park was near the edge of the commercial district, right near the water. Walking over to look at the civilian boats tied up along the small pier, I discovered a shrine of black-speckled granite with an 18 by 24 inch framed photograph of an old-fashioned Japanese battle ship circa World War II. On a ledge beneath the photograph, a handful of fresh cut flowers lay, pinks, yellows, whites, in a cone of white paper decorated with Japanese lettering. Someone paying respect and love to one's lost in the idiocy of war.

Suddenly, without warning, fatigue hit me. I was tired. A tad of jet lag? I do not know. Making my way through the main gate with no problem with my orders, I pressed on to the BOQ, picking up a video on the way at the main desk titled *Independence Day*, a science fiction movie about blowing up the White House and everything else in the country. I would watch it after dinner. Hit the sack early.

The menu at the Officer's Club boasts an extensive dinner selection. I was surprised there were so few diners; probably the personnel living off-base were home and the ship's crew ate on the boat. I ordered a nice thick steak with big crusty onion rings and a bang-up salad—$4.95. No tax, no tip. No gratuity. No smart-assed "Service Person." The steak was large, barbecue-charred with enough carbon on the outside to pave eight feet of artery, and savory juicy red on the inside. It was a south Texas three-toothpick steak. *What is a three-toothpick steak?* It's one that takes three toothpicks to clean you teeth after eating it. What is a toothpick called in Naval jargon? Obvious: It is a "wood interdential stimulator." The onion rings were rolled in dough and deep-fried in a vat of boiling lard—probably not too many calories there, and the salad was of course fat free—some cut up lettuce, baby tomatoes, young carrots, couple pieces of cucumber topped off with some bacon bits and croutons. I crumbled on a chunk of blue cheese and a glob of Thousand Island Dressing made of mayonnaise, chili sauce, and seasonings. Didn't look like it weighed much—couple of ounces maybe. A good solid meal. Healthy. I wanted to keep the fat calories down per my daughter's instructions. *How do ounces of calorie metamorphosize into pounds of fat?*

I chomped and chewed, content as a white-faced heifer in tall clover, while listening to Jo Stafford belt out *Jambalaya* on the free jukebox. Peculiarly the Japanese, like the Egyptians, play a lot of American tunes popular in the fifties, not the forties, nor the sixties or seventies, but the fifties. Good swing dance music. Thailand also. In

Nongkhai, Thailand, two years later, I was at the top of the Nongkhai Royal Hotel having a beer while catching up on notes. It was about eight in the evening and two young Thai guys were playing country western music, twanging away on guitars bigger than they were. The lithe, lovely Thai waitresses were wearing bulky, ill fitting Levi's and red-and-white checked lumber shirts; someone's off-the-wall idea of a western theme. They were not comical, just sad looking—they are so beautiful in their traditional skirts and bodice—and to put them in Paul Bunyan's hand-me-downs is akin to painting a Greek marble statue with bright acrylic paints, something I have seen the Arabs do. In Beverly Hills, there is a fenced, gated mansion with green lawns, reproductions of Greek and Roman marble statues, and Greco-Roman architecture. An ex-movie-great manor. Beautiful in it's simplicity, like a beautiful woman wearing an elegant simple black dress with little jewelry. Well . . . after an Arab gentleman purchased it, he decided to spruce it up a bit: the white stucco fence was painted pink, the marble statues were re-clothed in acrylic gowns of blue, greens and lavender; crimson adorned curving stone lips and cheek, and eyebrows painted black! Even pubic hair was painted on. Gross!

Everyone to his or her own taste said the man as he kissed a cow!

After the Thai duo finished Jambalaya, they started in on *Lost in Lodi Again!* For you people in the east and the mid-west who are not country-western fans—I'm not either—Lodi is a small town just south of Sacramento, California's state capitol. Known as a grape-growing center in the hot Sacramento Valley, Lodi, . . . Well! . . . That's about it, Lodi grows grapes. Drunk—or sober for that matter—and in *Lodi . . . again* . . .is no one's idea of R&R.[9] Beer in hand, I walked over, said *Sawadee Krop* (Hello) engaging the Buddhist git-pickers in conversation. They had never heard of Lodi, had no idea it was a town, in fact, they weren't quite sure where California was. But, they sure did a good job on the song. Learned it phonetically.

After finishing my three-tooth picker steak at the restaurant, I engaged in smiling good-byes to the diminutive waitresses following my appeased tummy to the BQ. Jet lag and lack of sleep were eroding the ol' body that used to pole vault twelve feet in high school; now climbing two feet onto the bed was the physical event of the day. As Bob Hope once said, *"I don't have to jog: I just sit up in the morning and my flab does it all by itself!"*

---

[9] Rest and recuperation.

Watched a bit of the alien's lasering the hell out of Washington, toasting the White House before blowing it to smithereeens. Too bad a couple of our ex-presidents weren't there at the time; they would have been, as they say in south Texas, *"disconceited real fast!"* Speaking about the controversy on aliens. I know that there are some around. I have seen them. Go into any bar in Los Angeles after midnight; you'll find them all over the place.

Watching the movie *Independence Day*, brought to mind another science fiction movie *Contact,* staring Jodie foster based on a book by Carl Sagan. In this science fantasy, little Jodie is looking for extra-terrestrials as in, *ET Come Home*! And when evidence of extrater-restrials is discovered, everybody in the film jumped around in excite-ment, happy as a South Georgia cracker in hot pursuit of a female cousin with a reasonable prospect of overtaking her. (One Georgia farm lad was asked what kind of girl he wanted. He said, " . . . it don't matter none, long as she wasn't part of the 'emeegite' family." I think he was one of the ejits my Mom knew so much about.) The American Indians got all happy when Columbus dropped in on the beach as did the Aztecs did when Ol' Cortez rode up. Big Mistakes by the indigents. Even the Incas whooped it up at first when Francisco Pizarro dropped in, but changed their minds later when his men boiled a couple of the locals to get grease to shine up the soldier's rusty breastplates!

Do you see what I am getting at here?

There are 400,000,000,000 suns in our Milky Way galaxy; and there are 50,000,000,000 galaxies give or take half-a-dozen. Now, given the number of stars in the galaxies and what we know about planet formation, the probability of intelligent life existing elsewhere in the universe, even in our own galaxy, is a statistical certainty. Given the immense distance between the stars, it is probable that there is no one else—life—within a thousand-light years of Earth. Therefore, hope-fully, nobody from *out there* will come nosing around misnaming us Indians, Kotozens, or Klingons. That is probably just as well for us for ,given the lessons taught by Columbus, Cortez, and Pizarro . . . Well! . . . You can figure out what is going to happen when those maybe-not-so-good-ol'-boy aliens land here! Some Seven-Day Adventists are going to run out throwing down the welcoming mat and immediately start to convert someone or something 13, 783 and 1/2 years old, hol-lerin' at them to join up with J. C. and the Boys. Benny Hinn is going to reach out with his collection buckets yelling "Heal!" "Heal!" (Give MONEY!) then some Pecker Head from Shitville High school yell

"I doen wanna any green-headed three-armed Ail-yen marrying up with LuLu-belle where's my shotgun Billy-Joe-Bob?"

Hell! We cannot even get along with half the world and ourselves now! We had a Civil War and killer a few hundred thousand of our own folk! The Muslins are fighting the Jews, the Irish the English, the Turks the Kurds, and Saddam everybody else. Remember that old saying: *"You'd better be careful what you ask for, you might get it."* Let E.T. *stay* home in the first place, then he/it/she will not *have* to go home again. I, for one, do not want to wind up on some alien's menu.

Before bed, I decided to drop a line to Dr. Sherry Bates, the administrator who arranged for me to come over here; I thought I would kid her a bit. She told me to keep her informed.

So:

Dear Dr. Bates:

I made it to Japan okay—just an hour late. Someone had efficiently put my name down on the bus list; I assume it was you. The navy hasn't been very friendly to me however. On my way to the Independence, I picked up a bedraggled seagull smeared with oil. As I walked up the brow, the Officer of the Day said to me: "You can't bring that filthy hog aboard ship!"
"I said that it wasn't a hog, but a seagull.
He said, "I know. I was talking to the seagull!"

Happy Valentines Day

Lord Jim

I went to bed.

****

COMMAND HISTORY

USS Independence CV-62 was commissioned as a "Forrestal Class" attack aircraft carrier (CVA-62) at the Brooklyn Naval Shipyard, on January 10, 1959. She is the fifth U.S. Navy ship to bear the name *Independence.*

Since her commissioning, "Freedom's Flagship" has been on the cutting edge in projecting naval air power and protecting U.S. national interests around the globe. Called on by President John F. Kennedy during the 1962 Cuban missile crisis, *Independence* provided a strong, visible reminder of U.S. determination and resolve as a key participant in the U.S. naval blockade of Cuba.

In 1964, the ship deployed for more than seven months, including 100 days in the South China Sea off the coast of Vietnam. In 1973, President Richard M. Nixon delivered his annual Armed Forces Day address from the decks of the *Independence*.

In 1982, while based in Norfolk, Virginia, the ship provided critical support to the multinational peacekeeping force in Lebanon. In 1983, aircraft from the embarked air wing flew missions in support of Operation URGENT FURY, the action to liberate the Caribbean nation of Granada. Returning to Lebanon that same year, the ship's air wing conducted air strikes against Syrian positions.

In June 1988, *Independence* completed the Service Life Extension Program (SLEP) at Philadelphia Shipyard. It was fitting that the ship should be rejuvenated in Philadelphia, home of the Revolutionary War's "Liberty Bell," which figures prominently in the ship's crest. Later in 1988 the ship transited around the tip of South America and arrived at her new homeport of San Diego, California.

In August 1990, with Carrier Air Wing FOURTEEN embarked, *Independence* acted to deter Iraq aggression during Operation DESERT SHIELD. She was the first carrier to enter the Arabian Gulf since 1974. The ship remained on station for more than 90 days and permanently reestablished a U.S Naval presence and provided ready response capabilities in the region.

Independence changed homeports again on September 11, 1991—this time to Yokosuka, Japan, embarking Carrier Air Wing FIVE and becoming the navy's only forward deployed aircraft carrier and flagship for Commander Carrier Group FIVE.

Since that time, the ship has made three deployments to the Arabian Gulf in support of Operation SOUTHERN WATCH, and has participated in numerous bilateral and multinational exercises, including exercise RIMPAC in Hawaii. On June 30, 1995, *USS Independence* became the oldest ship in the U.S. Navy's active Fleet, and as such, proudly flies the First Navy jack from her bow. In early 1996, *Independence* found herself in the media spotlight during heightened tensions between Taiwan and China and during a visit by President Bill Clinton as part of an official visit to Japan.

First view of the USS Independence.

Lifting a A-V Harrier to the dock.

Chapter 4

"Intellectually, I know that America
Is no better than any other country;
Emotionally, I know that she
Is better than every country."
Military quote of the day.

Officially on board the *USS Independence* today!

Still, I did not check out of my rooms. I kept the billeting at the BOQ; I may need a backup if a bunk is not readily available.

I finally feel rested. I should be, I went to bed early enough, eight o'clock last night—Opps! I mean hit the sack at twenty hundred—2000—military time. But the mind decided to rummage around its attic trunks around 2:30 this morning, brushing away mental cobwebs to probe into antique memories, some faded and torn, others fresh as if they only happened yesterday. I told it to shut up—the mind telling itself to shut down—to go back to sleep, that the old body was tired, that it had lugged the mind around all day doing its sometimes ridiculous bidding, but the mind wouldn't listen to itself. It was as lively and raucous as a Los Angeles Latinoamericano pinto jumping bean doing the Mexican Hat Dance in a skillet greased with hot Cristo lard right out of the bucket. It wanted to be up and at the day; it kept saying, " . . . *the early bird gets the worm! The early bird gets the worm!*" Then, answering itself with *"Who in the hell wants a worm anyway?"* At last . . . gave it up. Got up. When your own mind starts arguing with your own mind . . . well, remember ol' Don Quixote running around jousting with windmills or Vincent, thinking his head was a Thanksgiving turkey, whacking off parts of the anatomy—you know where that can lead.

Wandered downstairs to see what were the conditions were for coffee.

They were bad.

Black thick syrup.

The coffee simmered so long it could be used to resurface the tarmac outside—I believe it is the same coffee I had on the carrier *Carl Vinson* and the destroyer *John Young*! They just ship it around place to place. The Navy runs on jet fuel and black coffee in equal amounts.

When I was on the *Carl Vinson*, off the coast of Mexico, 6,200,000 gallons of jet fuel—JP-4—was burned; I believe the consumption of coffee beat that. To paraphrase Henry Ward Beecher . . . "A cup of coffee—real coffee—home-browned, home-ground, home-made, that comes to dark as a hazel-eye, but changes to a golden bronze as you temper it with cream that never cheated, but was real cream from its birth, thick, tenderly yellow, perfectly sweet, neither lumpy nor frothing on the Java: such a cup of coffee is a match for twenty black nightmares, and will exorcise them all".

A bit long-winded, but Hank no doubt liked his coffee.

The biscuit-faced duty petty officer gave me a nonchalant "Mornin' Sir!" Guess he was used to people wandering around at all hours. Sleepy-eyed, his class-A uniform rumpled, he was standing at the entrance counter shuffling papers about, probably thinking about LuLu-Belle's panty-line showin' through her cotton dress back in Whistle-Stop, Kansas. *Should-a-had-been over there at the table making up a batch of fresh coffee. Lazy bastard! Boy! "You sure are hard on people now that you are old and crusty! Forgotten how it was, Gyrene? Remember, you had that kind of boring duty back there in the fifties!"*

"Yeah! Well . . .."

I couldn't think of anything to answer myself. I will come up with a snappy retort after I have had some hot coffee. Early in the morning is not my time for a keen encounter of wits; in addition, after the flight across the Pacific with little sleep, I felt as dull as ditch water in a cotton patch.

Peaked at the darkness through the entrance door curtains. Bleak and cold out. The dead wintreness grass glowed luminously with hoarfrost. White and frosty. Winter in Japan. My buddy Jack Thorne never heard of hoarfrost. He thought it was a prostitute left out in the weather too long. City boy he is. I never figured there was a winter in Japan, just as I never thought that most of the rain and snow falls in the oceans. "Brrrr . . .It is *cold!* " Like the guy said, "It was so cold I almost got married."

Back up the bleak concrete stairs, reperked yesterday's java, ate a couple of granola bars, watched part of *Waterworld,* with Kevin Costner, then burrowed back under the covers until 06:30. It was now *0600*. It is redundant to write 06:00. Military time is 0600. I liked the movie *Waterworld.* Have not met anyone else who did.

0700. Eggs Benedict were calling across the lawn from the officer's mess: the same breakfast as I ate yesterday . . . Heck! . . . I am not finicky. One time I had a tuna club sandwich five lunches in a row. Still my favorite sandwich. Goes well with a frosty Coke in a glass. Not a can or a paper cup; Coca-Cola must be drunk in a glass if one is to savior the quintessence of the bouquet. Tried a tune sandwich in five different hotels in Los Angeles; the best was at Great Western just outside the L. A. airport. The potato salad served with it had little pieces of bacon and walnuts . . . Umm . . . Umm! *Notice I said, "Tuna sandwich." I did not say, tuna fish sandwich." When I order a ham sandwich, I do not tell the waitress to give me a "Ham pig sandwich or ham mammal sandwich," nor do I order a "chicken fowl sandwich."* Upon informing my mother (Mom) of her incorrect use of the term tuna-fish sandwich, she sent me out to eat with the chickens and hogs. Said that was where I belonged—adding succinctly the hogs wouldn't mind, but the chickens might be put off their feed a trifle. Serious mistake on my part as she was serving up homemade cinnamon rolls with a creamy topping that afternoon and my brother got first shovel at the pan.

Today I was officially scheduled to go aboard the *USS Independence CV 62,* nicknamed the *Indy* so the sailors told me back at the airport. I dug out a black turtle neck shirt, tan trousers with about fifty Banana Republic pockets, dark brown Tiger hiking boots (inside, on the heel, is imprinted "Hike like a Tiger!" —No kidding! —Must have been fabricated in China: but they were good boots!) —My beat-up soft felt hat with a low crown creased lengthwise and a brim that can be turned up or down. I have used the hat as a sunshade, water receptacle, pillow, towel, and weapon—slapped a big, ugly Great Dane—dog, not person. Topped off the whole outfit with aviator sunglasses. Talk about a fashion statement. Everyone would know: *Indiana Jones is in the building! . . .Uh! . . .On the carrier.*

During the saunter from the morning mess, I walked over to a cliff face to closely examine something I saw the day before, something that seemed out of place. Carved out of the black-speckled granite was an indentation about nine feet deep, high and wide enough for a small truck, something like a Toyota half-ton. Then I saw several more openings along the face of the cliff. One opening had a half-inch round steel grid cemented into the rock wall at the back of the short tunnel. Shielding my eyes and peering in I could see that the tunnel had been sealed off at that point. Miniature train-type rails, rusty, pitted and bent, led into the tunnel; it was evident that they continued into the mountain, past the sealed off back wall. I thought the small railway cars carried something, something like ore or . . . then I realized . . . beneath the bushes and trees of this whole mountainside there was once been a fortified military position.

Standing back and gazing up, shielding my eyes from the morning glare, I could see remains of old concrete bunkers higher up, near the top, all facing out to the harbor and the open sea beyond. These were the remains of heavy gun emplacements from World War II. Artillery pieces were rolled out from the interior of the mountain, where they were protected by hundreds of millions of tons of mountain, let loose a barrage of shells from the long-range guns, each explosive projectile the size of refrigerator, lofting in a high trajectory to hit an expected American battle ship or carrier fifteen miles out to sea, then rolled back in. Impressive!

Remembering the tunnel that the semi-flatbed truck had hauled the jet fighter through, I came to the conclusion this whole area was most likely honey-combed with underground passage ways: burrows, and excavations; places to store ammunition out of harms way; rooms for personnel, a hospital—a man made stronghold that could take a severe pounding from big naval guns. Japanese soldiers manned weapons up there, waiting, looking to the sea for the U.S. forces to invade the beaches. The final invasion did come, however, it did not come from the sea where it was expected, but from the sky. The initial attack on the mainland of the Empire of Japan was on April 18, 1942, when 16 B-25 bombers from the U. S. carrier *Hornet,* under the command of Major James "Jimmy" Doolittle[1], raided Tokyo and went on to bomb Yokohama and other cities. Some of the planes on the raid made it to China. Some. Not all made it. Three American flyers died in crash landings on the mainland of Japan. The Japanese captured eleven others; the captured fliers were executed as war criminals.

America exacted a terrible retribution on the Japanese peoples for Pearl Harbor and the execution of the airmen—prisoners of war—from the Doolittle Raid. America does not execute prisoners of war. As a

---

[1] U.S. Army Corps Lieutenant James Harold Doolittle, when 25, made the first coast-to-coast flight in a single day in September, 1922, flying a DH4b plane 2,163 miles from Pablo Beach, Florida to San Diego, California in 21 hours, 28 minutes flying time. The National Aviation Hall of Fame in Dayton, Ohio, inducted Doolittle honoring him as an "Outstanding Pioneer of Air and Space."

result of Germany and Japan's treatment of prisoners and civilians, four conventions were adopted in 1949 to strengthen and codify earlier treaties. Hiroshima was a commercial and industrial center manufacturing ships, motor vehicles, steel, and rubber. On August 4th, 1945, American planes dropped leaflets over the city of Hiroshima warning, "Your city will be obliterated unless your government surrenders."

The warning was ignored.

At 8:15 the morning of August 6th, the city of Hiroshima disappeared into a bluish-white glare.

"And he will stretch out his hand against the north,
And destroy Assyria; and will make Nineveh a desolation.
A dry waste like the desert."
—Zephaniah 2:13

Hiroshima was the target of the first atomic bomb ever dropped on a city. The *Enola Gay*, a U.S. Army Air force Boeing B-29 piloted by Paul Tibbets, flew from the atoll of Tinian dropping the bomb from 32,000 feet. Exploding 660 yards above the city, producing millions of degrees of heat and an atmospheric pressure of several million pounds *per square inch,* the bomb destroyed four square miles of Hiroshima. Code-named "Little Boy", the atomic bomb was ten feet long weighing 9,000 pounds with the explosive power of 20,000 tons of TNT. Casualties numbered between 100,000 and 130,000 civilians and military personnel. 90% of the city was leveled. Besides the number of people killed outright, another 100,000 eventually died from burns and radiation sickness.

Most of Hiroshima has been rebuilt. An area of the city has been left in its devastated state as a "Peace City", as a memorial in honor of the dead with the inscription "REST IN PEACE, THE MISTAKE SHALL NOT BE REPEATED."

We hope so.[2]

Checking out of the BQ, I had the clerk telephone for a taxi; I was not going to attempt to haul four pieces of baggage a quarter mile. The fare was $3.15. The other night the minimum was $5, the base mini-

---

[2] **Civilian deaths World War II.** German bombs killed 70,000 British civilians. Some 100,000 Chinese civilians were killed by Japanese forces in the capture on Nanking. The Russians, Americans, and Free French killed hundreds of thousands of Germans, as did the bombing of Japan. Some 45 million people lost their lives in World War II.

mum price said the driver. I guess the base price depends on who is driving the taxi, what time it is in the middle of a cold night, *and* how pickable the pigeon.

At the wharf, it was all business today. Last-minute supplies were being swung in large nets to the flight deck of the carrier as well as being loaded through the elevator openings. Dozens of civilian and military trucks rumbled up, disgorged their loads and left, bouncing over the rough concrete as little yellow forklifts tore about toting crate after crate from huge stacks along the road. Military and civilian personnel were going up a one-way brow, down another in a constant antlike stream. It seemed nobody was directing this swarm! At least I could not see anyone who seemed in charge. The wharf was organized chaos—which is not an oxymoron however—the navy often works like my desk looks: disordered debris. However, I know where everything is on my desk; in my mind it is in order. *And*, in the navy, if everyone follows the book, rules, and guidelines, an immense amount of organized tangled work gets done amid considerable noise and demoniac activity.

Cranes swung loaded pallets, dangling them about like yo-yo's, pallets of Coca-Cola—cases by the hundreds, boxes of toilet paper, sanitary napkins, camera film, clothing—everything you could find in a small town . . . except perhaps a bowling ball and I am not sure about that. I've never encountered a bowling ball on a carrier, but I bet you doughnuts to a dollar there is one there someplace. I mean, there are plenty of golf clubs, fans, televisions, radios, and trout fishing gear hand-carried up the brow; I saw a guy take a bicycle aboard the *Carl Vinson* once, and I on one occasion I steeped in a makeshift hot tub on the *USS John Young* bound across the Indian Ocean, so you never know what you'll find on these big guys.

Unloading from the cab, the tiny wheels on one of my suitcases seemed to have an affinity for every wandering crack in the concrete; I felt like a clumsy boob struggling up to the portable plywood security shack at the base of the officer's brow. Not my orders, my FBI clearance papers, nor the Raiders of the Lost Ark outfit I was wearing impressed the torpid Seaman Apprentice, a two-striper, running the desk. It took some time for him to make the effort to take his feet off the government issue green metal desk, scoot his chair forward, scratch his balls, and reach for the phone, moving almost as fast as cold Louisiana molasses. *Navy squib. Probably from South Texas . . . No! . . .*

Probably South Georgia. They needed a Leatherneck with some "Yes Sirs!" running this shack! Finally, Speedo got someone on the line—it seemed troublesome for him to undergo the effort required for thinking. I think it fatigued the little darling—languidly dialing the telephone and getting hold of some one named Pierson in the ESO office. This Pierson would be right down to "Git Yo!" Speedy Gonzales said.

Ten minutes dragged by, taking thirty minutes to do so. A young, slim sailor stood directly across the street from me on the other side of a fast-food booth locked in brace with a youthful Japanese female pressed the length of his body, her arms locked behind his neck. Husband and wife—maybe. Or lovers—probably. Saying their good-byes. I learned later that many of the enlisted men were married to Japanese ladies. Yokosuka is U.S. Navy homeport of the *Independence* meaning it was here year round except when on deployment. Many of the personnel lived permanently ashore, the enlisted as well as the officers. The young sailor would be gone four months. Leave-taking is rough, rougher for the young because hormones and emotions are high; rougher for the young married couples because of young children and just-starting-homes. No one else was staring at the young lovers; they were detached, alone in their own private world. Not for me to eye ball them. I left them alone. Good luck to them.

A click of heels and a thump of feet came from behind me as I waited by the security shack. A Japanese female carefully made way down the brow carry a load of manila office folders. A Japanese female schoolteacher? Evidently, for about twenty-five miniature Japanese—first graders? —trailed behind, all in line like a gaggle of ducklings, each clutching a white rope that ran the length of the little column so they would not get lost. Cute. Wearing little ball caps.

PN 3[3] Pierson, the ESO clerk, hastened down the steel brow, introduced himself to me, grabbed some of my luggage, led me up the brow, into, and across the wide hanger deck, up several steel ladders all the while feeding me information that I promptly forgot, then through a labyrinth of identical passageways and more stairwells to a cabin. Actually, it wasn't my cabin at all; I didn't know it at the time, but I lucked out. Of all the roommates I might have been bunked with on a boat of over 5,000 inhabitants, I beat the odds by being paired

---

[3] PN denotes administration. The 3 a third-class petty officer.

with the main enlisted honcho of the boat, the Chief Bo'sun[4]. What is a bo'sun? The definition was defined in the days of tall ships as " . . . one who took care of the systems of ropes, chains and tackle used to support and control the masts, sails, and yards of a sailing vessel." In other words, he was in charge of the deck crew. Imagine transferring that job from a sailing ship to a modern-day carrier with 5,500 people; 3,400 sailors, the rest the Air Wing. Well . . . the guy that has the job on the *Independence* is Master Chief Petty Officer Robert Yoder. The Big Maa-Moo. The Big Cahuana. Bob Yoder. He was to become a good friend as well as a good mentor.

Chief Bo'sun Yoder is a bit over 6 feet, full head of dark hair, always clean-shaven with a neat, dark mustache. Few people wear a mustache as well as Bob. Hospitable and courteous to a fault, he never complained about sharing his personnel quarters with Ed—another instructor—and me, a couple of clowns who were generally ragging his ass, eating his candy, miss-placing his magazines and, always, in his way—you know—just generally being a pain in the lower posterior extremity. By being in his way, I mean he was on constant, twenty-four-hours-a-day call. In contrast, Ed and I worked about three hours—and not too diligently at that, screwing around the rest of the time.

Meeting Bob and Ed changed my attitude about being on a carrier. On prior Navy ships, I mostly did serious work without getting personally involved with the crew. On the *Indy*, while enjoying the fascination of watching the jets land and take off plus all the other sights to see on a modern day ship of war, I did the same work with a lot of jollity thrown in. Ed and I were perfect counter jokers generally using Bob as the butt of our tomfoolery, but as in the game of life, Bob often jammed the bat up our ass.

Although he often shook his head at our tomfoolery, Bob was proud of ol' Ed and Jim. Once, in the mess, while talking to a group of officers as we were eating evening chow, Bob turned to me to clarify a point. When—luckily, I knew the answer—I gave a little discourse on the subject at hand and when I finished, Bob beamed a *see what a couple of intellectual roommates I got*! Smile. He was satisfied to have us bunking with him. Feeling silly about this miss-placed adoration, I said, "Yeah Bob! You run this whole ship, and Ed and I don't

---

[4] Boatswain. A Warrant Officer or Petty Officer in charge of ship's rigging, anchors, cables, and deck crew.

know shit-from-Shinola about motorcycles" (about which he knew a hell of a lot) and we got him to talking about bikes while we wore our identical chicken-shit grins pasted across our mugs.

I like Bob. I like his favorite greeting. Because of his duties, he is constantly all over the ship like holy on the Pope and whomever he meets, be it the lowest enlistee or the Captain, Bob will usually come out with "Hi Shipmate! How you doing today?" In addition, if you wanted to stop and tell your real or imaginary woes, he would listen. A colorful, blue eagle tattoo nested on his left forearm. The insignia of a Master Chief—a spread-wing eagle, with two stars above it's wings, perched on crossed anchors, with three stripes below— adorned his shirt collar points and a rainbow of ribbons colored the left breast of his always freshly pressed khaki shirt.

Despite the fact he was the chief enlisted honcho on the *Indy*, Bob's cabin was the smallest I had yet to occupy on an American warship or would occupy in the future, even on the destroyer *USS John Young*. Three of us shared this little prison cell; a cubicle so narrow that when I sat at my fold-out desk by the doorway, I had to stand and move my chair to let someone in. The *USS Independence* was commissioned in 1959, the year I graduated from college, so, being over 40 years old, she did not have the space or facilities as do the more modern, super-phenomenal, nuclear big-boys. No big, wide bunk with a three-quarter sized mattress as I slept on aboard the *USS Abraham Lincoln*; here the three-tier bunks were narrow, had a thin mattress on a steel shelf and a blue draw curtain for privacy: convicts in Vacaville prison, where I once taught, have better sleeping facilities, but not as good food.

The first time I met Bob, I was standing in the cabin jail-cell, luggage piled at my feet, pondering what my next move. The Chief Bo'sum came in to change—he changed clothes about three times a day—introduced himself, said that the top bunk was for me while cleaning out a cabinet for my gear. He then invited me up to the officer's wardroom for coffee remarking we would get settled in later as he graciously introduced me around. I met Chaplain Ross, a Lieutenant Commander[5], who was to later become a breakfast companion and good conversationalist, and a couple of academy graduates who played football at the Naval Academy: one played fullback and the

---

[5] Chaplain Ross became a commander in charge of all the chaplains in the Coast Guard on the East Coast.

other linebacker. Big dudes! The ESO came in, joined the conversation, and I felt as if I belonged; everyone was so friendly and accepting. Sipping our coffee, the ESO and I discussed my classes—I am to do pretty much as I want; just the way I like it! I was beginning to believe that the *Indy was* the Friendliest Ship in the Navy!

Listening in on the table conversation, I heard one of the officers, one of the Academy ex-jocks, exclaim that he was a mite miffed at a female officer. She has a degree in psychology and was chairperson of a goal-writing group this officer was assigned to. The group had something to do with formulating goals of evaluation of possible conflict as the result of bringing women into combat situations aboard ship. Evidently, from the ex-jock's story, she was hyped on using politically correct educational words—you have heard them if you work in a government office or taught school—words such as *interface* and *prioritized*. He was showing his buddy a memorandum she wrote and passed out to the members of the Formulating Goals Group. I eavesdropped as he read it aloud. I think I got most of it.

"The primary aim of this research project is to examine the role of psychological dependency as an antecedent to interpersonal attraction, particularly, through not exclusively, in heterosexual relationships, in which the individuals involved label their attraction 'romantic love'."

Shaking his head as if to clear it of jumbled thoughts, the buddy said, "What the blazes does that mean?"

Ex-Jock replied, "I think it means, 'Why do you love somebody,' but I'm not sure."

Neither was I.

I did not catch all the particulars of the conversation, but I did hear *his* evaluation of his chairwoman/officer. Leaning over to his buddy he lowered his voice. "She-all thinks she's hot shit on a gold platter, but she's jist a cold ol' turd onna paper plate!"

Well . . . . I thought . . . *he certainly does have a way with words. I mean, I understood his summation clearly. And, as for her, anybody goes to a psychologist ought to have his head examined.*

The other ex-jock, the buddy, said that he knew the woman the first ex-jock was taking about. He didn't care much for her either. Besides, he thought that she had a *temperamental bustline*.

Temperamental bustline?

I didn't ask.

Listening to the disgruntled officer tell his tale of gobbledygook language, I was reminded of a retelling of an incident that I got from an impeccable source—a fellow Marine—in Korea in 1953. A few of us, Corporals and Pfc.'s, were sitting around a pot-bellied stove in a tattered squad tent on the DMZ (Demilitarized Zone) during a Korean winter trying to keep the chill off our blains when, George Nasser, a nineteen-year old rifleman in my 3rd squad, mildly tipsy on two cans of near-beer, related the following. Seems this Marine company commander, a Captain, had remnants of his command left after a few altercations and subsequent mauling with the communist hoards in the latter months of the Korean "Conflict."

The Captain was in a partially capsized bunker on a ridgeline, when a ROK soldier (Republic of Korea) came in hysterically yelling, "The en'my is comin! The en'my is comin'!"

"How many?" said the Captain turning to the enlisted man's ROK Captain sitting by the stove drinking cold coffee.

The Rok Captain went out and came back in.

"Sir! There is a rather multitudinous contingent of the adversary advancing in the direction of our foreground local."

Unperturbed, and still not knowing how many people were out there, the Marine Captain looked over to his British attaché and asked, "Percival ol' fellow. Be a good chap there—would you mind toddling out and checking on how many gooks are out there?"

"Quiet all right ol' boy," replied the nattily-attired attaché, picking up his swagger stick, checking his cap, and giving a two-fingered salute, ducked out of the sandbagged doorway. Immediately the Englishman, excited and agitated, returned exclaiming, "There's positively a multitudinous progressing in congruent contact with our immediate situate Captain!"

A mite piqued, the Captain nodded acknowledgment, went on with his paperwork lazily saying to a Marine private who has just wandered in. "PRIVATE! Get yo' ass out there an' see how many them God-damned gooks are a-comin'!!"

"Aye! Aye! Sir!" The enlisted Marine shouted. (Marines, being a part of the Navy, often use navy terms.) The private came running back like a bat-out-of-hell shouting:

"SIR! THERE'S A WHOLE SHIT-POT FULL OF GOOKS OUT THERE SIR!"

"OH MY GOD!" Shouted the Marine Captain.

"WHY DIDN'T SOMEBODY SAY SO! LET'S GIT THE HELL OUTTA HERE!"

When I signed in San Diego to go aboard the *Indy*, Cynthia, my liaison at the Central Texas College office, said that the *Indy* was headed for Australia—she thought. One surprising thing I learned about the Navy: when you are on a navy ship, no one really knows where the ship will eventually wind up for sure—not even the captain, not even the Admirals who sent them out. Once, on the *USS John Young,* I was originally slated to finish my tour in Bahrain; I liked that idea for I was anticipating a stop over in Rome on the way home. My flight to the *Young* took me from California via London across Europe to the Persian Gulf and, after checking with the airline, I could have a stop-over in Rome at no extra charge on the return route. I have never been to the Eternal City and thought it would be pleasant to spend a few days there since the Navy was paying for the flight. Instead, because of a change of orders, I took a dreary two-week trip across the Indian Ocean, completing my tour in Perth Australia, halfway around the world from where I expected to wind up. The skinny[6] in the wardroom about our present destination was that . . . yes . . . we were going to Australia, but would stop over at Guam. That was interesting to me; Guam has figured prominently in World War II stories of the sea war in the Pacific. There would be memorials and graveyards to visit. Let others rush to see Planet Hollywood (there is one in Guam); I find the monuments and graveyards absorbing. Besides, one meets a more interesting quality of people there then at Planet Hollywood.

Bob left the wardroom, his food half-eaten, in answer to a call over the loudspeaker, speaking over his shoulder as he left that he would see me later to get me settled in. I left the wardroom right after Bob to get to know the ship better. I wondered around, up and down, winding up at the end of the hanger deck opening out to the fantail.[7] A few yards away, on the concrete pier, there were people saying good-bye, mostly young couples, hugging, kissing, and holding tiny hands of tiny children. The older couples were not in evidence; they probably said their good-byes at home with the little ones still in bed or hanging around the legs of Mom and Dad. They had said goodbye too many

---

[6] Skinny: News, gossip.

[7] Fantail: The overhanging stern of some ships.

times before to bare their heartbreak in front of strangers much like their counter-parts in San Diego.

The tempo around the great ship began to decrease, the supply trucks were dwindling, the cranes sliding away on their rails. The ship was going to leave port soon. I thought I would stretch my legs one last time on Mama-San earth before taking to sea. *Would I get seasick? I had not yet.* Leaving the wardroom and wandering the labyrinth of passageways and stairwells to the cabin to pick up my Indiana Jones leather jacket, I noticed a fresh pillowcase on my pillow and a clean, fresh towel hanging on the end of my rack. The chief Bo'sun had taken me under his wing. I was now one of his charges, one of his people. I was to learn that he looked after his people.

Walked around a bit thinking about how many times I had been to Japan, but had not seen as much as a one-week tourist. I did see a snow-capped mountain west of Yokosuka that resembled Mt. Fujiyama.[8] I was sure it was Mt. Fuji for I knew Honshu was in that direction and the sacred dormant volcano is in central Honshu. Rising 12, 387 feet, its perfect cone can be seen from many of Japan's prefectures (districts).

I came back on board at 1530. For a departing ship, the quay was strangely empty. I stopped off for a piece of chocolate cake in the wardroom (worse cake I have ever eaten) and a cup of coffee (just awful!) Found the ship's store where I purchased a cloth *USS Independence* emblem and later sewed it on the right side of my blue, cold-weather-deck windbreaker; on the left side is the one from the *USS Carl Vinson* with a few others scattered around. Ed Morris, the other instructor, has twenty-three patches for twenty-three ships; he's an Old Salt.

Ed Morris teaches math and English. He was late to the ship: officials at Narita Airport detained him because he has an entrance stamp in his passport from his last trip with the navy, but no exit stamp because he departed by military ship—the same as I was doing today. They fined him a few bucks for their problems (suspicions). A year or so later I was to have the same problem in Thailand. I came into Phu-

---

[8] Mt. Fujiyama, also Fuji-san, is the most celebrated dormant volcano in Japan. It last erupted from November 1707 lasting until January 1708. Many sects in Japan regard the mountain as sacred and numerous shrines and temples are on its slopes. During the Korean War, my friend mike kanocz, (a Marine Corporal, now a retired Captain) said that when he hiked up Mt. Fuji he purchased a hiking staff at the base, and as certain heights were reached the staff was branded to show what height the hiker achieved.

ket, Thailand on the *USS Peleliu* debarking the ship there simply by taking the liberty boat to the dock. No Thai officials were present—only an American MP saluting me as I walked out the shipyard gate. I visited Phuket and Bangkok for a couple of weeks flying from Phuket to Bangkok with no one asking to see my passport. Then, when I attempted to leave Thailand, I was held up forty-five minutes at the airport until I could get someone to understand my orders. Immigration officials wanted to know how I had entered the country with no passport stamp. It seems they couldn't understand exactly what I was doing on a navy ship. When I first explained to the immigration officer that I came off an American ship, he said, "No. You to old!" Also, I thought that someday I will be going back to Japan and, I'll have the same problem as did Ed. (I didn't however. The next time I came through Japan I had no problem. Ed must have looked more sinister then I did.)

Going up the brow, I heard a whistle. The American flag—Old Glory—was being run up the flagpole. I like the way the morning flag is raised here. At 0800, the bugle sounded and everyone comes to attention—no matter what one is doing, one stops in mid-stride and come to full parade attention. Then the National Anthem is played over loudspeakers. When it was finished, I expected the bugle to sound "Dismiss" as usual and started to walk off, but . . . before I had taken three steps . . . more music: The Japanese National Anthem was being played. Great idea.

The ship is buttoning up.

Engines are starting to rumble.

Rainbow-colored bubbles were breaking the surface around the stern of the ship.

I made way to the stern anchor station beneath the flight deck. Hawsers were being cast off, splashing in the water. Two enlisted men next to me are saying goodbye and blowing kisses to their Japanese wives or girlfriends—I know not which—forty yards away, all four speaking Japanese at once. One girl puffs her cheeks, extending them like a Blowfish, and deliberately blows at the ship—Why? I have no idea! Hesitate to guess. Conjuring up a wind? Maybe.

Music blasted over the con.[9] Then the Captain speaks, his voice booming out, reverberating off the hillside and the buildings:

[9] Con. A wired communications system.

"TO OUR GOOD FRIENDS AND FAMILY ON THE PIER, THE INDEPENDENCE WOULD LIKE TO SAY GOODBYE. SEE YOU IN ABOUT FOUR MONTHS."

The *USS Independence* slipped her hawsers; her wake churned mightily as the wharf disappeared into a blanket of cotton-gray, wet fog. In ten minutes, Yokosuka and Mt. Fuji were no longer visible. Shadows lengthened; the con trumpeted forth a lively tune; *Indy* came up to speed leaving Truman Bay, transiting into Tokyo Harbor, then made a wide starboard sweep, and pointing the bow southeast, began to ride the swells of the Pacific Ocean.

*****

July 7, 1998 A year and a half later. Military News.

Yokosuka, Japan—*USS Independence (CV 62)* departed its forward-deployed base of Yokosuka, Japan, for the last time July 7 amid a sea of media, distinguished visitors and onlookers. The aircraft carrier is relocating to San Diego, (California). Before *Independence* departed Japan, a ceremony was held on the pier to commemorate the historic day.

"This is a sad day for all *Independence* sailors," Captain Mark R. Milliken, *Independence's* Commanding Officer, said in his speech during the ceremony. "For the past seven *years Independence* has called Yokosuka home."

Independence, the oldest ship in the U.S. Navy, arrived in Yokosuka on September 11, 1991. Since then, she has been to the Arabian Gulf three times in support of Operation Southern Watch and was the stabilizing presence during the heightened tensions between China and Taiwan in March 1996.

The only permanent forward-deployed aircraft carrier, her most recent call to duty was this past January when she departed on a very short notice deployment to the Arabian Gulf. "Of the 12 aircraft carriers in the United States inventory, *Independence* was the only one that could respond at such short notice to further enforce U.N. sanctions," Milliken said. "This short notice deployment took teamwork, not just from the *Independence/CAG-5 (Carrier Air Wing FIVE)* team, but from the entire Yokosuka community."

This positive relationship and teamwork between the Japanese community and the *Independence* crew is nothing new. "*Independence's* relationship with the Japan Maritime Self Defense Force (JMSDF) and the city governments have been second to none," Milliken said. "Our annual bilateral exercise with JMSDF called *'Annualex'* and our multinational exercise, '*Rim of the Pacific,*' shows how training between our two navies pays great dividends. You all are true professionals who exemplify the best in the world."

In the next ten days, *Independence* will be in Pearl Harbor, Hawaii, to turn over the reign of the only forward-deployed status to the *USS Kitty Hawk (CV 63)*. The *Carrier Group FIVE* staff, *CAG-5* and hundreds of *Independence* sailors will cross-deck to *Kitty Hawk*.

Independence, in her 39th year of service, is scheduled to decommission in Bremerton, Washington, September 30.

I received a letter from a group representing reunions for people who had served on the *USS Independence CV 62* inviting me to attend the decommissioning of the ship in Bremerton, Washington. I was in Thailand at the time, so could not do so.

Chapter 5

"Older men declare war. But it is youth
That must fight and die.
And it is youth
Who must inherit the tribulation.
The sorrow, and the triumph
That are the aftermath of war."
Herbert Hoover

The Pacific Ocean is big! I mean REALLY BIG! There is lots of water out there, a whole bunch! With an estimated 64,000,000 square miles, it is the largest body of water in the world. I have been across it a whole lot of times and there is a whole lot of nothing out there except water. Aqua. $H^{2}0$. Hydrogen and oxygen molecules with a whole bunch of other chemicals thrown in. Understand there is tons of gold in seawater. I know there is lots of salt. Tasted it. Have not seen any gold however. Nor tasted any. Not many birds far out at sea, not much fish life—just lots of water, lots of sky, and lots of loneliness.

And, paradoxically, I have never been in a storm while on the ocean. Any ocean. I have read a lot of storm stories, but never been in even rough water. I am a fair-weather sailor I guess. One of the definitions of the word Pacific is "mild of temper" and this seems to fit the Pacific Ocean—most of the time. But, not all the time as we well know. I like the legendary Chinese philosopher Lao-Tzu's definition of water, which I like to apply to the Pacific Ocean. In the 6th century B.C., he wrote, "In the world there is nothing more submissive than water. Yet for attacking that which is hard and strong nothing can surpass it." [1] I am sure the cliff dwellers at Pacific Palisades in southern California agree with old Lao; one stormy winter I watched several homes and a 52 unit apartment building slide into the ocean as the Pacific waves undercut the cliff along the Pacific Coast Highway.

---

[1] Lao-Tzu (6th century B.C.), Legendary Chinese philosopher. *Tao-te-ching* bk. 2, ch. 78 (tr. by T. C. Lau, 1963).

From Japan to Guam, it is about 3,200 nautical miles in a straight line. A nautical mile, scientifically called an International *nautical mile* is equal to 6,076.103 feet. A mile on land in your car, riding a moped, or on foot by that matter, is 5,280 feet, more correctly called *a statute mile*. So of course, a nautical mile is longer than a statute mile. Why? I don't KNOW! [2] As you do know from high school science, there are no straight lines when one travels the surface of the globe: it's all curves and bulges. Nothing is flat. They say that the earth is not even round, that it is *pear shaped*. Hard to believe. Never particularly liked pears. When you travel on this pear, you have to go over or around everything, and that includes the surface of the sea (I do not know about submarines). Sometimes going around is shorter than going straight across. I know. Confusing! I understand it I think; I just do not want to try to explain it. (If you want more information on this, dig out your encyclopedia or go on the Internet; somebody on there will know.)

When the "Freedom's Flagship", the *USS Independence* departed Truman Bay, sailing into Tokyo Harbor, she headed out into the Western Bulge of the Pacific Ocean. Big, large, enormous—none of these adjectives conveys the immensness of the Pacific. Compared to land surface, the Pacific Ocean is several million square miles larger than the entire land area of the world; it is over two times the size of that little puddle called the Atlantic Ocean. (Atlantic: Middle English from the Latin *Atlantik* and *Atlas*, so Atlantic—I think—is Atlas's sea?) Maybe not. Try the Internet.

Even with spy satellites constantly circling the pear-shaped globe, a nuclear carrier can still hide out in the vastness of the Pacific Ocean, snaking through island groups, hiding in rainsqualls, and staying out of the paths of satellites. And as for finding a nuclear sub, the chances are very slim indeed! In the eighties, it was estimated that the United States had 41 nuclear submarines, the Soviet Union, 62. Each country was limited to this number by the Provisions of the Strategic Arms Limitation Agreement of 1972. They are all out there, lurking around,

---

[2] "I do not KNOW!" My old buddy Bill Solenberger and I developed a method of handling people who kept asking what we thought were stupid questions or redundancies. We would say simply, "I don't KNOW!" stress on the last word. This worked so well that in Pattaya, Thailand we had caps made up with "I don't KNOW" sewn on the front. When someone invariably asked a lamebrain question, we would simply point to the message on the cap. Once in a while, a particularly insistent questioner would say, "Why don't you know?" We would rejoin with, "I don't KNOW why I don't KNOW!" !" It's a good system. Try it.

drifting down into dark sea canyons, hiding. We do not know where the Russian nuclear subs are; they do not know where ours are. (*Red October* aside)

The *Independence* was charting a course from the Northern hemisphere, off the coast of Japan, sailing directly south, cross the Tropic of Cancer at latitude 23°27' north of the equator, the northern boundary of the Torrid Zone, and the most northerly latitude at which the sun can shine directly overhead. Then over the bulge of the equator to pass the Tropic of Capricorn at latitude 23°27' south of the equator, the southern boundary of the Torrid Zone, and the most southerly latitude at which the sun can shine directly overhead, on to the Southern hemisphere and Sydney, Australia.

The sky was a dirty, cold gray as we departed Japan's territorial waters—the air wet, the temperature frigid—every metal surface glistened with a sheen of oily condensation. Although Japan is about the same latitude as Northern California, it does not have the Golden State's climate. Since leaving Yokosuka, I had been at the rail a couple of hours watching the scenery when suddenly weary of the ashen sky, the leaden sea, and dingy, gloomy fog, I sought the ship's warmth and light inside.

The cabin was vacant. As usual Bob was working somewhere, Ed was gone. I grabbed a towel and searched for the showers where I spent awhile figuring out the shower system, an unfamiliar faucet set-up of one lever that controlled everything. Applying my best mental and mechanical aptitude to the problem, I managed to scald my skin and cook my nether parts in the process doubtless knocking off a few millions little sperm guys. The heads[3] were old, the metal dented and rusty, not as modern—naturally—or as clean as the *Vinson's*. The showers had another idiosyncrasy I discovered later as the ship neared the equator and the days began to really warm up. When it got really hot outside, the whole metal ship heated up over a period of days, the metal ship retaining the heat throughout the night. We could get *only* hot water—no cool or tepid—after the first five seconds of the shower being on. After that, it was Scald City baby. That made for some fast showers with considerable negative evaluations of the ancestry of the engineers in charge of the boilers.

At 2030, I was wet from my half-assed shower. Donning clean, cotton jogging clothes, soft and warm, I climbed Ed and Bob's bunks to

---

[3] Head: Navy term for bathroom, toilet, and shower.

my top one, scooting down into clean, soap-smelling sheets. Turning on the diminutive reading light fastened to the iron head railing six inches above my head, I opened up a paperback and promptly dozed—half asleep, half awake.

When at sea a ship is always a noisy environment. Always. It is ceaselessly moving when afloat, either going someplace, coming back, or just wallowing around. And a ship is crowded no matter the size. Noise—movement—people! Constant—sustained. Movement, noise and people assail your muscles and brain. Sustained over time, I believe that these three factors debilitate the human body. It is common agreement among the sailors that I talked to about it, that one is more easily fatigued on shipboard than on land; you are tired but don't know why.. Noise is a twenty-four-hour-a-day phenomenon and one is continually reacting to people. The body and mind rarely are at a complete rest. So, I hit the rack at 2030, tired, and sleepy. Ed comes in, turns on his desk light, drags a chair up to his desk, and does some paper work—trying to be quiet. At 2130 Pearson—the ESO clerk—bangs on the door with the information there will be a Man-Overboard drill the next morning at 0800 (That was the third warning I'd had this day.) At 2200, the evening prayer is read throughout the ship over the intercom—read loudly. Every cabin has a speaker on the bulkhead or the overhead; *they have no on/off switch*. Without exception, announcements blare into each and every cabin, each and every passageway.

I doze. The ship shudders. Something overhead clangs.

The ship rolls a little as it makes a sharp turn. The body rolls a little in synch. Earlier I noticed a broad, braided white band attached to the frame of my bunk; I don't have to ask what it is for: I figured that one out real fast—it's to fasten your body to the bunk so you don't do a swan dive to the deck when asleep or just trying to keep from becoming airborne in unkindly weather.

A jet takes off.

And another.

Another blasts off.

And another—and another is launched—for two hours jets are launched, practicing take-offs and landings. Each time one thunders away the metal overhead a few inches from my nose flexes, doing the hootchy-koochey in two/four time.

Finally, there is quiet, well, quiet in this situation is a relative term as temperature is relative. Put your hand in a pot of hot water, then put it in a pan of warm water; the warm water feels almost cool. The same with noise: when the jets stop their blasting and the overhead is not bucking, it is "quiet". The voices in the passageways, the creaking of the bulkheads, the footsteps overhead, the hum of a thousand generators is soothing, almost peaceful, practically silent, serene . . . At length, after going to bed a couple of hours ago, sleepy, but not sleeping, I snugly drift off. Then . . . Oh No! The curse of the older guy! I mutter a blasphemy under my breath tempered with hope, "I'll just ignore it—maybe it'll go away." Nope! The pain smolders. The bladder stretches—complains. The discomfort intensifies. *Shit!* Throw back the warm covers, in pitch dark hang a leg over the side of the bunk, catch the toes just on the edge of Bob's bunk, then a long leg reach to the deck. *Watch out for Ed's arm*! Find the shower clogs. *Where in the hell did I leave those floppy bastards! I gotta have a robe*; *you can't go into the passageway in shorts.* (I was told this several times. Can't walk around in my shorts scratching my balls like at home. This is a co-ed ship!) *Where's the damn robe?* I bump into a metal locker. *Shit! Gonna wake everybody*! Fumble for the doorknob. *What they do! Move it?* A shower clog falls off. *Damn!* Find the shower clog. Open the door. Light blasts in hurting scalding my retinas. Clop down the passageway, bumping the bulkhead—still half asleep. Find the head. Stand swaying, half-asleep, an overhead asbestos-wrapped pipe clutched in one hand for balance, the other fumbling. A dribble, then relief. . .Aaahhh. Put shorty away. Retrace my route down the passageway—*shit! Dribbled on my robe*! Open the door flooding the cabin with light again. Off with clogs and robe—put 'em somewhere where they wont be stumbled over—back up the tiers of bunks stepping on Bob's arm—he mumbles, rolls away. Hit my head on the overhead pipes that encircle my bunk like a rectangular spider web. Crawl into twisted sheet and blanket, dig the paperback book from beneath my back . . . *How in the hell did that get there?* Pull the curtains closed; the little hooks catch in the groove and hang up. I tug and struggle with the *stupid curtain. God damn it!* Finally—*sigh*—all straightened out. The sheets began to warm from body heat. I think back half-dreamingly about high school football and Janice—my high school blonde girlfriend—going to school dances. Trying to gear the ol' high speed cerebrum down to idling...planning on what I'll do for Classes . . . tomorrow . . . to sleep. Boy! . . . Am I tired . . . wish ol' Jan.i.c.e . . . was here n-o-w . . . Then! . . . a little twinge, NO! NOT AGAIN! Suunofabitch! I gotta pee again! A ship is hard on a man's sleep.

The nuclear carrier *USS Carl Vinson* is a 1992, eight-cylinder Cadillac Baritz with all the extras: the *USS Independence* a 1959 Studebaker straight-six, standard shift. Conventionally powered, the *Indy* has four engines producing 300,000 horsepower and uses about *120,000* gallons of fuel *each day*. At 82 cents a gallon, that is somewhere in the neighborhood of $98,000 bucks per day, *and that's a pretty damn good neighborhood*! Not only does the liquid fuel propel the ship, the same fuel is burned providing desalination of seawater: 380,000 gallons of fresh water produced in a twenty-four hour period. It also provides electricity for cooking over 15,000 meals a day and operating the giant airplane elevators, electricity to process 200,000 lbs. of laundry washed per month, electricity for operating all lights on the ship, electricity to operate 2,300 telephones and supply a 50-bed hospital, operating room, an x-ray suite, and the reading lamp over my bunk.

After my first night at sea the ESO and I tackled the class schedules. Being a conscientious teacher *and* an experienced one, I plan ahead and *always* try to have more material than needed. I learned this valuable lesson the first class I taught in college. Thinking I would have all kinds of class participation—it was after all, *a college class*—I planned material for an hour. I was of course naïve in those days. Thirty minutes after the class started I was done, dead, nada. I had yet to learn how to get a class going, get some reaction, some input. I extracted myself from that particular situation by surreptitiously announcing, "Since this is the first class, I really do not want to get into the subject until you have done some reading." I let them out early: they were happy. I was relieved. As I said, now, I was experienced, hardened, been there. I was going to be overly prepared for these swabbies! I planned for these classes on the *Indy* by acquiring the 7th edition of the text provided to me on the *Vincent*. I typed the test master's sheets ahead, spent hours on individual study sheets, which lend themselves to teaching in the situation encountered at sea, as well as writing lectures based on the text chapter progression. I even pencilled in a few "spontaneous jokes" in the margins of my lectures. For example, when we study genetics I would throw in *"The way men and women dress to today, the only way to tell them apart is what is their genes!"* (Jeans) Get it! I know! I know! How about this one? *"Incest: A game the whole family can play."* And when we study political systems: *"Definition of POLITICS: Poly means many and tic (k) s are a blood-sucking parasite, hence—politicians are . . .?"*

Well! . . . Give me a break. They seemed funny at the time. Didn't they?

Anyway, everything was based on the 7th edition text. I was prepared. Red-dy to gooo . . .! The texts arrive in cardboard boxes by helicopter mail, usually about a week after the class starts. Sometimes they are aboard ahead of time. That's rare. When they arrived for these classes, I eagerly unpacked the bright clean cartons, pulled out a brand new textbook neatly labeled *8th edition. Damn!* Everything I prepared was based on the 7th edition. *Double Damn*! *Lost in Lodi Again!*

The administrators ashore—administrators, not teachers—allotted 48 college hours of instruction for three units of credit. *No way, Jose*! Class starts: People are missing because they have the duty. During Flight Ops, the overhead shakes, and all conversation stops as a jet comes up to full roaring power and launches. The classroom shakes like a chorus of fat ladies doing a St. Vitus' Dance; they launch about every five minutes though and say that they can do it every two minutes. There are also fire drills and man-overboard drill disruptions. The original concept of having college classes aboard has merit—but the environment, facilities and schedules make a preferred attainment of goals dubious. At best, the students will get a watered-down version of the subject as taught on a college campus. Also, there is no college library, limited audio-visual materials, and no quiet study areas, no labs.

Notwithstanding all that, I like the PACE program. PACE stands for Pacific Academic Educational Program. The students aboard ship are getting their appetites whetted to further their education and learning, after all, is an individual thing—the instructor is just a guide. Many will learn to like formal learning and go on to further education in the navy or out.

The very first day of class there was a man-overboard-drill. Usually we know ahead when a drill was to be held, but we did not get the word this time. Ed and I headed for the ES office since we were closer to it than our cabin—we had to be counted in one of those two places. If we were in the cabin, we would just phone in to be counted. A man-overboard drill is to account for every body aboard—not an easy task when there are over 5,500 people working, sleeping, or wandering around. The Captain wants the count made in less than twenty minutes. This one took twenty-seven minutes. Four people unaccounted for.

"Let's do it again, people." said the Captain over the speakers.

The second man-overboard took over thirty-minutes to count everybody, longer than the first time. Perturbed, but still in a refined voice, the XO (Executive Officer—second in command)[4] gave a little pep talk and held a third man-overboard drill. Ed and I took a nap. Over twenty minutes later—no luck! *Still over the twenty-minute limit!* No more drills today, just some ass-chewing. I wagered to myself that there would be another drill before the night was over.

It was Saturday, no classes today. I wandered around finding the post office, the library (three rooms—lots of religious and action books), and another store. Found Bob in his shorts at his metal wall locker changing clothes. Bob changed clothes three times this day—once into full dress blues for "leaving port" flight deck photographs. Bob is number one enlisted Honcho on board of course—I stick around him a lot so people will think that I am important.

The ESO Ray took Ed and me up, high up the "island" into admiral country to meet some higher-staff. You know when you are in admiral country: the floor is not the battleship gray found elsewhere; here the deck is tiled in Royal blue, the walls were a brighter, cleaner white and there is lots of shiny brass around—the metal kind, not the human kind. Come to think of it, that must be why they call the higher-up officers "The Brass." They have so much brass on the handrails, doors, and their uniforms. I met Captain Tom Fellin, a gentleman in all respects. He chatted with us, welcomed us aboard, and asked: "Is the EO treating you okay?"

Well Sir!" I said. "His office staff is great; they've given everything that we need. But Ray . . . well . . . he won't tell us where the hot tub is!"

The Captain turned to Ray with a serious frown on his face saying, "EO. You are derelict in taking care of these men. Now you show then the hot tub and take them to the bowling alley too!"

We had a laugh and left him to his work. A gentleman. It is Satur-

---

[4] XO. An XO who most likely is a Lieutenant Commander is usually called Commander rather than Mister because of his position. However, if he prefers to be addressed simply as XO, he is addressed that way. On large ships e.g., carriers, battleships, LHAs, etc., the XO may be a Captain in rank, in which case it would be proper to address him by his rank. However, usually he will prefer to be called XO to avoid confusion with the commanding officer, who is also a captain in rank and captain of the ship.

day evening. I am standing on the fantail letting the sea air wash over me, washing away the stale air from inside the ship. Being stuck inside a steel box smelling like the inside of a oil can foster an appreciation of the evening air. The sun is a red-orange orb sinking into gray-green waters. Off to the right, shadowing us like a predatory gray shark is the *USS Mobile Bay*. Saturday night is usually just another night on a carrier, just another work day. I came on deck to rid my body of the stale air of the closed-up ship breathing in fresh salt-laden air into my lungs as well as to watch the sunset. I have a routine of watching sunrise with Bob Yoder as we are both like old farmers, early risers. At sun down, there is always a group out appreciatively watching old Sol sink into the watery horizon. The *USS Mobile Bay (CG 53*), one of our constant companions, is always around somewhere, protecting the flank of the *Indy*.

The *Mobile Bay* is an AEGIS Guided Missile Cruiser. At 567 feet, the *Mobile Bay* is half the length of the carrier, is 55 feet wide and will ht 30 knots plus. The *Mobile Bay* and the *Reuben James*, another companion on this trip across the Pacific Ocean, can keep up with the *Independence,* as the carrier is not nuclear-powered. Were she nuclear—we would have to slow to their top speed. The crew of the *Mobile Bay consists* of 37 officers, 33 Chief Petty Officers and 339 enlisted. The cruiser's Aegis Combat System is designed as a total weapons system from detection of the enemy—primarily submarines—to destroying them. The heart of the AEGIS system is an automatic detect and track, multi-function radar, the AN/SPY-1. This high-powered radar system is able to search, track, and guide missiles to over 100 targets *simultaneously*. The Aegis System can also perform against a multi-mission threat: anti-air, anti-surface and anti-submarine warfare concurrently. Pretend, for example, there are a few dozen Bin-Laden bees swarming about, a few Khadafy scorpions crawling on the ground, and a couple of Saddam water snakes gliding along the surface. With a twelve-gauge shotgun loaded with number 12 shot; you take them all on together, hitting over 90%. That's what the Aegis system does; only the 12 gauge shot are MK torpedoes, Harpoon quad canister launcher missiles, MK 45/54 caliber guns, MK 41 vertical launch missiles, MK 36 Super Rapid Blooming Off Board Chaff System and four 50 caliber machine guns. Little Red Riding Hood should have had a shotgun gun like the *USS Mobile Bay;* it takes care of the tyrannical wolves of this world very effectively.

Latitude 20 degrees. As we near Guam we see off to the port 16 volcanic islands, fringed with coral reefs, paralleling *Indy's* course. Inhabited for over 3,500 years by a people called the Chamorros, a sophisticated matrilineal society, the islands were first brought to European awareness by Ferdinand Magellan who sailed through them in 1521. Spain annexed the islands in 1565. Still, these tips of underwater mountains were largely unknown by the so-called civilized world—Europeans did not move into the area until over a hundred years later, in 1668. During World War II the islands became known world over for some of the bitterest fighting between the Empire of Japan and the United States. These volcanic tips dotting the Pacific Ocean in a line are called the Marianas.

The Marianas from north to south are, Pajaros, Maug, Asuncion, Agrihan, pagan, Alamagan, Gugan, Sarigan, Anathan, Medinilla, Managaha, Tinian, Rota, and—the most well known to the western world—Guam. From the air the islands resemble giant stepping stones extending in almost a straight-line north to south from 13 degrees to 20 degrees latitude. In 1899, Spain, at the end of the Spanish-American War, ceded Guam to the United States. Magellan sailed into a bay at Guam in 1521 "discovering" the island and claiming it for Spain without consulting the indigenous Chamorros. Under Spanish rule, the Chamorros dwindled from 80,000 in 1668 to 1,500 in 1783, partly because of infectious disease, partly because of Spanish brutality. Spain was a big player in the Pacific until the USS battleship Maine was blown up in Havana Harbor, allegedly by the Spanish—then, Commander George Dewey's navy destroyed the Spanish fleet in the Philippines, and Teddy Roosevelt took Cuba with his troops shouting "Remember the Maine!"

"Ye who remember the Alamo,
Remember the Maine!
Ye who unfettered the slaves,
Break a free people's chains.[1]

The U. S. wound up with Guam, the Philippines, and Puerto Rico. After kicking Spain's ass, the U. S. paid them off with $20 million

---

[1] Richard Hovey, "The Word of the Lord from Havana," *Along the Trail*, 1903

ending Spain's colonial presence in the Americas. There was controversy that perhaps the blowing up of the Maine ws not done by the Spanish, but by Americans, and was a pretext to take Cuba from Spain. With two hundred and fifty-eight "Brave" American sailors and Marines killed, no one gave cr4dance to this counter-argument. The rest of the Northern Marianas claimed by the Spanish were sold to Germany and eventually taken by Japan in 1914. In 1941, during the beginning days of World War II, Japan took Guam. After fierce fighting, with heavy loss of lives on both sides, all of the Marianas were captured by the U.S. in 1944.

Now the Marianas are a Trust Territory under the United Nations. Guam became an unincorporated territory of the United States in 1950. The islands became self-governing and the trusteeship was terminated in 1978. However, the United States provides defense and has an extensive—very extensive—military establishment in Guam.

On July 21, 1944, the Marines assaulted the bitterly contested beachheads of Guam. By August 10th, the Marines, reinforced by an army division, had cleared the island. Arms folded on the rail, watching the ship's white furrow wake widening to the horizon, I contemplated the refuse of war that lay on the cold, dark ocean sediment two miles beneath the keel of the *Indy*. Broken aircraft carriers and riddled battleships of the Japanese and American navies, unknown submarines, crippled airplanes, loads of trucks, ammunition, howitzers, jeeps, foodstuffs: cargoes from sunken transports ships sunk, their cargoes scattered, littering the silt-muddied carpets and steep canyons below crushed under tons of sea water. I could not even begin to comprehend the waste of sailors, Marines, pilots, and civilians; both countries sent them here, never to return to loved ones. They are still there, young life mostly, young men mostly, lost forever, entombed in chilling, dank mud, sealed in black iron coffins—lost in the icy blackness, like tear drops lost in the rain.

"It's so easy to forget them,
Only a few sang their praises,
Of our Bob's, Jim's and Johnny's,
Only a few remember their graves."

I experienced this same feeling of sadness when I visited the military graveyards at El Alamein in Egypt. Hardly any of the grave markers had an inscribed age over 24. But there were markers there to joggle the memory, to spark an interest; flowers are still brought there today. But here, near the Marianas, there is just the sky and the sea. There are no graves I the sea. There are no monuments for those lost loved ones below. My generation remembers them; we were impressionable youths at the time. My children will not remember them for they never knew of them. Their bodies and their spirits will be lost in memory eventually, like raindrops scattered in the vast waters of the oceans.

There are no tombstones in the sea.

Boatswain Robert Yoder

Chaplain Derrek Ross

The author and students at General Quarters.

Chapter 6

"If there is no wind;
Row."
Military quote of the day.

Conversation in the Chief Bo'sun's cabin somewhere in the Western Pacific Ocean heading for Guam—everyone bored by routine.

I am all read out. Bored. Ennuyé flows through my body—apathy abounds. I am my bunk, hands behind my head, staring at a teacup saucer-size spider web up among dusty asbestos-covered pipes. A small black spider sits patiently in the center of the web, waiting, watching for a meal to come by. A nautical spider. A sailor spider. I have seen no bugs aboard so I wonder what it is it eats. I hope it does not nibble on people. A spider is an Arachnid. Some people study spiders. Spend their whole life doing so. Get advance degrees in spiderology. Strange people no doubt. "I have a Master's in Spiders!" *What? Ya marry a Black Widow?* Actually, the study of spiders is not called Spiderology; it is *Araneology.* Beyond that, I know little about spiders. Do not want to know too much more about them. I know that a grasshopper's blood is white and that elephants can be pregnant for 24 months. Have not made much use of the information though. Also, I know that human hair grows at a rate of one-hundredth of an inch per day; the same rate at which the continent is sinking into the ocean. Must be a correlation there someplace? Do not know what it is.

Bored.

Ed is at his desk correcting papers. Bob is in his chair reading motorcycle magazines.

Jim: "Hey Ed! " I said, speaking a bit louder than necessary in the small cabin. "Our esteemed room mate, Chief Bo'sun Robert Yoder has his name on the door. Printed on a *big* plastic card"

Ed: Looking up says, "Yeah! I saw it. Nice job."

Jim: "Very nice. *Professional*

Ed: "Without a doubt."

Jim: " We live here don't we Ed?"

Ed: "Yeah." Ed replied, looking up again, figuring something is going on.

Jim: "Well . . . I was a-wonderin' Ed. Why don't we have our name on the door."

Ed: "Beats me. Prejudice I guess! We be *Cee-vil-yuns*!"

Jim: "An' the Navy hires us—I mean 'don't we have some rights?'"

Ed: "We are just as good as any body else!" Ed replies, knowing now that we are going to rag Bob—again.

Jim: "Well then . . . How come we don't have *our* name on the door like some other people do?"

We know that Bob is listening, but he pretends he doesn't. He's reared back in his chair, ankles crossed, looking at a glossy magazine, concentrating on photographs of big, fat Harleys' with half-dressed ladies supporting over-sized mammary glands sprawled on them.

Ed: "Pure discrimination I guess. Just like some guys git to fly ahead to Guam with the Admiral while we have to stay in this shit hole!" (Bob is to fly ahead to Guam with the Admiral to see if it is feasible to bring a carrier into the bay at Guam.)

Jim: "We don' git to go to Guam. We don' get to hobnob with the Admiral. We don' get our names on the door. We don' count around here that's *pretty plain* to me!."

Ed: "Pure discrimination—plain and simple. Don't take no genius figure that out!"

Jim: "People crap ALL over you."

Bob "*Screw you guys!*"

Jim: "*Wha . . .?*"

Ed: "*What?*"

Bob: "I said, 'Screw you Screwballs!'"

Ed: "Well! I never!"

Jim: "Limited vocabulary that's what it is. Crude. Man doen hav' nuthin' to say—guy doen have nuthin' good to say . . . just cusses."

Ed: "An' me with my girl's picture in my pocket." He patted his ass.

Jim: "Crude fucker!

Ed: "It's the Navy way."

Jim: "Jus' like the Marines. *Semper Fi!* Hooray for me and screw you bucko'"

Bob: "PUT YOUR FRIGGIN' NAME ON THE DOOR!"

Ed lisping: "WEELLL . . . I J'ST DON'T KNOW! If you're just going to be *THAT* way!"

Jim: "Crude. Just crude. What ya gonna do?"

Bob: "I'll have the shop make up a couple name tags, assholes!"

Jim: "I'm a professor ya know! I prefer to be called "*Professor Asshole.*""

Bob: "Print out what you want. I'll have the shop print 'em up."

Ed: "Weeelll . . .If you *DO* insist, you *Daarrrling* you!"

Jim: "We never doubted it for a minute Bob. We love the Navy."

Ed: "Want somethin' done jist ask the navy. That's what I always say."

Jim: "Me too."

Bob: "Screw you guys."

Day after monotonous day the *Indy* 's wake followed behind, a two-mile, dirty white streak, pointing straight as an arrow back north toward Japan. We were headed almost directly south, oftentimes under squally ugly gray clouds—limiting our vision, cold and miserable. Nevertheless, when the squalls passed, you could tell that the days were getting hotter, daylight longer. Approximately 1,500 miles to the west was the great bulge of China intruding into the ocean, and 6,000 miles to the east, across the vast Pacific; Northern Mexico. Guam is dead ahead.

In deep ocean, routine prevails. Each day is much the same. The *Indy* rides easily, rocking gently on the long, broad ocean swells.

There is little outside the ship's environment other than sunrise and sunset to divert the senses. Sometimes the *Reuben James's* silhouette would show on the horizon. *The USS Reuben James*, a frigate, is one of the *Indy's* bodyguards, along with the *Mobile Bay*. An Oliver Hazard Perry-Class guided-missile frigate (FFG), the *Reuben James* is 453 feet long with a 45-foot beam run by a crew of 214. The frigate packs a hefty wallop with armament of two helicopters: one anti-submarine and one armed attack helicopter. Additionally, it supports 2 Mark 26 twin-arm Harpoon launchers; two 5 inch deck guns; 2-20mm Vulvan Phalanx—spewing out 3,000 rounds per minute—and 2-25mm Bushmaster cannon. Mainly, the *Reuben James*—like the *Mobil Bay*—super structure is festooned with huge antennas of the most sophisticated command and weapon control system developed by any navy—the Aegis Weapons system named after the shield used by Zeus, chief of the gods, in Greek mythology.

The Aegis system was designed as a total weapon system from detection of the enemy to the kill. It combines the naval task group's total weapon systems to react quickly and with efficient firepower to destroy fast targets in severe conditions. Aegis, using automatic detect and track, multi-function radar, can cover and engage over 100 targets at the same time. The Aegis system allows the battle group a 500-mile protective umbrella.

Today the *Reuben James*, whose home base is Hawaii, is a black paper-cut silhouette on our horizon.

No birds roam the sky. No fish break the unruffled surface of the sea. It is said that at any one time there are upwards to twenty thousand ships on the Atlantic Ocean. I would assume then there would be a pretty fair number plying the Pacific. But shipboard vision is limited to 11 to 15 miles from the deck depending on which level you are standing, therefore there could be a number of ships around, we just couldn't see them. Routine is the order of the day as it was yesterday, as it will be tomorrow.

Routine.

Doing the same thing everyday. Days of the week become not isolated units but a continuum—one relies on the calendar, otherwise whole days are lost. No television stations come this far out; we have some movies, all canned. Neither commercial radio nor television. The daily newspaper printed on board is a welcome treat; its four pages are devoured quickly along with the morning coffee. Sometimes the treat is tempered by bad news.

> *"A S-3B Viking with a crew of four from the USS Roosevelt (CVN-71) is missing. The aircraft from the Sea Control Squadron 22, was on anti-submarine warfare training 90 miles west of Haifa, Israel when it disappeared Tuesday afternoon. The crew was:*
>
> *Lt. Cdr. Mark Ehlers, 36, Fla.*
> *Lt. Mark Eyre, 29, Fla.*
> *Lt. Mike Weems, 27, Fla.*
> *3rd Class Wendy Potter, 24, California."*

Third-Class Wendy Potter. Twenty-four. Someone's daughter.

No word.

Flying jets is a hazardous profession. Flying jets off a carrier is a deadly dangerous profession. Flying jets is beset by a dozen ways to die.

A jet fighter must move fast to stay in the air. Broken down in simplest terms a jet—particularly a jet fighter—is a tube with flames shooting out the back. A controlled rocket. Rockets are of two types: solid fuel and liquid fuel. A jet fighter plane is simply a pilot-controlled, liquid-fueled rocket. For its size, a jet fighter has relatively small wings surfaces, hence, the slower it goes the less control the pilot has. Carrier jets land fast. They have to. There is no floating in at forty miles an hour as you see John Wayne do on the Late Movie about World War II landing planes such as Hurricanes and Buffaloes. Jets carrier planes have to land fast for two reasons: one; they lose control at low speeds and two; they must have enough speed to take off if the tail hook misses the restraining wire. This is why, as soon as the pilot feels his plane touch down on the moving steel deck, he slams the throttle full ahead; he has a short take off strip and little time. If the wire doesn't stop him, he's got to go—and go *fast*!

A crashing jet fighter breaks up in different ways. Crashing on the ground, a high-speed impact at ninety-degree angles guarantees small pieces in a circular hole. The twelve-foot long engine may be compressed to three feet and be—depending on soil consistency—twelve feet down.

According to Mark Berent in Rolling Thunder[1]:

"Lesser angles of impact splash the wreckage in the direction of flight and balloon billowing clouds of greasy black smoke and red flames. A near-zero glide angle on smooth terrain is another matter entirely. Unless the aircraft cartwheels, which it often does if one of the landing gear collapses, the wings usually remain intact, although probably separate from the aircraft. Large sections of the tail assembly and fuselage remain. If the wreck does not burn."

"Usually they burn."

Usually they burn.

Why?

JP-4.

JP-4 is jet fuel—mainly kerosene. JP-4 is a mixture of hydrocarbons commonly obtained in the fractional distillation of petroleum. A jet engine compresses air then mixes it with jet fuel that produces greater exhaust than intake velocity. Under compression, it is highly volatile. *Burned beyond recognition* is a common phrase in accident reports made of jet fighter crashes. When jet fuel—JP-4—explodes, it creates a heat so intense that everything but the hardest metals ignite. Everything goes: rubber, plastic, film, clothing, flesh, bone, minerals, hair,

---

1 *Rolling Thunder* by Mark Berent. A JOVE BOOK. Published by arrangement with Berent-Woods, Inc. 1989

blood and protoplasm. Every form of fetid chemical gases is released; one can smell the black horror of flaming death.

The jet fighter, the S-3B Viking, that was missing from the *Roosevelt* is standard on most carriers, usually about six planes per flattop. Classified as an "attack warplane," the Viking is typed as "a carrier-borne anti-submarine warplane." Its mission is to locate submarines, track them, and if the situation warrants, destroy the target. Powered by twin-engine turbojets, the "Hoover" is capable of a cruising speed of 518 miles per hour. Called the "Hoover" because of the modulated resonance of it's engines—some compare it to the Hoover vacuum cleaner—it is nowhere as noisy as the Tomcat. The Viking hunts submarines using three methods: One is to drop a sonobuoy—the plane carries 60—with a battery-powered microphone to listen to the sea and a radio to "talk" back to the plane. The S-3B also has APS-116 search radar for locating surface boats, and a MAD sensor in the tail of the plane to detect tiny distraction in the earth's magnetic field caused by the passage of a steel submersible. I mean they are very mean about searching for a sub, and once they get the scent, they are very difficult to lose.

Like the Viking that went down off Israel, the flight and mission crew is composed of four—pilot, co-pilot, and two systems operators—in tandem side-by-side pairs and all have ejector seats. I climbed inside one experiencing immediate claustrophobia. The insides are so packed with electronic gear there are only small seats for the crew. Moreover, there were no discernible toilet facilities for the mixed crew of three males and one female who are sometimes aloft for many hours. What do they do when they must micturate? —fancy word for pee—I did not ask. I mean astronauts do something; fighter-pilots do something when they are in the air a long time so, I assume the Viking crew do to, but I do not know what.

The Viking is versatile in its armaments: It can carry up to 7,000 lbs. of disposable ordinance including a 10/20-kiloton B57 nuclear weapon, or four 1,000-lb. free-fall bombs or mines, or four *depth* bombs, or four torpedoes. On wing attachments the plane can carry six 500-lb. Free-falls bombs Rockeye cluster bombs[2], and has multiple launchers for unguided rockets.

Sunday came and drifted away with little difference in routine except the lines at the ship's stores were longer, stretching down the narrow passageway and around a corner. Some of the enlisted men waiting, mostly younger guys, sat on the deck, their backs against the bulkhead reading books, writing letters. The inevitable in the service "Hurry up and wait!" Every ex-service man knows what I am talking about. I bought toothpaste and a deck of cards; Ed wants me to teach him blackjack; how a cosmopolitan human being like he can reach forty and not be degenerate enough to learn blackjack is beyond my comprehension . . . the guy is lacking in basic chauvinistic male education.

Monday was rainy and gray day—sunless. Apprehension was in the air. Planes were not landing as well as they usually do; there are more flybys. One day is hot as hell, the next cold and gray—maybe that is the reason landings are not up to snuff. Changeable weather. Nobody seems to know.

Read a couple of books. One called, *A Ride Along the Great Wall* by Robin Hanburg-Tenison, is about an English couple who rode horses along the Great Wall of China. Can you believe it! The English are always doing things like that.

"What are you doing today Dearie?"

"Oh! I dunno ol' girl. Maybe take a walking-jaunt aroun' the coast of England ya know? Clear out the ol' pipes."

"Jolly Ider, lov'. Do you a world."

"Tally Ho!"

"Back for tea are ye?"

"Righto!"

Although I heard it said that the Great Wall is the only thing visible from the moon with the naked eye, NASA astronauts say this in not so. They looked. Read it in some article. Do not believe that I will ever get a chance to check it out. On the ship people read books they normally would not read at home because the number and topics are limited. To someone like me, who is used to knocking off a book every two to three days, the lack of books becomes a scavenger hunt.

---

[2] Cluster Bombs can be dropped from any height and at the optimum height over the target, break open to release submunitions (bomblets) of different types against personnel or armor.

When not reading, eating, or teaching, I sleep. Bob complained that I snore. That rotten, backstabbing Ed backed him up! It's the same lie the guys on the *Vinson* used to tell as well as my kids at home and a couple ol' gals I used to bed down with. Some kind of mass hallucination I think. Bob said that I snored because I didn't eat right.

"Whardda ya mean I don't eat right. Where'd ya read that?—in one of them sex-filled motor cycle magazines?"

Bob's got one Harley-Davidson motorcycle magazine with a half-glad gal on it toting breasts that would make a Oklahoma sweet water melon think it was a cantaloupe—The caption on the magazine says, *"She's got five hundred pounds of hot steel between her legs!"*

"What the Sam-fuckin'-Hill does eatin' have to do with snorin'?" I went on.

"It's a scientific fact." He said in his best father's voice, wrinkling his brow. "Ya eat that fried stuff, yo gonna build up flim in the throat an' when ya breathe, it resonates."

Scientific fact?

Resonates?

"Well! . . . Well! . . . Screw me sideways! First of all—*Chief* Bo'sun—I do not snore. I have never heard my self snore—ergo—if no one is in the forest; the falling tree makes no noise. *Uh Ed?"* I didn't know what point I was trying to make, maybe Ed could make something out of it.

"Hell if I know" said Ed. "I don't even know what *resonate* means."

"Besides that *Chief* Bo'sun," I went on, "I eat that green pappy goopy yogurt toast *goop* you have ever mornin' why . . . Uh . . . I'd gag like a maggot!"

Bob has only papaya, yogurt, toast, and coffee—every morning. The same thing every day and it looks exactly like green baby shit.

"We doen git to eat with the Admiral!" threw in Ed, for what reason I don't know.

"That is because *Gentlemen*—an' I use the term loosely—you ain't cultured. Edjicated you might be, but no class! Definitely!"

I shot back with, " . . . Uh . . . I . . . hmm."

Ed said, "I got a dish that the Admiral would like."

I replied, " . . . Uh . . . I . . . hmm."

"What?" asked Bob.

"It's called Baked Stuffed Chicken,"

He gave me a grin.

"Actually, it is a perfect recipe for people who are just not sure how to tell when the chicken is done all the way though but not dry it up."

"You ought to write this down Bob" I said, handing him a pen. "Admiral might like it."

"You take six to seven pounds of chicken, one cup melted butter, one cup stuffing, an' one cup uncooked popcorn" said Ed.

When Bob heard the word "popcorn," he stopped writing. He knew something was coming.

"You salt an' pepper to taste," went on Ed. "Then ya preheat the oven to 'bout three hundred an' fifty degrees an' brush on some melted butter. Afta that, ya fill the insides of the bird with the stuffin' and popcorn."

Bob began to slowly shake his head over this long-winded tale.

"Ya put the chicken in the baking pan makin' sure the neck end toward the back of the oven." Ed mimicked putting a pan in an oven and closing the door. "Then, ya listen for popping sounds."

Ed paused for effect.

"Then when the chicken's ass blows the oven door open and the chicken flies across the room, it's done . . ."

One day in the Wardroom Ed and I ate with a visiting Japanese sailor from the Japanese navy who came aboard to observe engineering practices. Although we conversed a lot, we didn't gain much ground with my inability to hear certain nuances and his English pronunciations. We established that he lives in Tokyo and I in Sacramento. At first, he thought Sacramento was a Japanese word. Why? Beats me.

The Japanese have always been an enigma to Westerns. Infatuation with Americana rises to extremes in modern-day Japan: near Odaiba, in Tokyo Bay, a Statue of Liberty replica stands tall and there is also one in Yokosuka. Baseball, adopted from America, is the national sport, and brides and grooms wear traditional American wedding dress ushered by costumed Mickey and Minnie mouse attendants. The long post-war occupation by the US helped give rise to a deep affinity for American pop culture, which has made Tokyo Disneyland the world's most visited theme park. The United States bombed Japan into submission and, while adopting American culture to a high degree, the Japanese still think of Americans as barbarians, shuns children of mixed American and Japanese marriages, and are very much the racist society.

Jack Theroux, the travel writer, and Ruth Benedict, the anthropologist makes interesting comments about the Japanese conundrum. Thoroux writes in *The Great Railway Bazaar*, "The Japanese have perfected good manners and made them indistinguishable from rudeness."[3] Benedict says, "The Japanese are, to the highest degree, both aggressive and unaggressive, both militaristic and aesthetic, both insolent and polite, rigid and adaptable, submissive and resentful of being pushed around, loyal and treacherous, brave and timid, conservative and hospitable to new ways."[4]

The noted writer, James Clavell, gives a fictional account of the Japanese dichotomy in his famous book *King Rat.*

" . . . In '42, autumn of '42, I was in a camp just outside Bandung, Peter Marlowe said. That's up in the hills of Java, in the center of the island. . . . Well, the camp was tough on the Javanese . . . their wives and children were living just outside the wire. For a long time they used to slip out and spend the night, then get back into camp just before dawn. The camp was lightly guarded, so it was easy. Very dangerous for Europeans though, because the Javanese would turn you over to the Japs and that'd be your lot. One day the Japs gave an order that anyone caught outside would be shot. Of course, the Javanese thought it applied to everyone except them—they had been told that in a couple of weeks they were all to go free anyway. One day seven of them got caught . . . they were put up against the wall and shot. Just like that, in front of us. The seven bodies were buried—with military honors—where they fell. Then the Japanese made a little garden around the grave. They planted flowers and put a little white rope fence around the while area and put up a sign in Malay, Japanese, and English. It said, *These men died for their country*. . .

"The Japs posted an honor guard at the grave. After that, every Jap guard, every Jap officer who passed the 'shrine,' saluted. Everyone. And at that time POW's had to get up and bow if a Jap private came within seeing distance. If you didn't, you got the thick end of a rifle butt around your head.

---

[3] **Paul Theroux** (b. 1941), U.S. novelist, travel writer. *The Great Railway Bazaar*, ch. 28 (1975).

[4] **Ruth Benedict** (1887–1948), U.S. anthropologist. *The Chrysanthemum and the Sword*, ch. 1 (1946

"Doesn't make sense. The garden and saluting.

"That's why I don't like them . . . I'm afraid of them, because you've no yardstick to judge them. They don't react the way they should. Never."[5]

I thought as I read *Marlowe's tale*, "As the Japanese say, 'The nail that sticks up will be hammered down.'"

As previously mentioned, the wardroom requires formal dress for eating. Certain rules are taught at the Academy about wardroom behavior. Wardroom Rules are posted on a back bulkhead by the trophy case:

"The wardroom of a Navy ship is an officer's seagoing home. It is a club, a reading room, a dining room, and an office. It is a place where the ordinary rules of propriety, common sense, and good manners should be followed. This includes certain rules of etiquette founded on Navy customs and traditions, most of which are the same as those you observe in your own home. The Navy's prescribed code of conduct is much more formal than our contemporary way of life and most of it is based on extremely close contact with others over long periods, something most of us seldom experience. It is wise to refrain from working there or spending too much time there during working hours. The wardroom is usually closed for about two hours each day for cleaning."

I spend a lot of time in the wardroom. Each morning I go there to have coffee while bringing my journal up to date, shake the night's cobwebs away, and find someone to talk to. I used to do the same thing when Dad lived next door. We never talked when Mom was alive. Now that he was alone, and he would tell me stories of his childhood, of times when it was a treat to run to the barbed wire fence just to watch a T-Model Ford leave a dust trail down the dirt road I front of their farm in Arkansas. The rumble of boiling water would interrupt his contemplation's and he would put two heaping spoons of coffee in the water adding a pinch of salt. As the water frothed, he would take it off the burner and wait until it subsided. I can smell the aroma now, the teasing bouquet always better then the drinking. He would pour in cold water to settle the grounds. He took it black as I do now.

The coffee is sometimes fresh at that time of day, in the early morning, in the wardroom and there are usually one or two people to

---

[5] James Clavell. *King Rat*. Dell Books. Pg. 76

gab with to catch up on the scuttlebutt. The scuttlebutt is a nautical slang term for a drinking fountain on a ship or, in the days of sail, a water cask used to hold the day's supply of drinking water. On the older sailing ships, the scuttlebutt was the water barrel. As a sailor stopped for a drink, he gossiped, passing on the news of the day. So, "What's the latest?" became "What's the scuttlebutt?"

One of the messmen, Kris knows that I will be coming in around four to four-thirty, so he pours out the "tar" in the pot that has been simmering for hours and makes me a fresh pot. Nice guy. I munch a roll and read the *Declaration*, the ship's newspaper. I liked the procedures of the wardroom except the one rule on the *USS John Young* (total crew of 336) where at all meals all officers would stand behind a chair until the Captain showed. Often he was late; he's a very busy man. Waiting for the Captain wasted a lot of time.

The uniform of the day is required in the wardroom. In port, the uniform normally includes a coat and tie. At sea, the requirements are relaxed somewhat depending on the ship's interpretation of the standards of what was going on that day. Sweatshirts, skivvies, shower shoes, fatigues etc., are not appropriate; civilian attire is okay if you are leaving or coming aboard. Hats, caps, and other covers are not worn, except under arms or on official business. Courtesies are observed. A gentleman's club.

On the ships I have served on smaller than the carriers —and they all are smaller—the presiding officer—usually the Commanding Officer—sits at the head of the table, but not always—he may wish to occupy a center seat along a side so all can hear. The rest of the officers are seated to the right and left of the presiding officer in order of seniority. On the carriers, the Captain had his own private mess, and Commanders on down to warrant officers and civilians, such as I, use the wardroom. However, as I believe I have mentioned previously, I can eat anywhere on the ship without violating military protocol exceptions being the ship's Captain or the admiral's mess. I've expected to be invited there—never have been! Pure discrimination. (Maybe it is the beard!) When you come to the table in the carrier wardroom you ask, "May I join you?" even if there is only one person at the table and even if the officer is of a lower rank. The senior seated person will say, "Please do." (If you are a buddy and there are no high ranks around nor civilians, me excepted, the seated one may say something a bit aside of military protocol such as, "*Sit down Asshole!*" or "*there a lot of empty tables over there by the garbage can Dick head!*")

At one breakfast Ed, Bob, and I were sitting with Chaplain Ross and a couple of other officers. The Chief Bo'son was bragging about breakfasts in Hawaii. Ed looked at me winking saying—

"Heck Chief Bo'sun! You orta eat breakfast in South Texas!" I had told Ed this joke.

"Why's that?" Asked the Chief Bo'son looking up from his usual morning mess of papaya, yogurt, toast and coffee. *As I said he ate that shit every morning.*

Ed looked at me.

I said: "Yeah . . . well, I've eaten it down there. I looked down at my plate. Serious.

" . . . They cook up about four pounds of stringy, ol' tough Longhorn steak, give ya' a fifth bonded of Old Crow whiskey an' a blue-tick no-good hound dog."

Long pause . . .

I didn't say anymore. Ed kept quiet.

We waited.

He fell for it!

"Why'd they give ya the Hound dog?"

Ed said, "*To eat the steak!*"

Bob wanted to address us with his favorite descriptions of our personalities, lifestyles, and ancestry back several generations but couldn't with Chaplain Ross sitting there. He shook his head, looked down at the colorful compost on his plate mouthing "*Assholes.*"

Whenever an officer leaves the table, he asks to be excused. Smoking used to have certain rules and was allowed after coffee, but never while eating. However, any cigarette smoking on today's Navy ships is strictly regulated to "safe" areas, usually on the fantail but always outside any completely enclosed area where fumes may accumulate. The rumor in 1998, was that within a year or so there will no smoking aboard navy ships; *no smoking period!* Good idea. A necessary regulation. Of course, I do not smoke cigarettes, or anything else for that matter, but any possible source of fire is extremely jeopardous aboard any ship. Fire is the major cause of maritime disasters. The carrier has over five thousand personnel and can carry millions of gallons of high volatile fuel—not to mention there is enough explosive ordinance around to wipe out a couple of major cities or a small country. Cigarettes are not sold at the ships' stores. Smokers are pariahs, and on carriers, hopefully, face the same future as the Dodo bird. I can hear the smokers now: *"We are discriminated against. We already pay $36 a cartoon. We have a right to blow germs and harmful chemicals out of our moist lungs into your face and that of your child. We have a right to stink up the place and throw our butts on the sidewalk. We have the right to die of cancer and emphysema."* My cordial answer to their logically reasoned rights is the same as always: "Tough Shit Lone Ranger!"

For a solid week, I taught three classes of cultural anthropology without a textbook; for the one Physical Anthropology class, I had the new 8th edition. The box of texts the ESO and I thought were for all the classes were for Physical Anthropology only. I guessed the book department in San Diego had a problem getting the new Cultural Anthropology 8th edition fast enough. I can handle the cultural all right—I have about twenty years of it stored in my head—but I was sure glad to have the physical anthropology textbook. Physical anthropology is another problem—it is not my specialty. Thank Bhudda I had the twenty anthropology videos I stol . . . borrowed from some college years ago to take up some of the slack. Just as I was running out of lectures the problem was solved. I was making way to the post office to get a money order for uncle IRS, taking a twisting walk through the ever-busy hanger bay when a couple of my students gave me a call. I saw Seaman Roland and Seaman Johnston standing waist high in mail and packages. Literally hundreds of pounds of mail had been brought aboard off a supply ship—the *Guadelupe*—enough to fill a couple of trucks—and there were several cardboard boxes from Central Texas College.

Roland and Johnston yelled to me. "Hooray! Mr. Gunn. The books are in!"

My name wasn't on the boxes but the guys knew what they were. They told me not to bother carrying them; they would bring them to my cabin. Nice guys.

At that time, the *USS Independence* was the largest afloat post office in the Far East. The Military Postal Service (MPS) is an extension of the U.S. Postal Service (USPS) and operates under an agreement between the Department of Defense (DOD) and the USPS. The goal of the MPS is to provide shipboard personnel, *at a minimum*, a level of service equal to that provided by the United Postal Service.

Moreover, they do.

On a typical deployment, the crew of the *Indy's* post office will receipt, dispatch and sort over a half million dollars in money orders and postage stamps. Mail is sorted at the ships post office, but is not picked up there by individuals; a designated mail orderly picks up mail for his division and passes it out during Mail Call. Mail Call can be daily or weekly or even bi-monthly depending on accessibility of the ship to aircraft. Throughout the carrier there are eight mailboxes where the mail is collected and postmarked daily. Hence, not only does the carrier have a daily newspaper; it has a complete postal system. All Navy mail at sea is addressed the same: first is the rank and name, then Divison on the second line. On the third line is the name of the ship and on the fourth the Fleet Post Office designation. For example, the shipboard address of my old friend Master Sergeant Joe Maher on the USS Peleliu is:

MGYSGT Joseph Maher
CE 11th MEU (COMM)
USS Peleliu LHA-5
FPO AP 96618-2760

I learned a valuable lesson about postal service—money wise—when I left the *Independence* in Sydney, Australia. I wanted to mail a heavy briefcase to Sacramento containing class records. The local post office down the wharf from the ship wanted to charge $84. *Eighty-four dollars! They were out of their cotton-Australian-picking-mind!* That's twice what I paid for my first car! On a hunch, I checked with the ship's post office clerk; the charge there was *$6.40.* I asked the postal clerk why the big disparity? He said the reason was that the ship charged from its zip code, which was San Diego, California, so I was paying to ship from San Diego to Sacramento although I was really in Australia and the *Independence's* home base is Japan! *Go figure!* Moreover, the suitcase did not have to go on the *Indy* to San Diego, which would have been another four months, the duration of the deployment, but would be flown from Australia as regular mail. Make sense? I guess so. Anyway, I liked the idea.

Delighted that I had texts, I left the post office making my way to the cabin. Ed was at his desk when I came in. He pointed to a note on my rack; it was a message from Bob informing me the textbooks were in. People on the ship look out for one another.

Deck crew laying out safety net.

Safety net in position.

The author in Navy togs.

Big Bertha

Crowded flight deck.

UNREP

It was the 23rd of February and Chief Boatswain Robert Yoder's birthday. Forty-three today! Forty-three and the tall dog of the enlisted crew—not bad for a forty-three year old! However, Ed and I did not tell him that; we told him that he was *Over The Hill*! We put a big hand-lettered sign on his locker saying—

"43 SUCKS!"

Back home, on the other side of the International Date Line, and the other side of the world, it is still the 22 and my son Jim's 33rd birthday. Hardly seems possible my son is thirty-three; it was just a little while ago that he would ride on my shoulders. I went up to the mess hall and told the messman, Bryon Rivera, that it was the Chief Boatswain's birthday. He motioned me to follow him to the kitchen where he sliced off a hunk of warm, flat, breakfast pastry. I stuck three pieces of red and white colored candy on it, wrote "Happy Birthday Chief" on a napkin and took it to the cabin.

When I got to the cabin, Bob was in his rack with the curtains drawn, trying to get a few minutes rest. (He was up and down all night preparing for today's Un Rep—resupplying the ship). I placed the slab of cake on his desk. Ed took off for hot coffee for the three of us. When he came back, Ed called to Bob to come out for a note from the Admiral. When Bob crawled out, sleepy eyed, standing in his skivvies, scratching his balls while searching for his shower thongs, Ed and I sang "Happy Birthday to You" ending with "WE LOVE YOU BOB!" Heads poked in from the passageway, nosy, trying to figure what the ruckus was.

Ed dug out some trinket he had in his pack; he had all kinds of gewgaws in there, stuff he used to get into girl's panties. He gave it to Bob and shook his hand; I kissed bob on the cheek. Then we begged him to let us eat some of the cake.

"Screw you guys," he said. "Git your own cake sport fans!" He said as he began dividing the pastry into three equal parts with a letter opener. The Chief Bo'sun is a hard man. I think I detected a slight moistening at the edge of his eyes.

Yeah!

Ol' Chief Bo'sun is a mighty hard man.

May he always have fair winds and following seas.

Chapter 7

"Any person who is prepared for defeat,
Would be half defeated before he commenced."
Military quote of the day.

Sitting on the edge of my bunk dangling my legs a good five feet above the steel deck thinking I have corrected all the class papers, prepared for the next lectures, and so what is there to do the rest of the afternoon. Ed was at his desk writing a letter to a girl. Ed writes lots of letters to lots of girls. Being at sea, as much as he is, he has to keep in contact; he has to keep them primed for the short time he will home. Right now he has three girls that he is true to: the others he just sees from time to time when he wheels his little red sports car around San Diego. I told him that I almost had a psychic girlfriend once.

"What do you mean 'almost?'"

"Well . . . like I said, She was psychic an' dropped me before we met!"

The last date Ed had in San Diego turned out to be a disaster he tells me. He answered one of those "WOMEN LOOKING FOR MEN" adds and received a letter well written, in a beautiful flowing feminine script in lilac-lavender ink. A correspondence developed and he called her on the telephone. Her voice was low and throaty just as he hoped. He lowered his. They talked. They laughed over the electronic line, his voice a nucleus, hers an electron; they were elements of the universe of love beginning . . .

" . . . breath to breath, where hushed awakenings are beginning to stir . . . "

They would meet.

Coronado Hotel. San Diego.

At the bar.

"Sevenish," she breathed.

"Hell! . . . She could-a played linebacker for the Rams if she hadin'a been so damn FAT!" exclaimed Ed, his voice rising in indignation as he related the ill-fated date to me. She hadn't combed her hair in a week, and all she talked about was her asshole husband who did nuthin' but support her fat ass for eighteen years while she laid around watchin' television, eatin', an' readin' True Romance magazines."

"How'd the unblissful date end?" I asked. "Did ya git her in the sack? On the other hand, was there not one around big enough? "I giggled.

"Hell no! I said I hadda go to the head, so I cut out."

"Cut out?"

"Out through the kitchen. Even let her pay for the drinks."

"Boy! You are *tough!*"

"Yep!" He leaned back. "She an' I were like two ships sinking in the night."

While Ed and I were jabbering away Bob is in his bunk with the curtain drawn, but he's not sleeping. His light is on; I think he is reading a letter from his wife. I can hear the rustle of the pages.

"*Hey Ed!*" I said loud enough to be heard in the cabin next door.

"*Yeah,*" He said, looking up, raising his eyebrows questioningly.

"Awhile ago I was coming down the passageway an' I smelled popcorn. FRESH POPCORN, ED. The kind ya smell at the movies, you know . . . when ya first go in?"

"Yeah! Yeah!" More interested.

"I checked it out. Guess what? Those guys in F-7. They got a *microwave oven!* They showed it to me. Brand new . . . ! They pop popcorn. They gave me some. An' they can have popcorn whenever they want. They doen have ta go all the way up to the mess deck like we do."

"Yeah. I'll be damned!"

"We don't have a microwave oven, do we Ed?"

He looked around like it might be hiding somewhere.

"Nope. Don't see none."

"How come?"

"I dunno. What's their rank?"

"Hell, I don't know." I said. But, I know one thing—they don't have the rank the Chief Bo'sun does—. They only got some 3rd class Petty Officer. Guy name Jenkins."

Ed said "You mean they can get a microwave oven, have nice fresh popcorn any old time, just pop it up all hot and buttery, just put some salt on it, a great big bowl of hot, buttery, salty fuckin' *popcorn*?"

"All they want!" I said, rolling my eyes and throwing my arms up in exasperation.

Ed paused for minute; he looked up from his desk over his left shoulder at Bob's curtain, I bent over from the top bunk, looking down between my knees. It was quiet. No paper rustling now—*he was listening.*

I nodded my head up at Ed saying, "I guess the guy in charge over there is a nice guy. He take care his men. 'Good Man'. You know what I mean?"

"Yeah." Ed replied. "Not like *here*! An' here, he the top guy! The *Chief Bo'sun* for Christ's sake!"

Nothing. His light was on . . . he *was* listening.

"The Big Honcho!" Ed, a bit louder.

"The Big Maa Moo!" Me, louder yet.

"*Fuck you guys!*" drifted a voice from behind the blue curtain.

"Huh?"

"Did you hear something, Jim?"

"Yeah! I heard some 'em. Sounded like a squeaky little rat."

"Sounded like a little queer rat to me!" Ed had a big grin on his face.

"*Fuck you guys!*"

"Well I never!" said Ed.

"Is they're someone in there?" I asked. "I didn't know anybody was there! Did *you* know somebody there Ed?"

"Who's in there?" I yelled down.

"Yeah!" Ed said. "Someone's there. Someone very negative. Somebody probably eat popcorn with the *Admiral*. God knows we don't ask for much. We sure fuck doen git to go to Guam like somebody. Somebody's Admiral's *asshole* buddy!"

"It's the Navy Ed" I said.

"It's the NAVY FUCKIN' WAY," said Ed.

"I never met a Navy squib who'd do anything for a buddy."

"Probably let ya' drown even you fall overboard. Guy drown, they doen care."

"Yeah! Jus . . ."

"SCREW YOU GUYS AN' THE HORSE YOU RODE IN ON!"

"Wha . . .!"

"Well! . . .That's just plain rude!" I lisped—something I had learned from Ed.

"Crude! Crude! Crude!"

"Crude fag!"

"Lack a vocabulary. I read it inna book, Ed. Guy doen know how to talk, he jist natural' use bad language. Alla damn time! No class."

"You know Jim . . . some Navy trousers don't even have pockets."

"You kiddin'!" I was astonished.

"Nope! Same as women's pants. No zipper neither!"

"No zipper? How 'bout buttons?"

"Nope!"

"How they pee?"

"Squat like a toothless Singapore whore over one them holes."

"No!"

"Yep!"

"Umm . . . How they carry money? Ain't got no pockets."

"Too friggin' cheap. Probably don't need 'em. Wouldn't loan no money to a buddy anyway. 'Prob'ly wouldn't buy a buddy no popcorn" (Ed is an English teacher. He slips into the vernacular easily).

"Just like the Marines 'Hooray for me and fuc . . . '"

"*JESUS! Donin' you guys ever shut the hell up!"*

"OH! OH! . . . Guy take the Lord's name in vain he lie to his mother!"

"It's a fact!" I said. "Positively—POS-EE-TIVE-EE-LEE—A FACT!"

"Scientific!"

"Probably go to hell . . .."

"Inna basket."

"Onna big, fat Harley. Like them Hell's An-gee-lls . . .."

"Ain't no round trip ticket from hell, I mean . . ."

"ALLRIGHT ASSHOLES! I'LL GET A FRIGGIN' MICROWAVE! ANYTHING! JIST SHUT THE HELL UP FOR AWHILE!! *OKAY?"*

"Is that Bobby?" said Ed.

"Yep." I said. "That's the *BOSS*!"

"He Number One my book."

"Gonna git us a mike-row-wave!"

"Nice guy!" I said. "He's the *Chief* Boatswain. Friend the Admiral."

"The best!"

"Couldn't ask for better."

"Like a brother."

"The Navy is *the best!"*

"You need a *friend*, you ask a *sailor*."

"Give you the shirt off his back."

"Best guys inna world; that's what I always say."

"An' Bob. By the way. You git the microwave, you spring for the popcorn too. Okay?"

Gray days faded into grayer days. Sometimes you thought it was the next day, but it was still the same day, or was it yesterday? What the heck did sailors on Columbus's ships do poking along at three to four knots day after languid day—no television, no contact with home for months, or even years—how did they keep sane? Probably went nuts. Must have had a different mindset.

Daily routine blurred, sleeping times varied. No one on a carrier has a regular sleeping pattern: you don't go to bed at ten and get up a six—not everyday anyway. You nap. You nap in the morning after shower, or you nap after breakfast; you nap in the afternoon, you nap on a pile of life jackets off in a corner someplace. Flight operations might start at 0200, so you are up for a few hours, sleep a few hours, eat, go to class, nap, workout, shower, study, nap . . . fall asleep in the head.

Journal Entry—Up at 4 AM—0400. Watched a spectacular sun rise dripping a bucket full of gold out of a slate-gray sea. Angry eight-foot waves caused the *Indy* to rock gently as she sliced into them effortlessly. At 1400, the sea still ran high; there was a hell of an angry wind somewhere pushing a front toward us. There is always a period of curious quiet between the first sweet-smelling breeze and the time when the rain comes cracking down. Held classes. Napped. Dined with Edward, the ship's physician, and a male nurse. To bed at nine.

Journal Entry—The day is rising, the sun coming up fast. Had a cigarillo on the fantail. The morning palette splashes reds, yellows and violets on an eastern canvas sky at the edge of our horizon, the colors constantly changing in intensity and patterns. If some of sunrises I have seen at sea were used in a movie, they would look phony, man-made—but man could never really duplicate the intensity of colors on the scale here. The overhead sky is blue—No . . . Not just blue . . . A dozen shades of blue—blues never before seen before by the lands-man, blues not available in a painter's oils. Now the sky is light blue; the sea, gray awhile ago, is now dark cobalt. The waves die down, subside into high, long ocean swells lifting the huge carrier gently, like an egg, then setting it down again in its watery nest. The swells come up, peak almost even with the flight deck, but stay mirror smooth, not a fleck of foam, no white breaks the unruffled mirroring surface. Sometimes the sea resembles cold black flowing lava. Today, the sea is a soggy desert, devoid of life—no birds dot the sky, no flying fish race across the living surface, no ships on the horizon—we are an isolated speck, a dark pencil dot on a vast ever-changing canvas.

Though we seem detached from life, life is all around the *Indy*. This particular stretch of the Pacific is alive with ships; we just cannot see them, but we know that they are there; their masts are down below the horizon. Radio, radar, sonar and our own Hummer's[1] tell us that the ships are there, below the curve of the earth seemingly so far away but, in actuality, less than fifteen miles; our straight-line vision is limited by the curvature of the earth. We know they are there for the *Indy* is participating in Tandem Thrust, a joint operation of the United States and Australia involving dozens of ships, and hundreds of airplanes and thousands of men plus a trio of nuclear submarines.

Bob tells me that he's going to be busy today. I thought: *"When the hell are you not busy?"* The Captain—who really is an Admiral . . . You see if your are in charge . . . But I have already explained that Captain stuff to you—told Bob they would probably start transferring fuel today from a Canadian supply ship. I plan to photograph Bob in his duties today using them to put together a montage for his wife.

> SHIP NEWSPAPER: *Calvin Graham was a hero of the Battle of Guadalcanel in August 1942. A gunner on the USS South Dakota, he helped pull fellow crewmen to safety despite his own shrapnel wounds. Many heroes emerged during World War II, but Graham holds a distinction among them. He was born on April 3, 1930, which makes him 12 years old when he rescued his shipmates. Graham had fraudulently enlisted at age 12.*

Tough little bastard. Would be in his early seventies today. Wonder if he is still around.

Journal entry: Cloudy/rain.

[1] E-2 Hawkeye. Reconnaissance and electronic warfare airplane.

"Mackerel skies and Mares tails,
Make tall ships wear short sails."

High 64. Low 58. NNE 15 knots. Wide-awake at 0235. I noticed that when the environment becomes tedious, I begin to put minutia in my journal—keeping the old brain sparks flowing.

Bored with reading, I climbed down from my rack carefully so as not to step on an errant leg or arm of Bob or Ed. Bob is in the middle bunk, Ed the bottom. Both asleep. *Lazy bastards. Teach 'em all I know, and they still don't know nuthin'!*

Pulled on black jogging trousers[2] with USMC (United States Marine Corps) printed in gold letters outlined in red with a red stripe down the leg. As I put on new white gym socks and stuck my tootsies into new, pearly-white running shoes, I remembered a bit of trivia about the red trouser stripe from Marine Corps boot camp days. The Marine Corps has many legends that persist as to the uniform of the Marine and the origin of traditional dress as well as names. Did you ever wonder why Marines were called such appellatives as "Leathernecks" and "Devil Dogs" in the movies? The red stripe down the outer trouser leg commemorates the courage and tenacious fighting of the men who battled before Chaputapec in the Mexican War and whose exploits added the phrase "*From the Halls of Montezuma* . . . " to the Marine Corps Hymn. The red stripe on the trousers of all Marine officers and the Non-commissioned officers is to symbolize the blood shed by those Marines of another century.

The term "Leatherneck" is well documented. U.S. Marines of three generations wore leather collars or stocks once worn around the neck by both American and British Marines as well as soldiers. Beginning in 1798, " . . . one stock of black leather and clasp . . . " was issued to each U.S. Marine yearly. This stiff leather collar, fastened by two buckles at the back, measured nearly three and a half inches high, and it supposedly to accomplished three tasks: it kept the neck rigid when sighting along a rifle barrel; it presumably improved military bearing by forcing the chin high—although General George F. Elliot, recalling its use after the Civil War, said it made the wearers appear "like geese looking for rain"—and it was to protect the neck against sword cuts. The collar was dropped as an article of Marine uniform in 1872.

---

2 Marines were trousers; women wear "pants" as in "panties!"

Marines are called "Devil Dogs" as a result of fighting in Belleau Wood during World War I. In 1918, the Germans received a thorough indoctrination in the fighting ability of Marines—which the Japanese would also experience in World War II. Fighting through supposedly impenetrable woods and capturing supposedly untakeable terrain, the men of the 4th Marine Brigade ferociously attacked time after time, and had the Germans referring to them as "Teufelhunden" meaning "fierce fighting dogs of legendary origin" popularly translated as "Devil Dogs."

Marines are still called Devil Dogs today, albeit, mostly in the movies. I personally have not been called a Devil Dog in the Marines. I will admit however, to being addressed as a *Devil,* and several ladies have come at me with the term *Dog* on more than one occasion. However, I do not believe they were connecting the term to the Marines. It may have been personal.

Strange about women using blasphemous words. I have been called a dog, a devil, and once a bastard—no, twice the female of the species has called me a bastard—. However, a woman has never called me a son-of-a-bitch. Not that I have not deserved it. I do not know why, but women just do not know how to cuss. They say—in modern times—"You dog! Or "shit!" And even "Fuck!" But that's about it. They do not know how really swear like a trooper. I mean, I have seen my Dad mash his finger with a two-pound ball peen hammer and, throwing the offending tool far out into the lumber yard—which by the way, he would have to go and hunt it up later—let fly with, "*God-Damn, sun-a-bitchin'-no-good, lop-eared, mule-headed bastard-go-to-hell!*" and he was an amateur compared to some of the lumberjacks.

I like what Ambrose Bierce says about cussing. He says, "Take not God's name in vain; select a time when it will have effect."

Women don't give the rough edge of the tongue when they say things like "Oh dang it!" or, "Shoot!" My mother, when she was really pissed would come out with the blasphemous "Oh Fuss!" *Oh Fuss?* Somehow, it just did not seem she was lashing out to tempestuously.

But they got other ways fellows.

I broke some of the tedium of the days by "working out." A black "T" slipover shirt emblazoned with a chalk-white human skull and a Marine Corps dress hat and the words " *I know there's a heaven 'cause I've been to Hell!*" under a black jogging jacket finished off my jogging outfit. Almost! Reaching up into my gray steel locker, I took down a brand new *USS INDEPENDENCE* officer's cap, with a mess of scrambled eggs on the bill. The finishing touch to my exercise ensemble was a pair of $40—on special at the ship exchange—aviator sunglasses. DAMN! *DID I LOOK HOT!* All these jazzy clothes and my black, neatly trimmed beard (there were a few white curly's in there; touch those little fellows up later with a little Berina Hair Color Cream, Dark-Brown A2.), *Sean Connery and The Hunt for Red October had nuthin' on this boy!* Cut quite a figure if I do say so; and I do say so! I mean, clothes make the man: naked people have little or no influence on society, although, come to think of it, if you go to work naked people will stop stealing your pens after they've seen where you keep them. There is another reason for dressing well says Ralph Waldo Emerson; namely: " . . . that dogs respect it, and will not attack you in good clothes."[3]

Journal Entry: Needing fresh air, I made way to the elevators. Hanging outside the ship, the elevators provide a spectacular panorama of the bow cleaving white furrows through the dark waters, the far away horizon, and the stern. The elevators are a place to escape heat for the ship's passage provides a stiff breeze right in the ol' face. The steel deck of the elevator is being swabbed, cleaning away oil and jet fuel. Just inside the bay a sailor, clad in spattered overalls, is spray painting a F-14 Tomcat while a few feet away four mechanics are changing a jet engine on a similar plane. A seaman was pitching brown paper trash bags into the sea from the elevator.

I was somewhat bothered by the amount of trash thrown into the ocean from the carrier. On the fantail, a continuous stream of sailors reacted to the speaker announcing it was time to dump trash. Most trash is contained in tall brown paper bags—biodegradable—and one of the big thrill of the day is to watch the bags go over the fantail, plop, splitting open littering the sea. Normally there is a guard with a polished broom handle, a hole drilled into the end it with a throng laced through it, poking into the bags searching for plastic—but he is often times not too effective—I observed plastic and many bottles go over. They will be there, littering the seabed or just floating, for a long, long time.

Journal Entry: Brass Balls: The *Independence* ,along with its battle group escort ships, got underway from Yokosuka, Japan, February

---

[3] Ralph Waldo Emerson. Entry written in 1870, *Journals*, 1909-1914.

15—and it was cold! Each day the ship left winter a little further behind as it inched toward the equator. Now the days were warming and would be come irritatingly hot as the ship made for summer in Australia. We were in the interim zone where one day it would be warm, the next drizzly with rain as the *Indy* made passage through microenvironments. Blackened jellyfish squalls trailed rain tentacles in the distance amid bright sunlit expanses of silver molten sea. I have seen one side of the ship with rain-wetted decks, while the opposite side was bone dry.

Fact.

Chief Boatswain Bob Yoder came in the cabin door wearing a plastic poncho mumbling, "Damn rain ruined my clothes" while slapping his cover free of water droplets. He continued grumbling as he took off the poncho to reveal rain spotted dress Khaki's.

"What's up, Bob?" asked Ed.

"Hot on deck . . . then cold. Freeze the balls off a brass monkey."

"Where'd that come from?" I asked. "I never saw a brass monkey with brass balls. I've seen a monkey with ugly balls 'specially them on oranoutangs an' on Ed."

"An' I saw Gunn once, naked in the showers. It was horrible! Somethin' I never want to experience again in this lifetime!" decreed Ed, the English Teacher of the Year—well . . . of the *Indy* anyway.

"HA!" yelled Bob, scaring the hell out of Ed whose ass raised a couple of inches off his chair. "You smart-asses college pukes don't know what 'freeze the balls off a brass monkey' means do YA?" HA!"

Ed looked at me, his eyes saying ol' Bob had finally slipped his moorings and was heading directly out to sea.

"You been smokin' coffee grounds again Bob? Better git some of that good marijuana next time" I said, moving over close to the hatchway in case I had to make a fast escape.

"HA!" He yelled again. "HA! Smart guy! What does it mean?"

"What the fuck does what mean?"

"Freeze the balls off a brass monkey!"

Hell. I didn't know. I shrugged.

"Well . . . it means it's so cold . . . a brass monkeys balls would freeze off. I guess"

I looked to Ed for confirmation. He shrugged.

"No way, O'say!" Bob said. "Listen and learn sport fans." He went on to say:

"Back in the days when sailing ships had nuthin' but iron cannon for protection, well . . . cannon of the times required iron cannonballs. Cannonballs had to be stored so that they did not roll around on deck, understand? One solution was to stack them in a square-based little pyramid near the cannon. The top level had one ball, the next level had four, the next nine, the next sixteen, and so on. Four levels provided a stack of 30 cannonballs. Even you two dummy's can count that high. To keep the cannonballs in place a brass plate with rounded indentations, one for each cannonball in the bottom layer was devised." He used his hands to show the square of the brass plate. "This brass plate was called a *brass monkey*. Brass was used because when the iron cannonballs rusted, they would not stick to the brass plate as they would to an iron one. Ya didn't know that, did ya shitbird?"

I looked at Ed.

"He's talkin' to YOU!" said Ed.

I shook my head, too entranced to be insulted.

" Well . . . when temperature falls to low levels, brass contracts faster than iron, and as it became colder, the indentations in the brass monkey would get smaller than the iron cannonballs they were holding. If the temperature became too cold, the bottom layer would pop out of the now smaller indentations spilling the entire pyramid all over the deck.

"Thus, it was, quite literally, 'Cold enough to freeze the balls off a brass monkey.'"

"No shit!" I gazed in wonder. He had said *"literally."*

Bob had a chicken-shit smirk on his mug.

"An' he said *'Thus!'*"

"I'll be fucked sideways!" Said Ed, dumfounded, stealing one of my sayings.

"Well! Slap me a sunburn." I echoed.

"*HE IS* SMART!" Said Ed, pointing a long finger at Bob.

"Shines like the evening star! An' that's a fact!"

"He is so bright, his Momma used to put him under a washtub so the sun could come up!"

"He didn't fall off no turnip truck yest'day"

"He is technically sound but socially impossible . . ."

"Screw you guys."

"An' sensitive."

'He's as sensitive as a cat with a feather up its ass!"

Bob got a shit-eatin'-grin on his face.

"I'll tell ya how sensitive I am," he said with a sly look. "I'm tired of living with a couple of hogs in a pig sty. I want you two PRO-FESS-EERS to give this place a field day. If'in this place ain't swabbed and picked up by 1700, yo are not gonna share in the cake messman Shaul gave me. You got that Sport Fans?"

He had cake? That was a different story.

"YESSIR!" I yelled, snapping to attention.

"An' you Morris" he said, looking at Ed. "Trouble with you is there was three kids in your family—one of each sex!"

I smirked at Ed. Bob got him that time!

"An' who lef' this pogey bait layin' 'round here for ants? Git that cleaned up too!"

"AYE! AYE! Chief Bo'sun" said Ed. "It wasn't me! It was Gunn!"

Rotten Ed. Turn in his best friend for some cake. His *only* friend.

"An' you Gunn. You stopped to think, an' forgot to start again."

I come back with, " . . . Uh . . . I . . . Hmm."

"Remember. This place not clean—no cake!"

"AYE! AYE" Chief Bo'sun! We both bellowed, saluting as Bob went out the hatch, back to work.

"WE LOVE THE NAVY!" we yelled around the corner.

"Screw you guys!" he threw back.

And so, under a sky dotted with fleecy mares tails scowling across the sky, we sailed on, inking our way across the map on a satellite determined path across the vastness of the Pacific Ocean heedless of fog or rain. No one need be at the helm; electronic circuits in the *Indy's* computers would communicate with electronic circuits in other ships and overhead satellites to plot courses, plotting imaginary lines across electronic oceans on the navigator's screens projecting where each ship would be in the hours ahead, plotting speed and course to warm of possible collidings. We did our little tasks, read our mail for, unlike the old whaling ships, the modern boat is serviced by that most phenomenal contraption the flying machine. The old Nantucket whalers would shout to passing ships "Ahoy! This is the Southern Star! We are bound where the leviathan goest! Send our letters to the Pacific Ocean . . ." And the letters might arrive in two or three years. On the *Indy*, the mail is brought in weekly or, at the worst, bi-monthly—and we complain.

The *Indy* made its way on across the Great South Sea toward the speck in its vastness called Guam, and we were happy for, like all sailors, we were delighted to go to sea, and, like all sailors—old salt, or neophyte—we anticipated once again being on land.

*****

The Pacific Ocean
By
Herman Melville

"The Great South Sea, the most lovely and serene of all oceans, it rolls eastward a thousand leagues of blue. There is, one knows not what sweet mystery about this sea, whose gently awful stirrings seems to speak of some hidden soul beneath; like those fabled undulations of the Ephesian sod over the buried Evangelist St. John. And meet it is, that over these sea pastures, wide-rolling prairies and Potter's Fields of all four continents, the waves should rise and fall, and ebb and flow unceasingly; for here, millions of mixed shades and shadows, drowned dreams, somnambulisms, reveries; all that we call lives and souls, lie dreaming, dreaming, still; tossing like slumberers in their beds; the ever-rolling waves but made so by their restlessness.

"To any meditative Magian rover, this serene Pacific, once beheld, must ever after be the sea of his adoption. It rolls the midmost waters of the world, the Indian Ocean and Atlantic being but its arms. The same waves wash the moles of the new-built California towns, but yesterday planted by the recentest race of men and lave the faded but still gorgeous skirts of the Asiatic lands, older than Abraham; while all between float milky-waves of coral isles, and low-lying, endless, unknown Archipelagoes, and impenetrable Japans. Thus this mysterious, divine Pacific zones the world's bulk about; makes all coasts one bay to it; seems the tide-beating heart of earth, lifted by those eternal swells, you needs must own the seductive god, bowing your head to Pan."

Chapter 8

"In war; the defense exists mainly
That the offense may act more freely".
Military quote of the day.

The canvas banner stretched all the way across the broad side of a one-story warehouse on the dock. Held aloft by steel cables it could be read a fair mile out to sea. In the red, white and blue colors of "Old Glory" words, man-high, spelled out a slogan—a motto we were to see often around the island:

"Where America's Day Begins—Paradise in the Pacific!"

Underneath the banner, a smaller white sign with a blue border leaped out from the side of the tan building:

HAFA ADAI
WELCOME TO GUAM

Guam, an enigmatic term unknown by Americans, prior to World War II in the Pacific, but infamously known by those who have seen an American war movie of that time or the rare teenager who diligently read their American history book in the eleventh grade. In the eleventh grade, sixteen year-old moi, was interested in football, looking up Miss Cheer Leader's Fench poodle embossed skirt, working on the 1936 Ford my brother bought me for $40, and hanging out with Carter Hamilton, Bill Lesher, and Odis Hunt—Mr. Brady's History 1 was way down on my teenage hormone planned list. I assume most teenagers' thought along the same lines—the males anyway. Most of the guys I knew in high school were interested in sports, cars, and sex—not with whom, but when. History and current events, outside the school, was practically non-existent.

Guam is a microscopic speck on a map of the Pacific Ocean 6,100 miles from the Golden Gate. A glimmering, iridescent green emerald dot, one of hundreds of such dots flung by an unplanned hand across this part of the Pacific, small and lonely in a sapphire sea, Guam has only 212 square miles of surface area. Although it looks like a grain of sand on a maritime chart, It is actually the peak of an immense underwater mountain. Only a few yards above sea level, the island barely escapes being a seamount.[1]

Once ashore, I discovered a paradoxical diversity packed into this small area: little farms of one and two acres, fishing villages, and quaint little hamlets ringed the island like a string of beads along the shoreline while in the interior, juxtaposed on this quaintness, there was a major university, sex shops, and a Beverly Hills neighborhood. Fashion emporiums abound: Gucci, Nordstrom's and other high-priced department stores. There is even a high-priced Planet Hollywood restaurant/movie star museum with glass-encased, waxy Sylvester "Rocky" Stallone—The Italian Stallion—hands clasped overhead; a mausoleum of remnants of old actor's paraphernalia inside and a huge revolving globe of the world outside. Well drinks were expensive, a Coke $2.50.

One landmark on Guam, that was talked about incessantly on board the *Indy* as we drew nearer Guam, a monument to commercialism that everyone planned to visit (I didn't plan to but I did!), was: **K-Mart!** Now this ain't just any ol' K-Mart, no common variety type! Guam has the honor of boasting *the largest K-Mart in the world!* Wow! Why this fascinated the crew so much, I never came to understand. They are all young of course; they wear civilian shirts with slogans, strange voluptuous trousers, weird shoes—some with seemingly four-inch soles—an' caps on backwards among other things*!* And ear rings! I mean, some of the clothing that the modern under and around twenty wear . . . well . . . if they'd worn them in the fifties when I was in high school they would have been sent to their guidance counselor! *And rightly so!* I mean, they are *weird!* At their age, I looked sharp in my 1950's khaki pegged-trousers with the little tab in back, Tab Hunter shirt with a little tab in the back, and blue-suede shoes with white socks. *And their hair!* I wore my hair in a nice sweptback wave—with a curl hanging over the forehead and a ducktail in the back held in place with Brill Cream. These guys are shorn up the sides with stubble on top. And these sailors, these *killer technicians* who, just hours ago,

---

[1] Sea-mount: A submarine mountain.

were handling million dollars of expensive electronic equipment and some of the most dangerous weapons in the world had, once ashore, become deranged dressers, wearing a gobbledygook of mismatched clothing, clothing that, had I put them on at home when I was a kid, Mom's ol' cow Bessie would have lowed[2] in incomparable shame. Or would have at least stopped giving milk!

Let's go shopping Mabel; let's go look at some things! "Things" and "Stuff" are what people who like to go shopping for in the malls at home. I understand that there's actually a living, breathing group of people in the world—mainly women—who actually *like to go shopping*! However, they are not to be blamed to harshly for this affliction—obviously it is a genetic defect, a missing DNA molecule or an under-achieving gene battered off its double helix by some errant particle from a video game played at the South Side Mall on a Saturday afternoon. This gene is passed by chromosome from female to female completely skipping the male animal. Men only shop for tools and only at Sears, who happened to have the best display of tools in the world. What about cars you ask? Men shop for cars don't they? Nope! They're just lookin'. You don't shop for a car, you look for one. A word of advice: Do not, I repeat: *Do Not* go looking for a new car with girlfriend or wife. They shop for color and care nothing about the fact the vehicle will do a hundred and fifty in eight seconds—you know—the important stuff! Some people shop for as much as *over an hour!* Not me boy! Fifteen minutes I've parked, done all my Christmas shopping for the year, picked up a couple pair of socks and shorts; brown or black—the socks, not the shorts—had a cup of coffee an' I'm outta there. *Save 50%!* Heck! I saved more than that! I saved 100% 'cause a lot of the time I don't buy anything in the first place!

I did go to K-Mart in Guam. I went to the big K-Mart in the sky! *Why did I do it?* I don't know! Everybody else did. It was packed with sailors from our ship; there was a bus every fifteen minutes from store to ship, a distance of about eleven miles; a free bus on a continual fifteen–minutes schedule picking up and disgorging sailors by the hundreds.

Before K-Mart took over, the island of Guam had been a United States territory since William McKinley,[3] as the 25th president of the United States, declared war against Spain in 1898. As a result of the

---

[2] Lowed: Moo or mood to you cement-bound city dwellers.

[3] (1843-1901)

Spanish-American War there was Spanish evacuation of Cuba and the cession of Puerto Rico, Guam, and the Philippines to the United States. Guam's people became full U.S. citizens in 1950: however, not all provisions of the constitution apply to the island since it is an unincorporated territory. As of our time of our arrival, the population stands at approximately 165,000.

A few days before making port at Guam, there was serious discussion on the *Indy* among the higher-ups in Admiral country—Bob attended—whether we would actually go ashore. The normal berthing facilities at the Navy Station on Guam are shallow and the entrance to Apra Harbor is splattered with coral heads, jagged and menacing, visible just beneath the water's turquoise surface. For a ship the size of the *USS Independence*, a big carrier, there are no modern-day berthing facilities. No ship the size of a carrier had ever berthed inside Apra Harbor—even during World War II. These statistics, and the fact that the Big Brass told Bob not to expect liberty for they weren't about to attempt to small-boat over five thousand sailors to shore, and back for three or four days—were of little interest to the Chief Boatswain. The scuttlebutt was however, that the higher-ups, still as nervous as a sinner newly turned saint after the Tailhook incident, were not that interested in turning loose five thousand—mostly young men—people loose to the bars and flesh pots of Guam, the Japanese's new Hawaii. This was gossip, however, and the Chief Boatswain paid little heed to hearsay. Robert wanted his people to go ashore, to have a liberty in a foreign land, for some of them their first time to visit an exotic region.

Other people's statistics are of little interest to Robert Yoder, Chief Honcho of the *Indy*. He did not get to be the Main Enlisted Man listening to other people's ciphers or paying too much attention to a couple of yahoos like Ed and me. Bob makes his own statistics. After his meeting with the scrambled-egg higher ups, Bob lugged in a sizable roll of blue prints to our cabin, pushed a couple of motorcycle magazines aside and filled all empty space with big drawings of Apra bay and the *Indy*. Spreading the blue prints and drawings out, he set to pondering. Ed and I watched him as he intently pored over the papers with ruler and pencil. We stayed out of his way, and kept Ed kept his yap shut—a hard thing for him to do. I, of course, was my usual smoothly agreeable and courteous self. The Admiral liked Bob, this we knew—that was not effortful, everyone of account liked him. Nevertheless, we figured he was nuts; he had about as much chance of changing the brass's collective minds as a used car salesman hawking a 1957 rusty Edsel at a Mercedes dealership in Beverly Hills; he was just going to get in disfavor with the Admiral if he kept this opposition to the Big Guys. But Bob had other ideas: he was a fellow who was intent on creating a bit of carrier history—he wasn't going to let a little thing like the absence of docking facilities keep his "peoples" from liberty.

Just before noon, after hours of sweating concentration, penciling in lines, and muttering, Bob called to Ed and me. "Take a look at this sport's fans!" he said, standing up, stepping back so we could view his desk. We did. He had penciled and ruled in enough lines on an exterior drawing of the carrier and a shore line that it looked like a gaggle of spiders at a square dance had started spinning psychedelic webs in drunken revelry.

"Yeah!" Ed said, looking down at the spidery lacework without an inkling of what he was seeing.

"Looks good to me." I said, raising my eyebrows while grimacing the corners of my mouth down to Ed as if to say, *what the hell is this?*

"I think that'll do it don't you?" Bob said, rolling up the sketches he'd made along with the big rolls of ship blue prints.

"Yep!" said Ed nodding his head sideways.

"That's it!" I commented brilliantly having not the least idea of what he had done.

Bob spit-shined his black dress shoes and got all fancied up in his Class-A uniform. Ed and I stayed out of his way and for keeping our mouths shut. Finally, Bob cleaned his glasses meticulously, set his jaw, and stomped off to see the Admiral.

Ed looked at me; I shrugged.

"Think they'll kill him?" he asked me.

"Without a doubt" I said.

Hell! I'd been on the boat 'bout a month and I had never even *seen* the Admiral—well once! Bob dropped in whenever he felt like it.

He spent an hour in the luxury of the Admirals quarters—paneled walls, bedroom and it's own mess! —Talking and flipping around blue prints. Ed and I decided that Bob was trying to change the Navy's motto "Welcome Aboard!" to the See Bee's "Can Do!" However, enlisted just do not do that with Admirals.

He came back about after an hour, face dark and clouded muttering " . . . he had told somebody off . . ."

Ed said, "Be careful Bob. When the elephants fight, it's the grass that gets trampled."

Not answering, Bob grabbed some papers and took off again.

I gaped at Ed. "Elephants fighting in the grass?" I said. "You been readin' Kipling again?"

Ed looked at me, shrugged, and sat down, contemplating the gray paint on his drop-down desktop, picking at it with a fingernail.

"Crappola!" I said.

"Yeah. You know it," said Ed.

Bob did not come back.

Later, at chow, Chaplain Ross mentioned that with no preamble, that the Chief Boatswain, and the Admiral helo-coptered to Guam to look over the entrance to the bay and study the docks. I looked at him, then at Ed. "Uh. What . . . what do you think they are gonna do?" I asked Derek, looking at Ed.

"Something about taking the *Indy* into berth" said the chaplain.

No shit! . . . mouthed Ed.

"Well . . . the . . . Chief Bo-sun told us . . . uh . . . he might . . . he an' the Captain might take it in" I said.

"Yes. I believe that is what they are planning," said Chaplain Ross nonchalantly rising from the table to bus his dishes.

I looked at Ed. He raised his eyebrows as to say *beats the hell out of me1*

"Maybe he did it" I said.

"I dunno if he did or not, but this worrying about Bob put me off my feed" said Ed, tall and lanky, who then proceeded to scarf down enough chow to feed a hungry Chinese family plus grandma for a couple of weeks.

"NOW HEAR THIS! NOW HEAR THIS! THE SMOKING LAMP IS OUT, THROUGHOUT THE SHIP, WHIKE HANDLING AMMUNITION. I SAY AGAIN, THE SMOKING LAMP IS OUT, THROUGHOUT THE SHIP WHILE HANDLING AMMUNTION.

Ed and I wandered down to the bow part of the hanger deck watching the ammo handlers bring up bombs and boxes of fifty caliber bullets from the depths of the ship using a brightly yellow-painted chain block and tackle. Bob usually supervised the Petty Officers who supervised the ammo handlers. He was not there today; things went off all right.

"MAN OVERBOARD! MAN OVERBOARD! MAN YOUR BATTLE STATIONS! MAN YOUR BATTLE STATIONS! I SAY AGAIN, MAN OVERBOARD! MAN OVERBOARD! MAN YOUR BATTLE STATIONS! MAN YOUR BATTLE STATIONS!"

Ed and I toddled off to the ESO office to be counted. During a "Man Overboard" drill, everyone on the carrier was to be accounted for in less than 20 minutes. The closest the crew came was 23 minutes. The skinny was that XO was pissed. He passed this mimeographed sheet out on three different occasions.

Man Overboard

When a person goes overboard, prompt action is essential. Anyone who sees someone go overboard must immediately sound the alarm "Man overboard, port (starboard) side," and drops a life ring or life jacket. If possible, the person is kept in sight. A smoke float or dye marker is immediately dropped if possible.

The officer of the deck then takes charge and maneuvers the ship to a recovery position. At the same time, word is passed twice and six more short blasts on the ship's whistle. The lifeboat crew stands by to lower away when directed and if available, a helicopter is to be launched. A helo has a better chance of spotting a person than a crew in a boat.

The Navy impresses on seamen, that the person overboard may be "you." If you go overboard, keep your head, do not panic or despair. Hold your breath when you hit the water; the buoyancy of your lungs will bring you to the surface. Do not swim frantically away from the ship; the screws will not suck you under, because they are to deep in the water. Keep afloat and try to stay in one place. The ship will maneuver right back down her track toward you.

Even if no one saw you go over, keep afloat. When a shipmate is found missing, ships, and aircraft began an intensive search along the track.

No one believed the part about the screws *not* sucking a person under.

"Hello Sports Fans!"

It had been three days. Ed and I had been dragging around, swathed in lassitude, off our feed—well . . .I was down to three meals a day and a couple of snacks and Ed could only eat half a pumpkin pie after dinner. My spleen was off, circulation sluggish.

I told Ed a joke.

"Hey Ed! Ya know when life begins?"

He looked up from some math papers he had been staring at.

"Life begins?"

"Yeah! This Rabbi says to this Catholic Father, 'Ya know Father, life begins when the sperm meets the egg.'"

The Father says, "No! Life begins when the fetus is formed."

" So, not knowin' which of 'em is right, I asked my Dad." Dad says, "Life begins when the kids leave home an' the dog dies!"

Ed looks at me blankly, grim about the mouth. He didn't get it. Lately, he has been about as fun as a coffin salesman at a Buddhist convention. No word from bob in three days.

So, we came in and he says:

"Hello Sport Fans!"

He's sitting at his desk, a Navy cup of coffee in one fist, a shiny magazine in the other, grinning ear to ear like the fat Cheshire cat in Alice in Wonderland.

"Bob!" bellows Ed.

"Chief Bo'sun!" I gave him a big grin.

He turned, smiling, laying aside the latest Harley Davidson publication.

"You been in jail?" I asked.

"You guys ready for liberty in Guam? Bob asked.

"Whatta the Admiral say?" Ed asked.

"WE GONNA GO? I yelled at him.

THE SHIP GOING IN?" yelled Ed.

Dragging out that broad cunning feline grin again Bob said:

"Was there ever any doubt?"

The Chief Bo'sun was back!

The Chief Boatswain convinced them all: The Captain, the XO—whom he had told off telling the young Commander in effect he didn't know his ass from a hole-in-the-ground, apologizing later—and the Admiral—his buddy. Bob said they had accepted his plans for docking the big carrier, that it was going to cost a bundle—about $800,000—and that he was flying in with some of his "peoples" to set the while thing up.

Later I told Bob the joke about "You Know When Life Begins!" and Ed laughed his ass off.

Just as he was reading to leave with his "peoples" for a week to fly to Guam, Bob's macabre subconscious *dark side* made itself known; his evil, mean side, lurking perniciously beneath his polished uniform; *his black, evil side*, just like Darth Vader in *Star Wars*. Ed said it was not subconscious at all, that he had noticed Bob's Dracula tendencies from the very beginning; that they were obvious as a black tarantula on a virgin bride's white wedding cake!

Animal treacherous to his roommates, Bob said to Ed and me that, " . . . while you turkeys are stuck here in this coffin of iron, I will be in a 'Tittie Bar' in Agana[4] suckin' on a few brewski's watchin' some of that fine ass dancin'." Totally shocked at this uncompassionate rhetoric, we *reparteed* that this elicitation was an unchristian attitude, that we—Ed and I—had been the most unobtrusive of roommates—never criticizing. An' did we *ever* ask for anything? No! We never asking for anything like a lot of his *peoples*, and that perhaps, with his present attitude, his time ashore might be more profitably spent in the library or church practicing virtuous deeds.

"Many are called but few are chosen," Bob, I told him. What did I mean? Phooey. I do not know. I was just trying to think of something

"You drink an' fool aroun' Bob, you gonna feel like the symptoms on a medicine bottle!" Ed said.

"What the hell that mean?" I asked.

Ed shrugged.

I looked at Ed with an, *"Is that the best you can come up with?"* His mouth puckered as he shrugged his shoulders again with a look of befuddlement.

"Well!" Bob held his hand to his ear . . . I hear them callin' and . . .What? " He cupped his right ear again " . . .it's one, ah . . .Yep! . . .It's one of them little brown nudies at the Tittie Bar. Gotta go!"

---

[4] Agana: Capitol and only city on Guam.

Although that is where we would certainly spend some time when ashore—Tittie Bars—we pleaded with Bob, we adulated; we told him it would lead to sexual thoughts, beer drinking, chawing and spitting of the vile plug tobacco weed; and God knows what other traps of Lucifer's a *married* man of Bob's sensitivities might be led into. (When we put stress on the word 'marriage' he flipped us the bird!)

He was finishing up his kit, checking his spit-shined shoes already polished like a piece of new obsidian. We suggested that he might follow the Christian Way and think of his poor buddies, captives in this iron box; we had no friend like the Admiral flying us around in his own personal helicopter. He, Bob, was our dearest friend an' as we were sorely derived of whiskey, he might find it in his heart even . . . even to find us a bottle of Johnny Walker Black Label, a germ-killing liquid which we would use for medicinal purposes; i.e. to fight chills and ward off pneumonia and other pernicious diseases(Ed called Johnny Black Label liquid panty remover.)

Nothing.

"Why'n don't we go with you, Bob. We could be your assistants."

"Yeah!" said Ed. "Tell the Admiral you need our math or somethin'"

At least this got a laugh, albeit a diabolical one and a "You sportfan's stay here an' eat popcorn outta the new microwave!"

I said, "We're sorry about the microwave Bob; we wont ask for nuthin' else," I whined. "Anyway that was Ed's idea, not mine." I had no qualms about blaming Ed remembering his telling Bob about me leaving candy laying around for the ants. "Maybe I could go?" (My English was deteriorating fast, reverting to lumber mill days.)

"An' remember Bob", said Ed. "Lookin' at those poor little naked girls is a sin." Ed was one of the hornest, pussy-chasing guys I ever met. He always stayed in his own room in any port so he could take pictures of all the naked strumpets he brought in—he kept a box of pictures of unrobed maidens in his desk. "You sin Bob, an' you'll burn in the abyss of hell!"

Abyss? Abyss! For Christ's sake! I gave Ed an exasperated stare. He shrugged.

"I doen know no ab-piss stuff. But while you yahoos is here, I is there! Yippe-ty-yi-oh! Yeehaaa! Them gals is warm for my form!" Whoo-aaw!

He sang:

"Rye whiskey, rye whiskey, rye whiskey I crrrriieee,

If a tree don't fall on me,
I'll live 'till I diiieeee."

Well! We learned.

We learned just how barbarous a man could be when he held the upper hand, how cruel he could be to his fellow shipmates in their time of need. Not even giving us the courtesy of a reply to our humiliating entreaty, Bob pursed his lips in a haughty, superior manner and, holding an imaginary cocktail glass in his right hand while cocking his little pinkie finger out into the air a couple of yards like some snobbish Grand Dame, replied in his most cultured voice, nice and soft:

"Screw you Bozos!"

"I take it that you are not amenable to our suggestion?" asked Ed.

"You got that right Shipmate! Ya can stay here an' eat all that stolen popcorn ya got stashed in your fart sack!"

"Hooray for me an' screw . . . " I never got it out . . .

"*Screw you Gunn*! I doen wanna hear any that Leatherneck shit! Friggin' Marines I.Q. is gotta stay in two digits or they friggin' wan' let ya in. Friggin' Marines 'bout as useful as a friggin' ashtray on a friggin' Harley." Ash tray on a Harley motorcycle—that was one of his favorite sayings. We'd heard it half a dozen times.

"This definitely is not a Christian attitude, Chief Bo'*sun*." I said. "Not Christain at all!"

"Just remember, Bob." Said Ed. "There ain't no round trip ticket from hell!" *We'd said that before.*

"OH Yeah? Well, while you an' this ape-lovin,' hippie-bearded pro-fes-whore are here *in* hell on this steel box, I'm gonna be *in* heaven *in* a tittie bar havin' a beer an' watchin' them little honeys shake them sweet littl' asses! *WHOOHAW!*"

Slinging his ditty bag over his shoulder, he went out the hatchway laughing gleefully like Jack Nickolson in *One Flew Over the Cuckoo's Nest*. The steel hatch slammed with a resounding glang. Ed and I stood there glassy-eyed like a couple of tick-infested South Texas steers that had just been pole axed with an eight-pound sledge-hammer. Bob stuck his head back in saying, " . . .An-na one of you pussy's make my rack; an' clean up this pig sty!"

With a lingering "A-Low-HAA!" he was gone.

"Damn!" I looked at Ed.

"Crap!" he said, "I'll make the bunk, you wanna sweep up."

"He got us that time," I said, looking for the broom,

"Yeah! I know." said Ed shaking his head. "Can't trust the crafty bastard! He's gittin' more like us ever day!

Bob was gone. Gone a long time. Gone for days.

We cleaned that cabin like a couple of self-pitying galley slaves, making Bob's bunk tight enough to bounce a quarter halfway to the overhead. We kept to the routine. I taught my classes, Ed, his. I began to notice a lassitude; I was dragging around, tiredness in my bones. After each class I seemed unnaturally tired and would sleep on and off all day. I began to suspect that the fatigue was caused by the body's constant adjustment to the ship's movements *and* the incessant background noise of the ship *and* boredom. I don't believe in boredom, but I was bored. I talked this over with some of the anthropology class members about this phenomenon of the constant boat and continual noise: they said, yes it was true. The body has to accustom itself to the ship; get in shape as it were; build up little muscles. Along with this malaise, I accidentally rubbed some chalk in my left eye and it almost swelled shut, reddening, and seeping liquid. After class, one of the enlisted men took me down a couple of stairwells, around a few left and right turns to the medical facility where another enlisted cleaned the eye with saline solution. Cleared right up! Nice guys!

Life aboard was even more monotonous now that Bob was not around—no one to pick on. Ed mostly worked on his English class papers, reading essay after essay, blooding the papers with miles of red pencil. He has sixty students: I don't know how he stands to read the same one-page "What I want to be" over sixty times. Drive me bonkers! His English students spoke well, but their writing was amateurish. It is a truism that we learn two versions of English: a spoken one and then, later, a written version. I once had a partner in the real estate business who obviously was intelligent and spoke well—he was close to a millionaire—a self-made man. His writing, however, was about the fifth grade level, scrawling without regard to correct use of grammar. He did not have to worry about it; he could just hire someone to all his correspondence.

One day, after evening chow, about 1810, I ambled back to the stern of the hanger bay, making way through the clutter and workmen in the jet engine repair and testing room out into the salt-laden evening air. One of my students had told me that he was going to be fishing off the fantail; he wanted me to come by. The angler was there, however, he had set his pole aside; the *Indy* was moving too fast causing the hook to continually flip into the air losing bait. From Texas, the fisherman was typical of some of the middle-rates. Early thirties, married and divorced, he joined the Navy young, got out and, not being able or not wanting to make it on the "outside," he "shipped over." Often the phrase "He found a home in the Navy" is used as a joke, but this fellow—and many others—did find a home; the Navy was their fireside. Some ex-convicts, who have spent a good portion of their 70 odd years behind bars, cannot take the freedom of the outside. I believe some sailors are the same; there is a comfort in the rules, the comradmanship, the routine, the security of being in the navy.

I snapped more photographs of the glorious sunset—I now have dozens; each night they are so beautiful, you snap just one more. A sliver of burnt orange sun hung on the horizon this evening. I blinked. It was gone. I tottered off below to shower and wash my hair: the water is so soft one can really work up lather. When I went to Korea on a troop ship in the fifties, we showered in seawater—no lather—and the body felt slightly sticky after. On the carriers, the evaporators can turn seawater into fresh water at a phenomenal rate—over 300,000 gallons per day. As much as needed for a small town.

Directly after breakfast the next morning, I was returning to my cabin when an announcement came over the intercom that a Lear jet was going to do a fly-by towing a dummy missile target on a thousand yard tow line and the Phalanx was going to fire at it. Not wanting to miss this, I quickly threw on some weather clothing, grabbed cameras heading for the flight deck. On the flight deck the loud speaker gave out that the first fly-by would be a practice one, the second *live*. The plane was fifty miles out, then ten, then five. Many sharp, young eyes saw it way long before I sighted the speck dancing over the sea. Swaying right at us, the plane was hard to make out against a background of scattered clouds. Suddenly it was there, then passing just in front of the bow, about three-quarters of a mile out and a thousand feet high. I had difficulty finding the target missile for the towline was about three times as long as I thought it would be.[5] The *Indy* didn't fire on the target—which I thought was very small—until the fourth pass. Someone said it was because the Phalanx was sighting in. The quip then

[5] The towline is long for good reason I found out later in the cruise. Seems that when the Japanese Navy fired on the same target with the same civilian Lear jet a couple of rounds went in the Lear.

was, "were they going to be able to 'sight in' four times in a non-practice situation, i. e., War! "

When a Phalanx fires a swarm of bullets it does not fool around; it gets right to the business at hand. The housing of the weapon looks like E-2 D-2 in Stars Wars—a white dome about three feet high—and when it lets go . . . "RRRAAAPPP!" . . . for about five seconds and 6,000 slugs fan out toward the target. Imagine an insect such as an ill-tempered wasp coming straight at you to put its nasty stinger in your fair soft body. You pick up Grandpa's ol' double-barrel persuader loaded with three thousand double-ought buckshot in each barrel and let fly dead on; that little bastard of a wasp's stinging days are over *as he has disappeared!* Gone to that little Entomology Land in the Big Bug Beyond. When the Phalanx fires, the same thing happens to an oncoming enemy airplane or missile.

The target was at twelve o'clock high in front of the carrier straight ahead of the bow; we were headed directly under it. After the RRRAAAPPP of the Phalanx, tiny pieces of metal rained on the bow deck. The Phalanx does not have to fire too long. It is designed as a "last ditch" defense against anti-ship missiles and attack warplanes at very close range. Once activated, the Phalanx Mk 16[6] operates automatically acquiring the closest target cycling out *three thousand rounds per minute.* The rounds (bullets) are made of depleted uranium which is about two and one-half times *denser than steel.* At their speed—3,600 feet per second—plus their solidity, the rounds go through a plane's armor like a 50-caliber elephant hunter's bullet goes through soft butter except for one not-so-slight difference: after penetration these babies explode. A desirable piece of weaponry—as long as you are on the friendly end of it. Goodbye wasp! Goodbye airplane. Goodbye missile!

Today it became *SCORCHING*! Hot! Hot! Hot! Tuesday, February 25 and the *Indy* is at latitude 14° north, longitude 154° east. Since Guam is at 13°-north latitude and approximately 145°-east longitude, we are just a little northeast of the island; it is a few miles away. ("I figured this out all by myself" as my three-year old granddaughter would say.) 95 degrees at 10 AM and the low tonight will only be down

---

[6] General Dynamics/General Electric Phalanx. Class: Anti-aircraft gun since 1980—ship-borne rotary Phalanx Mk 16 @ 3,000 rounds per minute. (cyclic) Weight: 13,430 lb. Horizontal range: 6,500 yards. Crew: One. Caliber: 20 mm.

to 75—and the metal of the ship is heating up, retaining yesterday's heat. We are definitely getting closer to the equator: the sun will soon be directly overhead at noon when we arrive there; the atmosphere thinner in relation to the sun and the earth and it will be *hotter!*

Bob came back.

It was late morning. Ed had eaten someplace; I chowed down in the "Dirty Mess'—the pilots mess. Bob came in looking as neat and crisp as a new hundred-dollar bill. He was all-aflame, hopped up from his visit to the "tittie bars" in Guam.

Grinning like a shit-eating ape, he began to tell Ed and me his latest escapade ashore with the Admiral.

"You homos wanta' hear what we had to eat?"

"No!" I said.

"Definitely not!" emphasized Ed.

"Well . . . First the Admiral ordered this fancy wine, ya see. Then, we had some of that horse's ovaries shit—hors d'oeuvre to you intellectuals. An' it wasn't jus' me . . . there were these other land-lubbing high brass dudes; there was stars and braid all over the place an' there was ol' Bob eatin' with the brass." He put the rolled up blue prints of the ship on his desk and started taking off his Class-A uniform; it was as neatly clean and creased as when he left days ago.

"Then the Admiral had this golden-brown duck; I had a big ol' rare steak with these choice little baby mushrooms an asparagus with *reel* butter."

I'd had half-warm "shit-on-a-shingle"[7] for breakfast. It had looked like light-grey vomit. Taste wasn't far off either.

Ed looked at the half-eaten peanut butter and jelly sandwich on his desk, the bread slightly hard from being dried out. He picked it up with two fingers and made a one-hander into the wastebasket.

Bob went on.

"I ate a bunch of French bread drenched with butter an' that garlic shit. Boy! That was *good!* Then this big fat-assed waitress aske' me I want some kruutons? I ask her 'What are these kruu-tons?' She said real slow—'kru...tons'. I said, 'Huh?' She said, 'c-r-u-t-o-n-s' like I was some kinda idiot. I said, 'What the hell are krutons?' She says toasted bread all cut up! Dumb broad! If'n it's toast, why don't they say toast!"

And he went on:

"Do yu wanta know what we had for desert?"

---

[7] Chipped beef and gravy on toast.

"No!" said Ed. "I definitely do not want to know! I am not the least interested."

"Screw you, Bob." I said. But I wanted to know. I am partial to lemon pie myself—no meringue—with steaming hot coffee. I prefer it at breakfast. I asked belligerently, "Whadda ya have . . . *Pussy Pie?"*

"Please! Please! No crudities among the troops . . . Well! . . . .The Admiral ordered this tray with all this flaming shit on it an' the waiter lit her up like a bonfire an' dumped the whole mess on some ice cream."

"'Cherries Jubilee?'" Ed looked up at him.

"Yeah. Somethin' like that!" He was rubbing his belly now a little more prominent then when he left.

"Sure was good! Even tho' you guys got no balls, you guys want me to tell you about the tittie's bar I went to . . .?"

"You gonna' tell us anyway even I say 'No" I asked him.

"Yeah!"

"Ed?" I gave him a quizzing look.

'I don't care" he replied dismally. "Screw 'im!"

"What about the titties?"

"Boy! You shouda seen this little Filipino gal with the big bazoo-kas! *Man*! I mean those babies just went each other way stickin' right out there all bouncy and' smooth with big ol' . . . "

"*Bob*!" I said, sticking my finger in his face. "We went to a movie last night with fifty other guys."

"A boring movie" said Ed. "It had hundreds of black and white spotted dogs runnin' around pissin' on ever thing . . . some Disney thing."

"There weren't no sex in it Bob." I said. "Jist dogs kissin".

"Well on her big ol' titties, she had these big ol' . . ."

"No!" I said. "I'm not going to stay here and listen to this sadistic bastard, Ed!" I grabbed a towel and headed out the door. Bob was grinning. Ed's faith in depravity was reaffirmed as Bob ticked off the names of bars and the perversive acts therein. I dreamed about food and sex most of the night.

Not until later did I find out the steps it had taken by our brave First Bo-sum to get the *Indy* and it's liberty hungry crew into Guam—but he pulled it off—one enlisted man up against all that Brass. The Admiral and other decision makers on the ship had, at first, thought about taking the carrier into the shallow waters of Apra Harbor, near the sprawling naval station, but had decided it was not feasible to do so. Bob worked over the blue prints of the ship and the drawings of the harbor crisscrossing both with red and blues lines, and then he took the blue prints with him to a final meeting with the Admiral and the XO. The meeting generated a little heat; Bob told the XO off in no uncertain terms, mentioning that perhaps the XO really shouldn't open his mouth to show his ignorance. Bob eventually apologized, losing the battle with the XO, but winning the war with the Admiral.

We were going in!

Here is how he did it. Spending—and this is rumor from the wardroom—$800,000 (that's U.S. of A. dollars) on a wooden dock built on a steel floating barge that was put together in two days—about a third of the length of the carrier. Therefore, instead of docking at the shallow water wharf, Bob just had them make one where the water was deep enough near a large park and golf course. He also had concrete bollards sunk in the ground along the beach. You do not tie up a ship the size of the *Independence* to a couple of trees. Three small tugs, ordered by Bob, showed up and began to worry around the *Independence* like small terriers around a black bear, guiding the carrier as her rudder became useless for steering for lack of speed after her engines were throttled down. As we came to the narrow approach to the docking area, the tugs began to churn up mud from the channel floor, pushing and nudging with little room to maneuver in the cramped channel; then the wind picked up blowing the wrong direction, working against the ship. The tugs held the carrier about a hundred yards from the park where the picnickers, golfers, and baseball players gaped at the goings-on. We were a good quarter mile from the regular docking facilities and the spectators must have wondered what the hell those crazy Navy people were doing now over there by the park and the golf course!

Knowing that you cannot tie an 80,000-ton ship to a couple of trees—if the wind came up the broad expanse of the carrier's side would act like a big sail and the carrier would rip the trees out by the roots—Bob had the Navy dig several deep holes in the bank near the navy golf course where they sank Volkswagen-size iron stanchions set with tons of concrete—concrete only two days hardened. Remembering my construction days, I thought *no way that cement is going to hold; it's still damp inside.* However, it did! While the tugs held the immense vessel steady, riflemen on the flight deck of the *Indy* shot lines landing in the lawn of the huge park bordering the water. These lines were used to hand-pull hawsers[8] that were then tied to some tractors, two dump trucks, and a couple of forklifts (forklifts for Pete's sake! I'd never thought of that!) and about five hundred sailors. They may even have had one of the park's riding ponies hooked up also.

These renegade tow-trucks, plus the sailors, began to take up slack on the hawsers—a giant game of Tug-o'-War was about to begin. The little tugs pushed, churning on the lee[9] side of the carrier; the fork lifts, trucks, tractors, men—and probably a couple of lawn mowers in there someplace—all of them began, at Bob's command, to pull on the other side, the windward side. Bob stood on an elevator with a hand-held radio coordinating, talking to observers strung along the flight deck, talking to officers and petty officers on the shore, yelling into the radio to the tugs out of sight on the other side of the carrier. Slowly the big lady inched toward the counterfeit dock; I could only tell when she began to over come her inertia and started to move by lining up a stanchion on the ship with a post ashore. Imperceptibly, at first, then . . . a movement. Pushing, props again churning the mud, the little tugs engines roared with diesel power; and cleat tractors[10], trucks, forklifts, men—some women sailors—and probably—those lawn mowers strained at the fat ropes, pulling, straining, pulling hard. Pushing and pulling—the Old *Indy*—the oldest ship in the fleet, nestled into the dock as smooth as a mother Red Wing sitting on her babies. Whew!

Cheers bounced off the ship and echoed from the shore as the big, heavy hawsers were rigidly made fast. The con blasted out with jazzy music loud and clear, a few sailors did a little jig, there was some laughter and then the music was cut. The Admiral's voice boomed God-like over the assembly:

"WELL DONE CHIEF BOTSWAIN YODER!"

Bob stood at attention, rigid in his dress whites, put his callused hand to his cap brim, snapping off a biting salute. My eyes moistened a little, probably from the wind.

Ed, on shore, gave me a wave of *Can you beat that?*

The Navy has a motto: "Welcome Aboard!"

---

[8] A large cable or rope used in mooring or towing a ship.

[9] Lee: the side away from the direction from which the wind blows: the side sheltered from the wind.

[10] Cleat tractors. Caterpillar tractors with hard rubber tracks that will not gouge the tarmac at airports as they pull air planes into parking spaces.

Chief Boatswain Robert "Bob" Yoder has a motto:

"The difficult we do immediately;
The impossible—
(After a couple of beers at a tittie bar)
— Takes a little longer."

Bob's "peoples" and Pro-fes-whore Jim went below to change into civvies—Ed was already ashore, on his way.

.

It was liberty time.

Chapter 9

"The wind and waves are always
On the side of the ablest navigator".
Military quote of the day.

Guam smelled like a sack of garbage, a big sack that has been rotting in the mid-day sun too long. The odor hit us at sea before land was sighted. The sky, cerulean clear for days, was now a dirty pall umbrella-like over the skyline at the bow. Oppressive humidity, rotting vegetation, and exhaust fumes from hundreds of automobile engines, nailed to the earth by a malevolent sun, put a slight damper on the clear blue skies of the past week and the verdant island. But that effluvium was not unexpected. I have responded to this olfactory stimulus before: Panama, Costa Rica (on the coast) and El Salvador—and the Amazon rain Forest— in the hot months—about 11 months of the year—all smell like an unwashed garbage can left out by the back porch to long.

Why the odor? *We are in the Tropics!*[1]

And the ol' *Indy* is letting the crew know we are in the hot country by becoming blistering herself—retaining yesterday's, the day before that, and last week's heat in her steel skin, conducting it along the framework to every cabin and passageway. In addition, the *Indy* was generally being cantankerous about her water and cooling systems. Last night I crawled out of my bunk twice, wet a T-shirt, wring it out, and put it back on to go to bed. Lay right down on top of the fart sheet[2] as soaked as a doughnut in a coffee cup in a South Texas greasy spoon cafe!

The men in the kitchens particularly have a rough time with the continual heat. Messmen—or more commonly, mess cooks—generally, do not stand watches, but do take part in drills. Standing over hot stoves the size of billiard tables, these guys put out *19,000 m*eals daily,

---

[1] **Tropic:** Either of two parallels of latitude on the earth, one 23°27' north of the equator and the other 23°27' south of the equator, representing the points farthest north and south at which the sun can shine directly overhead and constituting the boundaries of the Torrid Zone.

[2] **Fart sack.** Military term for the bottom sheet covering the bunk's mattress.

so they do not have much time to do anything but cook, sweat, and sleep.

The only cool water on board, other than that in the milk, soft drink, and cold-water dispensers in the mess, is water trapped in the pipes in the shower stalls. By cool water in this instance, cool means not boiling hot. The shower stalls are constructed of galvanized metal about the size of a small phone booth with a mildew-stained canvas curtain covering the doorway held by little hooks that are always snagging. To shower one turns on the cold faucet only; the water comes out tepid and in about eighth seconds is scalding hot—I am not exaggerating, it is *hot!* The *Independence*, besides being the oldest ship in the navy, is not nuclear, so it does not have the air conditioning power to cool a steel ship in the tropics as well at the *Carl Vinson* or the *Abraham Lincoln*. The enormous amount of steel in a carrier heats during the day, but because of the humidity and high temperatures at night—night temperatures as high as 85 degrees—it does not lose at night as much heat as it gains in the day. Consequently, each day, the ship gets hotter! To take a shower, you turn on the tap, get wet in three seconds, then quickly turn it off. Soap all over. Turn on the tap and you have five seconds to get the soap off before parboiling sets in!

All morning the ship's crew immersed themselves in an orgy of cleaning and waxing. Bob, his normally pristine khaki's stained with sweat, had been on the go all morning, grabbing a bite on the run, dropping in to the cabin to pick up a folder, grumbling and mumbling. After being the main principal in docking the carrier, he now was in the throes of hooking the sewage system from the ship to an outlet on land. As we neared Guam all sewage dumping at sea was ceased and stored aboard until docking. Consider the cost to dispose of the sewage of a small town in California with a population of 5,500 alimentary canals processing food all say! In addition, you will agree, each person does not go to the toilet just once a day; I mean *there is a lot of flushing going on!* Now from this small town there are three days of "collections." The cost to dispose of this waste on the carrier; a fee paid to the local Guam authorities comes to a crappy *$500,000*. Now that is not a lot shit, as in "I'm not shittin' you," but it is a lot of *crap*! Bank rolling a moving town like an aircraft carrier is an expensive proposition! High-priced one might say; and I do! $800,000 to dock; $500,000 to get rid of shit! That's over a million "dockshekels!" To be "crapped on" can mean "take it on the chin" and I believe that is just what the Navy was doing: taking it on the chin from the locals, i.e., getting crapped out! Being bamboozled. Consider how much a local economy like Guam is boosted when a ship with 5,500 young people come ashore with pockets full of moola, dinero, escudos, dockshekels—and eager to spend it. The local economy in Pattaya, Thailand, where I live, was reported by the local newspaper to have benefited by over $6,000,000 when the *USS Kitty Hawk* visited for three days on Operation Cobra Gold. It is said (rumor) that it cost $12,000,000 per day to run a nuclear carrier, $5,000,000,000 to build one. Six million here, Twelve million there, and five billion over there: It adds up to a pocket full of nice change.

No one can leave the ship for liberty in Guam until the work parties have secured the water and electrical lines—except the English teacher Eduardo who was already ashore. Everybody has a duty or a station, so nobody goes ashore except security, nobody that is *except* the ship's anthropologist. Who knows what mysterious and erotic artifacts the anthropologist is going to investigate in this tropical greenhouse. Hardly anyone knows what he does anyway. Probably going to look for some monkeys or apes. Anthropologists always wear a beard, some Navajo jewelry, an' they're all a little weird anyway. So, knowing this—which had a great deal of truth to it—I stuck a notebook under my arm and with a stride that booked no nonsense, strode right down the accommodation ladder not slowing pace, giving a brief nod to the armed brow guard—*Look! There goes the Anthropologist. Probably gonna visit some local Indians and bed down some monkeys!* —on to the dock and the fecund soil of the Territory of Guam.

Ed was an old hand at dealing with the rules and regulations of the peacetime Navy; he was waiting for me, standing by a bunch of new automobiles for sale parked in the grass near the entrance to the dock. I think he got off the ship before the brow was down.

A carnival atmosphere prevailed in the grassy area between the carrier and the park and the golf course. A portable commercial center appeared Aladdin-like overnight to service the carrier. Three new cars gleamed under a tarpaulin for delivery here or in the states; a couple of out-door beer booths with tables and benches were ready for business, and several souvenir stalls with sea shells, T-shirts, movie star photographs—Marilyn Monroe, James Dean, and Humphrey Bogart predominated—and lots of other "stuff" for sale, had expectant female proprietors—all with big "titties" trolling for customers. I am sure the fact that most of the sales clerks were of the female gender with generous cleavage and tight-butted dresses was no coincidence. Even if you did not buy anything, it was worth look . . . ah . . .shopping.

Ed and I were to old and experienced to be taken in by these female equatorial sharks; you buy all that souvenir junk and you wind up carrying it. Travel light that's my motto. You buy something; you have to lug it about, sometimes for weeks. Loaded with cameras and overnight bags, we hastened to get away from the ship and catch a ride to Agana before the flood of sailors was released from the ship. Immediately we met a congenial navy man dressed in civilian clothing who offered us a ride to the main part of the base a couple of miles away. He had a new Chevy Blazer and we where happy to pile in. Come to find out our benefactor was the acting commander of the base. He was great, very helpful, offering all kinds of advice until he found out who we actually were. He thought at first we were journalists, but when he found out we were not, he got rid of us pretty fast. The Navy Base Commanders like journalists; they do not care however, to associate with instructors and other low life.

The acting commander's directions were not very accurate when he dropped us off. However, we finally found the base travel agency, "Gato Travel" for what little good it did us. No hotels under a hundred bucks—the fleet was in, so up go prices—and no cars for rent at all. How come? Wiser heads than ours used the ship's R&R department to book ahead while at sea. Rotten swabbies! What to do? We walked. The base is well spread out with large neatly mown brown grassy areas. We saw a complex of buildings three-quarters of a mile or so away and headed off in that direction. There we found a large, modern shopping center much like home, set up with car rentals and banks of phone booths specifically set up for direct calls to the States.

Again, no cars were available for renting. We were out of luck. And it was getting hotter as we struggled around carrying our gear. Ed hailed a taxi—$27 for a ride to the capitol. Just as we were about to give in to the local pettifogger, I spied Smitty's Van with a sign on its side advertising a ride to Agana for $5. Ed and I piled out of the scoundrel's taxi—leaving him yelling Guamanian expletives at our fast-departing rear ends no doubt mad because we would not let him gouge us—and piled in with three enlisted taking off in air-conditioned bliss.

We found a passable hotel, the Hamilton Guest House, near the Agana Marina, on the edge of the city. $50. Nothing fancy, early Fifties decor with television, air-conditioning, shower, and a beautiful view of Agana Bay, just across the four-lane highway, with the turquoise

Philippine Sea beyond. We booked rooms next to one another; Ed disappeared into his, I took a shower sluicing away the days heat, turned on the television, lay down and fell asleep. The telephone brought me half-awake a few minutes later; some fellow wanted to know if I wanted a woman to come to my room to give a massage. I believe it was the old guy downstairs who had checked us in. I passed on the invitation.

The view from the balcony of the room was spectacular. Curved palm trees swayed in the ocean breeze; blue-green water with white breakers gleamed out on the reef, a photographer's dream, a honey mooner's paradise. Across the bay, a large pyramid shaped building seemed oddly out of place, most likely a resort hotel. I had never heard of the Philippine Sea nor the Andaman Sea, nor the Barda Sea, nor the Arafua Sea, but here they were, seas all over the place. Americans—including myself—know little of the geography of Oceania or of Southeast Asia—one could spend eons sailing the seas around Indonesia, the Philippines, and New Guinea . . . Well! . . . You could if you could avoid the pirates. Pirates still ply these waters. Modern-day buccaneers with assault rifles instead of knives, grenade launchers replacing swords, and high-speed jet boats. Standing with my hands on the balcony railing gazing at the turquoise sea and the cerulean sky, I recalled my grammar school years and the Sunday papers I read in the mountain foothills of the Mother Lode of *Terry and the Pirates* and the I-wanna-be-hero Steve Canyon. Then there was Burt Lancaster in *The Crimson Pirate*; that movie must have been in the early fifties. Hell! I could see them out there: Sea Rovers sailing their corsairs flying a black flag bearing the emblematic white skull and crossbones of the "Jolly Roger! "

There still pirates today. There are probably more pirates today plying the waters of the South China Sea, the Philippine Sea and parts of the Caribbean Sea than in the days of Captain Kidd and Edward "Blackbeard" Teach. The Malacca Straight between Malaysia and northern Indonesia and the Java Sea between Borneo and southern Indonesia are particularly noted for modern-day pirates. The newest boarding technique is for a high-speed jet boat to approach the bow of a tanker or freighter, board the ship, and set the crew adrift. Paradoxically, modern day commercial ships are manned by skeleton crews using computers instead of muscle to run the ship, and are generally not armed. Within days of the boarding, the cargo has been off-loaded in a pirate friendly harbor; the pirated ship has a new name or has been sunk, or as in several cases, ransomed back to the owners. Just recently in 2002, in Pattaya, a small tanker docked at Chon Buri, an industrial and port city just north of Pattaya and the crew and Captain took shore leave. They never returned. After a week or so, port authorities investigated the ship finding it was full of diesel oil and that the name was painted over. It was a ship from China that had been hijacked and sailed to Thailand. The original crew of seven Chinese never turned up nor did the hijackers as of the writing of the story in the Bangkok Post.

After my beauty nap, I was anxious to explore. Ed was not in his room, so I changed clothes, slung the camera bag over my shoulder, and took off up the beach toward the main part of Agana a mile or so away.

Immediately, I ran into three different groups of guys from the ship; dressed in civilian clothes, they were hardly recognizable. Under the modern policy of the Navy, no enlisted man under a certain rank can go on liberty alone—I believe it is E-6. He must have a partner; there must at least be two and the Navy prefers three together when in port, together *all* the time. It is a rule that has been drummed into each man so thoroughly that it is seldom broken. The top brass does not want any incidents involving American sailors in foreign ports since Tailhook and rapes in Guam and Japan by American enlisted men.

I walked a couple of miles along the park-like winding path of the shoreline stopping for a breather at an up-scale resort hotel just to sit in the empty, lavishly decorated bar, have a beer and gaze at the sea while listening to the piano music. It was nice to be in a room, with a view of the ocean, that was not moving. Waxed marble floor, oiled wood on the walls and enough plants to stock a small rain forest—a fancy place. The bottle of Coors was $2, not too bad for the ambiance. I sipped at the icy beaded bottle, ate a handful of salted peanuts, and listened to the piano. Had this been a movie, a willowy redhead or brunette would have undulated in, wearing a broad hat, elegant clothing with scarlet lips and equally red high heels. Although the place was empty of customers, just the bartender, a Hoagy Carmichael type wiping away at a bar glass, she would take the stool next to mine, leaning over with a cigarette in mouth asking, "Got a light?" And we would have taken it from there. Well . . . I have been all over the world—traveled in airplanes, trains, and boats and only once have this happened to me—once in Hawaii—a young lady from Canada.

No. I have not met many movie women in my travels. If I did, it would most likely go like this:

I would be in a fancy resort like this one. A gorgeous blond would sit down next to me. I would lack the nerve to talk to her, but suddenly she would sneeze and her glass eye would come flying out of the socket and I would reflexively catch it. "Oh my god, I am sooo sorry," the woman would say as she pops her eye in place. "Let me buy you dinner to make it up to you." We would enjoy dinner together, and afterwards she would invite me to her room for a nightcap. After a bit, she would lead me into her bedroom for a night of wild passionate sex. The next morning when I awaken, she would have my breakfast ready for me. I would say something like, "You know, you are the perfect woman. Are you this nice to every guy you meet."

"No," she would reply. "You just happened to catch my eye."

On down the beach boardwalk—made of concrete—amid the tattoo joints and massage parlors, I came to a steak house—a western theme bar and grill: saw-dust covered floors, a glassy-eyed, longhorn bull head over the doorway and spurs hanging on the wall—a joint touted by the ship's newspaper as the place to go for the enlisted people. The sawdust-covered floor was packed wall to wall with guys from the ship. Every one wore civvies, no one wore a uniform . . . Well, no one but a couple of MP's strolling around wearing Brossard and thumping a nightstick into a meaty palm. The guys—and a couple of female enlisted—were yelling to one another, throwing darts, feeding the juke box, eating platters of barbecued ribs and drinking beer from small pitchers—not glasses—pitchers holding at least a quart. I answered a few hellos thrown toward "that's my teacher" and "THERE HE IS!" Here a bottle of Coors was $3.75; however, one could throw peanut shells on the floor—and it was cheap for me; none of them would let me pay for a drink. The female waitresses (serving persons?) had red and white checkered, low-cut blouses strained by lovely, jiggling, over-sized mammary glands[3] and tight little butts in mini-denim shorts; when they walked it looked like two little piglets trying to get out of a burlap sack. Always was partial to pork, especially partial to the butt portion. I hung around with the crowd for an hour, but their young enthusiasm reminded me of college days—it was okay for me to visit, but too long and I would be a damper on their merriment. Another beer, a

---

[3] Bob would have said 'Titties'.

wave, and I was off. This was an enlisted person's place; officers and older people did not belong here.

I caught a taxi back to the Hamilton Guest House—$7.80 for one mile. The driver was a talkative, black-American, an ex-sailor from South Carolina. He said that he made a good salary, but living costs were high on the island. They were, as was everything else. Guam is very expensive; expensive they say because the Japanese now vacation here rather than Hawaii.

Ed was not yet in so I watched a little television. Just a few minutes after I returned to my room the bedside phone rang and a male voice asked, again, if I wanted a woman to come to my room. Envisioning a snaggled tooth, fat Melanesian-type woman waddling into the room gnawing on a taro root, I passed. As an ex-high school science teacher, I knew too much about syphilitic chancres, skin rashes, paresis, and Wassermann tests to dip into any of the local delights. Went to bed. Alone.

Awoke Saturday morning in a bed that was not as narrow as a surfboard, and was not moving. Luxury. Ed knocked on the door about nine—I had not seen him since we booked into the hotel. He hit a few tittie bars (shades of Bob) the previous night but was not too impressed. We rented a car—$65 daily—and drove out to the naval base where the *Indy* was docked and the shopping less expensive. I bought a blue polo shirt, some sundries and loaded up with film. We ate lunch on the base, then took a drive along the coast stopping at a little village that was having a celebration.

Banners hung across the narrow, pot-holed macadam road, varied colored balloons floated tethered to strings, and steel guitar Hawaiian music blasted from refrigerator sized speakers. A kids carnival—circa 1940—offered rides in little cars and planes; there was cotton candy, jet ski boat races, and beer: beer in tubs of ice, beer in hampers, beer in booths: there was mucho beer. The beer was $1.50 a bottle—tall neck—with a pair of sunglasses thrown in with each beer purchase. Why the sunglasses? I don't KNOW! Strange. I visited another beer booth and got a free disposable cigarette lighter with my brewski. Equally strange, but countryside pleasant.

We spent two hours talking to and watching the locals. The indigenous people do not call themselves Gaummanians as the sailors do; they are Chamorros, are of mixed ancestry, the result of intermixing between the original Micronesian population and later Filipino, Spanish, and American people. And although English is the language of business and commerce, the native people domestically, normally speak Chamorro[4].

Leaving the village, we took an alternate route, highway 17, cutting across the island. Expecting to see plantations of banana and extensive agriculture: we saw neither, scrubby brush interspersed with secondary-growth trees dominated. We dropped into the local tourist office and read a couple of brochures. The economy of Guam is now based on tourism—mainly from Japan—and U. S. government spending at the Navy and Air Force bases, and the export of fish and handicrafts. Both the fishing industry and tourism expanded greatly in the late 1980's. The rapid growth of tourism led to new buildings—Agana was completely destroyed in World War II—hotels, department stores (Gucci, Nordstrom's et al.) —and manufacturing. Burger King, McDonald's, 7/11 stores: they are all here, just like home. Guam exports textiles, clothing, and boats. Fruits, vegetables and pigs are raised for local consumption. Guam is a duty free port, hence it is a major distribution point for Melanesian trade. I do not really know what "duty free" means, for every place, in every airport I have been in, "duty-free" goods are invariably more expensive than at outlet stores in the U.S. They sure were expensive here!

Micronesia means "tiny islands," a region in the South Pacific northeast toward the Philippines, north of Melanesia and northwest of Polynesia, encompassing more than 800 islands. The average Joe-Blow American knows the name Micronesia—but that is about the extent of his knowledge as these islands are very isolated places—800 islands with a total land area of less than 1,000 square miles scattered across some 6 million square miles of sea water. Out here, you don't just run over to visit your neighbor for a Sunday barbecue.

If the geography of this vast ocean desert is alien to us, so are the names: Republic of Kirbati—independent since 1979; Nauru, a single island with an area of only 8.5 square miles is an independent republic;[5] the Commonwealth of the Northern Marianas; the Republic of Belau (Pelau); the Federated States of Micronesia; and the Republic of the Marshall Islands. Some of the names are known to us, exotic names, names in bold, dark print in newspaper headlines of World War

---

[4] Most Chamorros are Catholic. The birth rate is high, and the population has been increasing rapidly. It grew from 27,500 in 1950 to over 133,152 in 1990.

[5] A republic is a state in which the sovereignty is the people who elect the legislative or administrative leaders.

II chronicling the Pacific War with the Empire of Japan. But that is about all we know, the names. Of the people, the culture, the role in contemporary world affairs, we know zilch! nil!, nada!

In the center of the region are the Mariana Islands and most of the Islands of the Caroline group—Balu, Yap, Truk, Ponape and Kusaie. All are volcanic. These islands, with their towns and peoples precariously perched on their tops, are just peaks of undersea mountains and ranges, which rise steeply from some of the deepest ocean waters on earth. I say " . . . precariously perched on their tops" because of volcanic eruptions with great loss of life and property. Pelée, a 4,583 feet above sea level volcano on Martinique in the West Indies erupted in 1902 causing the death of more than 30,000 peoples and swallowed the town of Saint-Pierre completely. It is no more! Then there was of course the infamous Krakatoa. A continually smoking volcano in West Indonesia in the Sunda Strait between Java and Sumatra, Krakatoa blew its top August 27, 1883 in the greatest volcanic explosion since the eruption of Santorini in 1470 B.C. Although Santorini's explosion was roughly five times greater, Krakatoa's was heard nearly 3,000 miles away some four hours later, the dust it threw 34 miles into the air fell ten days afterward more than 3,000 miles away. The explosion created a tidal wave that wiped out 163 Indonesian villages and killed more than 36,000 people. In the 1900's alone, volcanoes have killed more than 65,000 people. 57 died as a result of Mt. St. Helens's May 18, 1980 eruption in Washington state causing $3 billion in damages. I like what Barbara Ehrenreich[6] writes in *The Worst Years of Our Lives* about disasters:

"Some of us still get weepy when we think about the Gaia Hypothesis, the idea that earth is a big furry goddess-creature who resembles everybody's mom in that she knows what's best for us. But if you look at the historical record—Krakatoa, Mt. Vesuvious, Hurricane Charley, poison ivy, and so forth down the ages—you have to ask yourself: Whose side is she on, anyway?"

Most of the islands in the Micronesia domain are low-lying—a few reach 2,000 feet—however, the majority are only feet above sea level—some as little as five feet. Fortunately the depth of the ocean in the region, and the absence of continental shelves, does not lend the area subject to tidal waves else all traces of habitation could be washed clean in a few minutes.

---

[6] **Barbara Ehrenreich** (b. 1941), U.S. author, columnist. *The Worst Years of Our Lives*, "The Great Syringe Tide" (1991; first published in Mother Jones, 1998.)

The folklore of most of the peoples of Micronesia speaks of local creation of their homelands, myths similar to our own Navajo and Apache Indian cultures. Nevertheless, linguistics studies of most of the island cultures show that they arrived in the area perhaps 4,000 to 5,000 years ago from Southeast Asia. With these early arrivals came domesticated plants, including the coconut and the breadfruit[7] and animals, including the dog and chickens.

Almost all Micronesians, until present modern day industries came along, lived on the coasts, exploiting the food resources of lagoons, reefs, and the sea. Some, particularly those from the tiny, low islands brought inter-island navigation and canoe building to an art form. To escape their tiny confinements, these peoples built canoes, some seriously large, either with double hulls or with outriggers, up to a hundred feet long. Since there was no large timber trees on the islands, the canoes and outriggers were laboriously handcrafted from small planks sewed together with braided cordage formed by braiding several strands of coconut husk fiber, rope fiber, straw, grass, or palm leaves to make into heavy string called sennit. The small planks were also caulked with the sennit.

These deep ocean travelers passed down by oral tradition, not just the maps held in their memories of the stars, but the detailed star courses and knowledge of deep ocean currents, wave patterns and bird habits that would guide them to a given island several hundred miles away. Their vocabulary of ocean terms is extensive; for example with the average modern North American, snow is snow; there is powder snow, and there is wet snow. That's about it. The Eskimos, however, have over fifteen classifications of snow since it is an integral part of their environment. The Micronesian, deep ocean traveler lexicon, is a word-hoard of wave, current and wind terms and conditions that imparts a mental image used as we use an automobile road map.

Why was the Micronesian interested in these obviously long, dangerous ocean voyages?

Well . . . travel was necessary to communicate with other islands, to trade, to secure scarce resources, and to "marry out," –to find conjugal partners so that the broad definitions of incest that had evolved would not be violated. Peoples, even as long as 5,000 years ago, al-

---

[7] The breadfruit of *Mutiny on the Bounty* fame. A round pebbly-skinned fruit of the moraceous tree that when roasted resembles bread. The English ship, the Bounty, was to bring back young plantings of the breadfruit tree as a staple for the slaves of that time.

though the did not know the rules of genetic determination, realized that inbreeding could produce extremely unfavorable results in the offspring and for small breeding populations, where an errant gene has less chance of being overshadowed by a dominant gene, the results could be extinction.

Winding around and through the island on the narrow roads Edward and I unexpectantly passed the entrance to where the *Indy* was having "Open House." The traffic and sheer number of people was overwhelming. When we tried to turn in the local traffic police would not let us take the car into the base. We could see why. Traffic was backed up for miles, people were standing around by their cars talking, eating and drinking, throwing Frisbees. We later learned that people were turned away and still over 30,000 people came to visit the ship.

After our drive, the heat and humidity was conducive to taking a nap. After our nap, Ed and I went to a local restaurant near the hotel for dinner.

Ed ate.

Ed ate!

I had a tuna sandwich, a small potato salad, and a coke.

Ed ate some more.

Ed had three glasses of water, an appetizer of fried squid, huge piles of rice and prawns—the seafood platter. He ate two baskets of bread with butter, a doughnut with cappuccino—two cups—and an ice cream bar! He was giving serious thought to ordering a second ice cream bar when we left. Ed is slim—clothes drape beautifully on him—and he is good-looking. I eat a potato what weighs a quarter pound; from it, I gained four pounds. I hate him.

When Ed was through stuffing himself, we drove to the main part of the city and on past to the giant K-Mart! —THE BIGGEST K-MART IN THE WORLD! Here was another carnival, a carnival of locals and American service men. The ten-acre parking lot was full of new Hondas and Toyotas. People were everywhere! Civilians, natives, and uniforms: humanity wandered—no swarmed—around the parking area, sitting in trucks beds[8], talking, smoking, drinking, eating—always eating—visiting in the tropical evening air. The front of the store had a couple hundred people looking at goods stacked on the sidewalk,

[8] 90% of the vehicles were of Japanese manufacture.

buying soft drinks, and eating pizza. Seeing Ed staring passionately at the pepperoni pizza, I asked kiddingly:

"Getting hungry, Ed?"

He paused, looked at the savory rounds of dough piled high with melted cheese and little smoking chunks of meat, thought a minute and said, "I'll wait a bit." I think he was seriously considering having a slice. What a trencherman! And he's slim. Did I say I hate him? If I consumed food as he did . . . I would be a blimp. Not to far from there anyway! Perhaps a small dirigible.

The store *is* BIG! And well stocked—but much more high-priced than at home. Ship or plane brought everything here hence the high price tags. We saw more of our people—sailors from the ship—clutching plastic bags, waiting for the free bus that ran every fifteen minutes back to the ship, always packed.

Leaving the social center of the island, Ed drove over to where he was last night: the "Strip." I was somewhat surprised to see out here in the middle of Melanesia, a little "Las Vegas." A Planet Hollywood, its colossal turning globe of the earth titled at an angle, big hotels—the Hyatt, Hilton and several others lined the strip—and many, many beer joints, little bars, their fronts plastered with girlie photos leaving nothing to the imagination: I mean nothing, nada, unclothed, nude, bare-asses-pussy galore!

We stopped in patronizing three eventually. In one we had a $5 bottle of sour beer while watching an attractive, lithe Caucasian girl at the edge of the stage, about 22, drape her legs over the shoulders of a sailor while he pushed a bill between her breasts with his teeth, her pubic hair tickling his chin on the way. She collected the bill by squeezing her breast together with her elbows, pulling the sawbuck out with her small pearly teeth; a method of bill collecting that would be a bust in most communities.

The circular performing stage was the size of a large bed with low seats all around, chest high, just perfect for the sailor's face to fit comfortably—Conveniently? Pleasantly? Warmly? Snugly? Cozily? —between the knees of the beauteous, bare-butted bill collecting *virtuosos*. On the other side of the round stage, her front to the bill collector, another innocent, callow, high-born, nude young lady was squatting over the head of a young sailor, who was leaning backwards with the back of his head on the stage. She pushed her vulva into his face so he could insert a bill held in his teeth into her. "Well!" I thought. *Interesting way to make a buck I guess, starting from the bottom and working your way up.* By the way, it gives a different twist to the old saying "laying down on the job!" Hope the lady is not prone to gas. *Not too romantic, huh?*

But, of course, the sad part of the whole spectacle . . . These were young men away from home and lonely, and this what is available to them. The only pussy they saw at home was their high school girlfriend's cat or a couple of heifers on the farm. And the girls, who actually seemed to like the work, were friendly and outgoing—not sleazy looking as is usual—however, the total situation was really just despondent; it certainly was not sex in a healthy sense. I never really enjoyed this type of erotica, even as a young hormone-charged young man. Following the acts I described above there was kissing by each girl on the mouth of a sailor, then on to the next mouth. I could appreciate the attractiveness of the young women, nevertheless, I saw sweat and spittle on their breasts, and visions of Guamanian tropical bacteria surfboarding around in unlimited hordes did not enhance *my* libido. If not tomorrow, then someday, this kind of "action" is going to cause some of these people real problems. Twenty minutes of this peccadillo "entertainment" and I was beginning to understand why people took up bowling or bird calling.

A Korean hostess, older than the girls on the stage—a bit long in the tooth—and several millenniums past her prime fighting weight, a person of the female sex that Ed had run into the previous night, came over and greeted him like an old lover, hugging and nuzzling. Her hair was lanky and long, hanging to her elbows and as varied colored as a rainbow. I thought why would someone want to do that to their hair. Her hairdo actually looked as if someone had stuck a firecracker up a parrot's ass and set it off. She was encased in a black sheath dress and nothing else—no jewelry, no under garments, little makeup and, in reality, was far from attractive—could have used a paint job! She sat down, uninvited, to "keep us company" she said, mouthed a few inane pleasantries, followed by a plaintive I-have-been-in-the-desert-for-months voice, " . . . *could I have a drink?"* I looked around for a canteen. Poor thing, dying of thirst. Then I saw the sign—hand-lettered, unobtrusively, just behind the bar stating:

DRINK FOR YOUR
CHARMING HOSTESS
$20.

Ed pretended to not hear her watery plea. She asked Ed again for a drink. She was *thirsty.* The Sons of the Pioneers came to mind singing "Ol' Dan an' I, out throats burned dry, an' *stiillll we crryyy* . . . for waatteerrr . . ."

"Please" she intoned, head lowered, eyes peering plaintively up at Ed. Poor gal was gonna die of thirst right there in the middle of the sawdust if Ed didn't save her life by shelling out twenty bucks worth of coin for a watered-down beverage. Ed said, "He would see . . . "

Giving up on ol' cheap pockets Ed, she turned and asked me "If she could have a drink?" Without thinking, I told her, *"Sure!"* Through with Ed forever, she turned to her new savior. *" . . . If you are old enough and have the money!"* I continued. My mind was aghast at what my mouth blurted out. Ed glanced at me horrified, then turned to see if the bouncers were coming with their bolos or whatever they used to carve wise guys into steaks around here. I did not think the words, they just were hanging out there, thrown out by my autonomic nervous system, the same one that makes your hand jerk back from a hot stove without thinking, the one that lets your ego write checks that your body can't cash.

The look she threw my way spelled . . . well! . . . I wasn't going to win any popularity contests around here—I was *too cheap*! *Let a girl die of thirst!* She flounced off contemptuously to troll, I suppose for other fish to save her from sinking towards a parched death. Poor thing . . . I would have sprung for a coke, but I am afraid 20 shekels is a bit high for ten ounces of H_2O. I guess she thought I was a cheap-skate. I hope so.

I was tired of this dump and so was Ed. We gave it up, hands in pockets we sauntered out glancing over our shoulders, and drove back to the hotel.

The next day was a Sunday. Up early, I took a constitutional stroll along the broad sidewalk that ran between the road and the ocean. Saw a couple of vans go by: *"Maid for you."* A cleaning service. Another: *"Happy Hooker!"* A tow truck company. *Original.*

A hand lettered sign at a service station: *"Why do the call a women's prison a 'PENAL' colony?"* Good question. *What should they call it? Perhaps a pussy pen.*

Another sign, in professional plastic block letters, was on a two-story billboard at another service station. It read: *"Why do they swab the arm of a convict who is going to get a lethal injection?"* I liked the conundrum; it had merit I thought, but does it really help sell gas?

Sailors, or I guess, anyone who plies the sea regularly (and is not prone to seasickness), develops a curious idiosyncrasy. It seems prevalent, that on a ship at sea, the mariner waits with joyous anticipation the next landfall. The ship's rail is lined at the first sight of the thin line on the far horizon; the heart revs up a few beats, and expectancy of a marvelous time is prepared for. Then after a few days ashore, one rapidly becomes tired of the uncivilized way of the civilians, the hustle and bustle, the "unregulated life". Even myself, after being home a few months, I'm ready for another pilgrimage to the ocean. Ishmael understood the phenomenon in the 19th-century when he said:

"Whenever I find myself growing grim about the mouth; whenever it is a damp, drizzly November in my soul; whenever I find myself involuntarily pausing before coffin warehouses, and bringing up the rear of every funeral I meet; especially whenever my hypos get such an upper hand of me, that it requires a strong moral principle to prevent me from knocking people's hats off—then, I account it high time to get to sea as soon as I can. This is my substitute for pistol and ball. With a philosophical flourish Cato throws himself upon his sword; I quietly take to the ship. There is nothing surprising in this. If they but knew it, almost all men in their degree, some time of other, cherish very nearly the same feeling toward the ocean with me."[9]

In one manner or another, this seemed how most felt as the stream of sailors flowed back to the *Independence* for the 1600 hours departure. No offense. After three days, we had had enough of Guam.

At 1600, on the nose, two tugs at the bow and one at the stern, pushed and pulled at ol' *Indy*, backing her out of her temporary mooring, spun her around and, in a half-hour, had us heading out into the channel, past the breakwater on the starboard side and crumbling granite cliffs to port, into the open sea.

---

[9] MOBY DICK by Herman Melville. International Collectors Library. Garden City, New York pg. 1.

Pacific Daily News
Guam
Tuesday February 25. 1997

"The arrival of the USS Independence and its attendant carrier battle group to Guam this week is fortuitous. The significance of the visit will likely be lost on some members of the mainland media who through innuendo, have insulted more than 100,000 loyal American citizens here by lumping us together with Asian operatives and lobbyists who contributed millions in questionable funds to Clinton-Gore and National Democratic Party campaign coffers.

"That implication, along with the assertion that more than $600,000 donated by Guam's Democratic Party has swayed administration policy toward Guam's commonwealth bid, was the subject of a Washington Post story written by John Pomfret last week. The article goes on to say that U.S. officials fear that if Guam is given control of immigration, we will i(n)mport thousands of low-wage Asian workers and subject them to poor treatment such as what has happened in the Northern Marianas.

"We have a newsflash for the Post. This is the westernmost part of the United States and we follow U.S. laws here—including minimum wage laws and fair labor standards. Those unnamed U.S. officials that Pomfret quotes apparently are not willing to admit that Guam has had more than 40 years of practical experience successfully implementing these regulations and dealing with various nationalities. If fact, if Mr. Pomfret ever gets around to reading our Draft Commonwealth Act, he will find that our aspirations for change of status actually promote a stronger relationship with the United States and reinforce immigration laws.

"Perhaps, Admiral Prueher, commander-in-chief of the vast Pacific Command, can help set the record straight when he returns from this historic voyage through American waters. This is an island that subscribes to law and order, and has the mechanisms and the will to enforce them for the benefit of every citizen, resident and guest of the community."

Even those that charge $20 for a drink of colored water for a parched Lady of the Night.

Me on the hotel balcony in Guam.

Beach on Guam.

Chapter 10

" It is better to wear out
Than to rust out".
Military Quote of the Day.

The flight deck of the modern day aircraft carrier, a warship of terrible power and manifold complexity, can be a hazardous region for the frail human body to venture. Even when nothing seems to be going on it is a dangerous place for, in reality, something is always going on. In the Persian Gulf one fine evening a young sailor strolls out for a breath of refreshing night air, the ship rolls, an undogged hatch swings, hits him in the back, and he spends the next eighteen hours floating in the dark, spitting up warm salt water with jelly fish and sea snakes as unwelcome companions. The danger is a reality, authenticated so often that the safety training is never completed. No matter how well trained personnel are, how rigid rules and subsequent punishment for infraction of those rules are applied, accidents happen. Metal becomes fatigued—it breaks. People become tired—mistakes happen. People get hurt. Sometimes people die. Sometimes lots of people die.

Last evening, while I was in my bunk reading, a crew member was almost blown overboard by the exhaust blast of a jet turning on deck—he was slightly injured. Another sailor landed in the hospital after being blown off the flight deck falling twelve feet onto the rough metal floor of a descending elevator. I used to think that working in a lumber mill was one of the most dangerous jobs in the world: in fact, I read an article in the eighties that said coal mining was the most dangerous, lumber mill work, with its buzzing saws, moving belts and machinery, and falling trees was listed as number two. Personally, my father lost two fingers at the mill from a band saw, my brother a large cut on his inner thigh from a double-bladed ax, and I, a jagged cut over the left eye from a twirling steel handle attached to a falling log. Our neighbor Johnny Morgan, a broken leg, the pond-man killed by a rolling log that crushed his head, and a friend's father killed when his Caterpillar tractor turned over. Lumbering is dangerous.

Now I think that the flight deck of an aircraft carrier must be the most dangerous place to work. On a busy day jet planes are landing at the rate of one every minute. Jets that have already landed are taxiing across the flight deck, while their wings are folding, weapons men are running out to put safety pins in missiles, and other jets are taking off while other jets are landing—coming in fast. People are literally running about amid deafning noise, volatile bombs, missiles, jet fuel, whirling blades, and sucking engines. Therefore, knowing the job, being constantly alert and always aware of what is going on is the way to possibly survival. There are safety nets around the edges of the flight deck. However, they are small, about three feet wide, and it is a long, terrifying drop to the sea rushing along the cold steel hull below, a maelstrom that would push a puny human body right along the hull to be sucked into the 4-28 feet high, 66,000 lb. churning propellers contrary to what the Man-Overboard drill says.

I was prepped about clothing colors when I came on board. I was asked to wear bland clothing: khaki, tan, or dark colors when on or about the flight deck and to not wear a cap that could blow off to be sucked into a roaring jet engine. I discovered later how important this color coordination is when the wardrobe was explained to me. Preparations for a launch very much resemble a well-coordinated ballet, albeit the music the jets make is a bit noisier than an orchestra. Personnel involved in the evolution have specific, clearly defined roles; these roles are recognizable by the color of the clothing worn called the "Rainbow Wardrobe."

People who run out dragging thick, black hoses to pump aviation fuel wear purple jerseys and are nicknamed "Grapes". Plane handlers, aircraft elevator operators, tractor drivers, messengers, and phone talkers wear blue. Green is reserved for catapult and arresting gear crews, air wing personnel, air wing quality control personnel, cargo-handling personnel, hook runners, and helicopter landing signal-enlisted personnel. Yellow is for aircraft handling officers; catapult and arresting gear officers, and plane directors. Red, being a danger color, is worn by ordinance men, crash, and salvage crews, and explosive ordinance disposal (EOD). Brown is for air wing plane captains and air wing leading petty officers. White is for squadron plane inspectors landing signal officer (LSO), safety observers, and medial personnel.

At first glance, to the unenlightened such as me, the Rainbow Wardrobe color-coded jerseys swirl in a hodgepodge of confusing movement. Sit at an ant hill long enough and you will see a pattern of coordinated movement; watch long enough on a busy flight deck and the colored jerseys define corridors, routes of movement, and silent communications.

The colored jerseys—sometimes vests—double as a life jacket—a flotation device. A water-activated-activated strobe light is attached to help find a person swept overboard at night.

When jets are landing on the flight deck, there are only three places I am allowed to watch the activity. One is on television in my cabin, one is on vulture's row, sometimes called vulture's roost, the other is the starboard side of the island. However, missiles and four-wheel carts loaded with practice bombs are usually stored in this area between the island and the railing marked off by rectangles painted on the deck—lines over which I am not to transgress (although I sometimes do)—so I am constantly in the way there. Besides, the view is much better from vulture's row where, when I am wearing my blue weather jacket and gold-braided cap, I can pretend that I am the Captain.

Today, the first day we had full landing exercises, I was fortunate enough to be on vulture's row to watch the *Tomcats* come in. I say fortunate, because if I am far enough down in the ship's innards, and there is no announcement over the con, I might not know a whole air wing is coming in.

The F-14 Tomcat, nicknamed "*Turkey*" by its flyers, is the world's most popular long-range fighter/bomber. First flown in 1970, the Tomcat is built by the Grumman Corporation. Grumman's technical representatives (Tech. Reps.) are well represented aboard ship standing behind the jet mechanics to give advice on keeping the complicated craft flying. Anyone who has watched the movie *TOP GUN* or any other modern day flight movie about the navy has seen an F-14 with its distinctive twin vertical tails (rudders) and separate engine nacelles[1].

As a child, during W. W. II, military planes fascinated me: especially the *Flying Tiger, the P-38,* and *the B-17,* the *"Flying Fortress."* The flying fortress has played many a role in the movies about World War II. *"Twelve O'clock High"* with Gregory Peck; *"Air Force"* with John Garfield; and *D-Day: the Sixth of June"*, with a whole bunch of movie

[1] The nacelle is a structure on an aircraft containing the engine—a covering. Usually the nacelle is placed on the wing, but not in the case of the Tomcat, which has retractable wings. The twin nacelles are amidships, between the cockpit and the starboard and port stabilizers.

stars, honoring the Flying Fortress. A news article written by Richard Williams in the Seattle Times on July 17, 1935 reads:

> "Declared to be the largest land plane
> ever built in America, this 15-ton
> Flying fortress, built by the Boeing
> airplane Company under Army specifications
> today was ready to test its wings . . ."

Boeing built the first flying fortress, the B-17, then went on to build the B-29 Superfortress, both of which were of great importance during World War II. Designed as a long-range heavy bomber, the—at that time—giant aircraft carried a crew of ten men whose job it was to carry a heavy—at that time—load of bombs for strategic strikes at military targets. Although over 9,000 different fortresses were built, the main workhorse was the B-17G of which over 4,700 was in front-line service by mid-1944. The B-29 was devised as a replacement for the B-17 and first flew in 1942, mainly seeing service in the Pacific Zone. The Enola Gay, which dropped the first atomic bomb on Hiroshima August 6th, 1945, was a B-29.

"My God!"
An exclamation by a member
of the crew of the Enola Gay
on August 6, 1945.

The other vintage plane that smitten me as a youngster was the *Lockheed P-38 Lightning*. The P-38 was the first American-built fighter to escort B-17s on a mission. They were used extensively in North Africa. The P-38's wingspan was 52 feet; fuselage: 37 feet, 10 inches. Powered by two Allison liquid-cooled engines its top speed was around 400 mph; range: 1,500 miles and ceiling 40,000 feet.

Another ship I like is the *USS Star Ship Enterprise* MK-IX Star Fleet Division, Heavy Cruiser Starship Class 1,NCC-1701. 895 feet long, 394 feet wide with a gross deadweight of 190,000 tons. With a crew of over 500 and a speed of over 186,000 miles per second this a flying machine to be reckoned with!

This bit of nostalgic rambling about aircraft of old and new is to illustrate that the *F-14* Tomcat is to the planes of World War I and II as the fictional space ship Enterprise is to us today. The P-38, a fighter, was 37 feet long with a crew of 1. The Flying Fortress, a heavy bomber, was 75 feet long with a crew of 10. The tomcat is a *fighter/bomber, 63 feet long with a crew of 1 or 2.* A P-38 carried two bombs and twin 50 caliber machine guns. The fortress—a heavy bomber—had an empty weight of 36,000 lbs. gross weight of 40,000 lbs. The Tomcat has an empty weight of 40,150 lbs.: gross weight of *74,500 lbs*! Top speeds: Flying Fortress: 302 mph; range: 3,750 miles. P-38: 400 mph; range 1,500 miles. Tomcat: *1,544 mph*; range*: 2,000 miles*. The F-14 Tomcat, a fighter/bomber, carries a much heavier load a lot faster than the Super Fortresses heavy bombers of World War II and can easily outrun the P-38 three to one.

One reason the engine nacelles are not placed on the wings of the F-14 is the "variable-geometry" wing concept. A plane such as the Tomcat, that can barrel along at almost Mach 2.34 at high altitudes—55,000 feet—over 10 miles up, cannot come slamming into a carrier deck like the supersonic plane it is. The variable-geometry, or "swing-wing" allows the wings to retract back along side the fuselage for accelerated speeds and to come forward providing more lift for taking off, cruising, and landing. The F-14 Tomcat is so heavy—loaded it can weigh over 74,000 lb.—it actually made the metal overhead (ceiling) of my stateroom flex whenever it was catapulted off the ship. (Remember the Flying Fortress of World War II, fame with its 10-crewmen, weighed 40,000 pounds while the Tomcat, with its two-crewmen, weighs 1.8 times the Fortress.)

Flight Operations can go on all night so trying to sleep in my cabin—right under the flight deck—is like sleeping inside a washtub with someone banging on it. To launch such planes, the steam-driven catapults have tremendous power: it is said that the catapults on modern day carriers can throw a Cadillac half a mile—well . . . okay. As long as it isn't mine. (I would like to see that though!) Even with the wings fully extended the heavy fighter hits the third wire at a touch-and-go 172 miles per hour.

The landing of a fast, heavy jet, like the Tomcat, is called a "controlled-crash" in navy parlance and for good reason. The pilot watches the "Christmas Tree" on his front left, lines the plane up with the "bubble," (Mirror)" watches the "pitch" of the flight deck, checks the number three wire and slams into the deck jamming the throttles to full forward! The oversize undercarriage—beefed up to take the jolt—smashes flat and the massive twin Pratt & Whitney turbofan engines scream in tortured agony as the jet, comes to a stop in less than the length of a football field. If it does not stop, if it misses the arresting wires, the roaring engines hopefully can drag it back into the sky. Often, when I see one of these babies land I think of the popular naval quatrain:

"There are some good, young pilots;
And there are some bad, young pilots.
And there are some good, old pilots;
But there are no bad, old pilots."

The F-14 Tomcat can inflict some appalling scratches with its armament claws. Firepower consists of one 20 mm General Electric Vulcan rotary six-barrel cannon; the Phoenix long-range missile; the Sparrow medium-range missile, and the Sidewinder short-range missile. The Vulcan cannon is located in the nose with over 700 rounds available. 353 rounds of ammunition are carried in two concentric spiral layers round the cannon which is fed by a double-ended (closed loop) system that carries away spent cases and makes possible the reverse-clearing system for the cannon. It can normally fire 2,400 rounds per minute with 3,000 rounds per minute possible; it is actually a four-barreled Gatling gun used air-to-air—against other planes—and air-to-surface—against ground troops and vehicles. The gun is not small: at nine feet long, it has the hard-hitting capability in the ground attack role of penetration of 29+ inches of armor at a slant range of 1400 yards. Enemy tanks get very nervous when a Tomcat carrying the Vulcan cannon comes around the neighborhood, knocking on their door, saluting them with an opening volley.

If the Tomcat wants to make a long range kill, it teams the long-range Phoenix missile with the "Hummer." The Hummer is a nickname for the E-2C Hawkeye, a two-engine propeller airplane. The Hawkeye is classified as an AEW or Airborne Early Warning platform. It has other names: Reconnaissance and Electronic Weapons Platform or Carrierborne and Land-based Early Warning Platform. It boasts a crew of five: a pilot and co-pilot and mission crew of three in the cabin. It is an all-weather aircraft, and with a wingspan of 80 feet and a fuselage length of 57 ½ feet, it is the largest and heaviest aircraft to operate from a carrier. Nuclear supercarriers such as the *USS Carl Vinson* and *the USS Abraham Lincoln,* carry up to four Hawkeyes providing 24-hour a day coverage. I once happened to get a launch off the Carl Vinson in a Hawkeye. I was strapped into a web chair facing the rear of the plane. As the two turbroprop engines revived up the plane began to shudder like a rabbit crapping peach seeds; the noise was deafening (they say they call it the "Hummer" because of the sound of its turboprop engines. I think they ought to call it the "Screamer."), then the catapult slingshot the silvery plane off the deck. As it slid into its right turn my stomach kept traveling straight ahead. Scary and noisy. Nevertheless, exhilarating! Hawkeyes have a ceiling of around 31,000 feet—almost six miles—and a range of 1,500 miles. When the Hummer spots a target, it relays coordinates to the Tomcat, and the Tomcat's pilot switches on the Phoenix missile's guidance system.

The Phoenix is an air-to-air missile, weighing 985 lbs, is over 13 feet in length, and can travel approximately *3,300 miles per hour* and that is movin' out pardner! Nothing is going to catch it! The swing-wing naval fighter launches the phoenix controlling it as it climbs to a peak altitude of 81,400 feet—15+ miles. At that height, the missile cruises under control of the onboard autopilot that is guided by reflections from the target back to the Tomcat and to the Hummer—a three-way action. Because of the lack of air resistance at high altitudes, the missile can range to 126 miles effortlessly cruising along at *55 miles per minute*, then nose dives toward the target. Nearing the target, the Phoenix's radar switches to the active mode for the final 20,000 yards. Increasing its vertical speed, the missile smashes its half-ton body-weight and 132 lb. blast/fragmentation explosives into the target. After launching one Phoenix that is guiding itself to the target, the Tomcat can turn away to avoid danger, or begin another engagement. Using its time-share radar system, the F-14 can engage six targets *at the same time*. If needed, the Hummer—Grumman E-2C Hawkeye—with its early warning radar working with the F-14 Tomcat, can extend the range of the Phoenix missile considerably.

The Tomcat can carry six missiles: four under the fuselage, two under the wing roots. The big, noisy, powerful brute of an airplane, that lacks any pretense of stealth or subtlety, and for over 20 years the leader of the pack of carrier jet fighters, is not without its faults; sometimes the Tomcat can be a real Turkey.

Sacramento Bee Feb. 26, 1996.
"On February 18, 1996, an F-14-D "Tomcat" fighter crashed and killed two crew members during exercises involving the Carl Vinson. That crash was one of 32 in the past five years involving F-14s and prompted the Navy to ground its entire fleet of F-14s through Febru-

ary 25. Each of the last three F-14s to crash was based at Miramar, although they were from different squadrons. The crew aboard the F-14-D from the Carl Vinson did not eject."

USA Today February 24, 1996.

"The Navy suspended all operations of its F-14 fighter jets Thursday after the third crash in less than a month. Early Thursday, an F-14A crashed into the Persian Gulf. The pilot radar-intercept officer ejected safely. The cause was not clear, but the Pentagon insists there's no link with the earlier crashes. "This is a mystery," said spokesman Ken Bacon. Admiral Jeremy Boorda, chief of naval operations, set a 72-hour worldwide "stand-down". "The goal here is to determine if there is something we can do...immediately." All three F-14s lost in the past month were based at San Diego, but circumstances and models differ:

"On Jan, 29, an F-14A crashed after takeoff in Nashville, killing both crewman and three on the ground.

"On Sunday, an F-14D practicing low-level flight plunged into the Pacific. The crew died.

"Thursday's F-14A crash occurred after a problem several thousand feet up.

"In the last five years, 32 F-14s crashed, 337 are left. The Grumman Jet, a star in the film Top Gun, costs $38 million."

In a recent book, author Gregory Vistica accuses the Navy's leadership of failing to replace the Pratt & Whitney turbofan engines on the F-14 model aircraft even though the Navy determined years ago that the engine was not adequate.

Defense Secretary William Perry said at a news conference in Sacramento:

"We found no evidence of a systematic nature in these accidents. They all seemed to be quite unrelated to each other." Perry called the F-14 "one of the finest fighter aircraft in the world. And it's very important to us to keep it in the fleet."

There were some temporary limitations put on the speed at which F-14s could be flown, and on the use of afterburners, which give a plane extra thrust by injecting fuel into hot exhaust gases. All F-14 pilots also were required to undergo refresher safety courses before they are allowed to fly again.

I have been most fortunate as a civilian to be on several nuclear carriers and not be in the military, free to roam and observe this airplane, this "Defender of the Fleet" do extraordinary things. I have seen it travel straight up while accelerating, porpoise along side the carrier seemingly to stand on its red-hot blasting exhaust flame, and watched the cockpit onboard camera of an F-14 record a simultaneous kill of two Iraqi fighters. On board we had an F-14A Tomcat of the VF-143 Atlantic Fleet fighter squadron nicknamed the "Pukin Dogs." This famous unit fought in Korea, Vietnam, and the Gulf War, and has flown the Tomcat for 20 years.

The Tomcat has been one of the great superfighters of the world since its first squadron took to the skies in 1972. It packs a massive punch, performs superbly, and is the warplane of choice for many aspiring military pilots. Nothing is more likely to worry an enemy than to know Tomcats are sniffing around his track. This tremendous fighting machine can operate from a football field strip or aircraft carrier deck, in all weather around the clock. Working with E-2C Hawkeye radar planes and using air-to-air refueling, a squadron of Tomcats can sanitize the airspace 400 miles out from the carrier battle group. This ensures that no hostile aircraft can get below this umbrella and threaten the 10-warship, $15-billion battle group manned by 10,000 sailors projecting as much firepower as England's entire armed forces.

Carrier Air Wing FIVE

A highly mobile and potent force

The main striking power of *USS Independence* is the carrier air wing, composed of eight squadrons and two detachments ready to respond at all times to any crises or conflict.

One squadron flies the F-14A Tomcat, a two-seat, twin-engine fighter, featuring adjustable wings for increased maneuverability. Capable of long-range air-to-air intercepts, the Tomcat can track up to 24 targets simultaneously with its advanced AWG-9 weapons control system, destroying them with a variety of air-to-air missiles or 20 mm cannon.

There are three strike fighter squadrons embarked flying the single-seat, twin-engine F/A-18C Hornet. The Hornet offers operational commanders flexibility by allowing them to employ the aircraft in either its fighter or attack role. Weapons include air-to-air and air-to-ground missiles, laser-guided bombs, and a 20-mm cannon.

The Carrier Airborne Early Warning Squadron flies the E-2C Hawkeye. With a crew of five, the Hawkeye is equipped with a power search radar and airborne tactical data link to send and receive information between similarly equipped aircraft or ships.

One tactical electronic warfare squadron is embarked and flies the four-seat EA-6Bprowler. The Prowler uses sophisticated receivers that can scan for enemy radar, confusing them with electronic jamming or destroying them with HARM missiles.

Two variants of the four-seat, twin-turbofan S-3 are flown. The S-3B Viking missions include anti-submarine warfare, surface surveillance and mine warfare. It carries torpedoes and the Harpoon missile. A variant, the ES-3A Shadow, provides the battle group with long-range electronic surveillance.

The C-2A Greyhound is the Carrier Onboard Delivery (COD) aircraft. C-2As provide a means to transport spare parts, mail, and people to and from the ship. This aircraft can carry up to 10,000 pounds of supplies at a time.

The embarked helicopter squadron flies the SH-60/HH-60-H Seahawk. The crew of four can use their sophisticated ASW suite and two MK-46 torpedoes to locate and destroy enemy submarines. The HH-60H provides Combat Search & Rescue (CSAR) capability as well as extra passenger and logistics capabilities.

Me and students

Rainbow Wardrob

Chapter 11

"A nuclear carrier is like
A six hundred-pound gorilla;
It can go where it wants."
Navy saying

USS INDEPENDENCE DEPARTS FOR TANDEM TRUST

"The aircraft carrier USS Independence (CV 62) along with it's battle group escort ships got underway to begin a deployment and participation in Operation "Tandem Thrust," a series of exercises involving all four branches of the United States Armed Forces and the Australian Defense Force."

The headline was the first item that I saw in the ship newspaper when sitting down to my Wheaties and milk.

I had heard of Tandem Thrust upon arriving in Japan even before boarding the carrier. Tandem thrust involves approximately 22,000 U.S. and 5,500 Australian personnel. The main attack area is to be held off Australia's coast and is designed to bring those forces together as a combined task force. The U.S. has an annual "exercise" with Australia, also annually with Thailand military forces called "Cobra Gold." Our ship and Carrier Air Wing FIVE is spearheading the training exercise—called a "Problem" in the Marine Corps—and is heavily involved with training on the interior and coast of Australia in addition to sea operations.

When we departed Guam, I was not totally sure of where I was going to wind up—finish my contract. Then the Captain spelled out the details over the speakers. We were on our way to participate in Tandem Thrust—sea military exercises—to link up with the Australian forces: the sea would be filled with ships and men attacking the Australian coast. If we were indeed a mighty task force of ships and men, it certainly was not evident from the deck of the *Independence*. As I mentioned previously, the majority of the time the *Indy* seems alone at sea. Depending on the height of the viewer's deck, the radius of sight is around eleven to seventeen miles so one sits at the epicenter of about a 34-mile circle depending on wave action. Considering the size of the Pacific Ocean, the area is a microdot on a planetary scale. In the (good?) old sailing days before radar, satellites, and all the other electronic marvels, an armada could be right over the curve of the horizon passing by without detection. I was pondering on this seemingly isolation as I stood on edge of the windy flight deck, after morning chow, taking my morning air and gazing out to seaward. Stinking Guam—fetid in more ways than one—had slipped below the horizon a couple of hundred nautical miles to our rear and, other than a few clouds and our trailing destroyer five miles to our right rear, the sea seemed uninhabited. In actuality, numerous vessels surrounded us—over twenty-five—all going in the same direction: a Carrier Battle Group (CVBG) headed for our rendezvous with the Australian forces and the land down-under.

No . . . the old *Indy* was by no means alone. Ranging ahead of the CVBG under the surface of the sea were two hunter-killer submarines—both nuclear. Overhead, way overhead, out of surface visual and radar sight, were the AWACS—Airborne Warning and Control System Aircraft—the E-2C Hawkeye's[1]. The Hawkeye is the Navy's all weather; carrier based tactical warning and control system aircraft that flies far and wide providing airborne early warning, command and control functions for the CVBG. The Hawkeye has a range of 1,500 miles plus; its mission includes surface surveillance—the carrier's television screens see the same thing that the Hawkeye cameras see—strike and interceptor control, search and rescue guidance and communication relays. The big radar-domed white plane operates high in the atmosphere, out of sight, high above the clouds, electronically looking down at the CVBG and the target miles below, —an unseen eye in the sky, searching for possible threats to its charges below.

We were in the middle of the pie, and along side, in front, behind, and below ranged frigates, cruisers, destroyers, and amphibious warfare ships, along with a nuclear submarine or two, providing a five-hundred protective umbrella: Anything unexpected is going to have a very difficult time getting near the Big Guy including the South Sea pirates! A typical CVBG incorporates the following:

---

[1] Wingspan: 81 ft, length: 58 ft, height: 18 ft, speed: 389 mph, range 1,500 + miles, armament: none, crew: 5. Names: Night Wolves, Fighting Escargot. Golden Hawks, Black Eagles, Liberty Bells, Sun Kings, Wallbangers, Greyhawks, Bluetails, Screwtops, Bear Aces, Tigertails, Seahawks.

Frigates:

Guided-missile frigates (FFG) are ships that bring an anti-warfare (AW) capability to the CVBG. Designed as cost-efficient surface combatants, the FFG 7 class is a forceful ship capable of withstanding considerable damage and still function.

Cruisers:

Modern U.S. Navy guided-missile cruisers perform primarily in a battle force role. These ships are multi-mission (anti-air, anti-surface, anti-submarine) surface combatants capable of supporting carrier battle groups, amphibious forces or of operating independently and as flagships[2] of surface action groups. The cruiser classes are the Ticonderoga-class and the California-class. They are equipped with Tomahawk cruise missiles for long-range capability.

Destroyers:

The destroyer's role is primarily anti-submarine warfare.

The types of destroyers are the Arleigh Burke-class, the Kidd-class and the Spruance-class[3].

The Arleigh Burke DDG-51 is a guided-missile destroyer that primarily performs anti-submarine warfare duty; they are multi-mission (anti-submarine, anti-air and anti-surface warfare) surface combatants.

(Ed says, "A naval destroyer is a hula-hoop with a nail in it". I have not yet figured what that means.)

Amphibious Warfare Ships:

Modern U. S. Navy amphibious assault ships are called upon to perform as primary landing ships for assault operations of Marine expeditionary forces: taking the troops to the beach. In a secondary role, using AV-8B *Harrier* planes and anti-submarine warfare helicopters, these ships patrol for submarines and provide close-air support for foot-slogging ground troops. I have landed ashore many times from AAS (Amphibious assault ships), slopping through the surf and mud with a forty-five pound pack, metal helmet, nine and half pound rifle, eighty rounds of 30.6 ammo, with fourteen inch bayonet and other assorted do-dads the Marine Corp loads on the infantryman so he can kill more efficiently—or die from exhaustion carrying so much gear. However, I landed from LCVP's (Landing craft, vehicle and personnel), not

[2] The flagship is the ship in a naval formation that carries a flag officer that is above the rank of captain, entitled to display a flag indicating his rank, generally an admiral.

[3] The author spent time in the Persian Gulf and the Indian Ocean on a Spruance-class destroyer, the *John Young DD-973.*

LCAC's (Landing craft, air cushion)—they were not invented yet. (As a Marine infantryman I've "foot-slogged" a bunch of miles. The poster at the Marine recruiting office read, "Join the Marines and see the world!" One little bit of information that the poster conveniently left out was that you had to *walk* to see that world! Walk and carry a lot of *stuff!* A whole bunch of stuff! These multi-mission assault ships transport and land assault troops by use of landing craft Air Cushion (LCAC), conventional landing craft, and helicopters. The classes of the Assault ships are the Wasp-class, the Tarawa-class, and the Iwo Jima-class[4].

Submarines:

There is support vehicle that is seldom seen *or heard*. We know that they are out there and, in a rare instance, a glimpse of the black, boat may be briefly seen. Only twice have I seen the shark-like ominous silhouette of a nuclear submarine: once in the Straight of Juan de Fuca as we were leaving Seattle, Washington—its conning tower broke surface briefly, then was gone, leaving only a swirl of grey-white foam to mark its passing. The other time was in deep sea; standing in an elevator bay of the *USS Carl Vinson,* I saw a shadow, a dark shape on the far horizon, as one of these leviathans drew up alongside and passed a Tarawa-class destroyer; the destroyer of this class is 563 feet 4 inches long. The submarine was longer.

Attack submarines are designed to seek and destroy enemy submarines as well as surface ships. Other missions range from intelligence collection and Special Forces delivery to anti-ship and strike warfare. Classes of attack subs are Seawolf, Los Angeles, Narwhal, Sturgeon and Benjamin Franklin.

The big boys of the submarine world are the Ballistic Missile Submarines; the most potent and deadly submarines afloat. Silent, impossible to locate, these enormous boats can hide beneath the sea and stay submerged as long as the crew can take the isolation[5]. A fearsome weapon, the Ballistic Missile Submarine can fire Polaris Missiles (SLBM's), each yielding millions of tons of TNT destructive force from the surface or submerged hitting targets up to 4,000 miles.

---

[4] The author was privileged to sail aboard a Tarawa-class Assault ship—the *USS Peleliu (LHA-5)* from San Diego, thence to attack Hawaii for five days, then on to Thailand.

[5] The giant 5,450-ton Triton (SSN, 586) In 1960, made an incredible underwater voyage around the world lasting 84 days.

The Carrier:

In addition to the naval power of the escort ships and submarines that accompany the *Independence*, there is the highly mobile and potent main striking power of the carrier itself: the carrier wing. Forward presence and domination of the sea and adjacent land areas are not possible without control of the area's airspace. The carrier's aircraft are multifaceted, capable of an extensive range of missions and payloads. The air wing is the key element in the Navy's ability to achieve its operational and tactical objectives.

Carrier Air Wing Five on the *USS Independence* is composed of eight squadrons and two detachments ready to respond at all times to any crises or conflict.

One squadron flies the F-14 Tomcat, a two-seat, twin-engine fighter featuring adjustable wings for increased maneuverability. Also there are three strike fighter squadrons flying the single-seat, twin-engine F/A 18C Hornet. The Hornet offers operational commanders flexibility by allowing them to employ the aircraft in either its fighter or attack role. Weapons include air-to-air and air-to-ground missiles, laser-guided bombs and a 20-mm cannon.

The carrier Airborne Early Warning Squadron flies the E-2C Hawkeye already mentioned. With its crew of five, the Hawkeye is equipped with power search radar and airborne tactical data link to send and receive information between similarly equipped aircraft and/or ships.

Another tactical electronic warfare squadron flies the four-seat EA-6B Prowler. The Prowler uses sophisticated receivers that scan for enemy radar, confusing them with electronic jamming or destroying then with HARM missiles.

Two variants of the four-seat, twin-turbofan S-3 are flown. The S-3B Viking missions include anti-submarine warfare, surface surveillance and mine warfare. It carries torpedoes and the Harpoon missile.

The C-2A Greyhound is the Carrier Onboard Delivery (COD) aircraft. C-2As provide a means to transport spare parts, mail and people. Powered by two T-6 Turboprop engines, this aircraft can carry up to 10,000 pounds of supplies.

The helicopter squadron on the carrier flies the Seahawk. The crew of four can use their sophisticated electronics and two Mk-46 Torpedoes to locate and destroy enemy submarines. The Seahawk provides CSAR (Combat Search & Rescue) capability as well as extra passenger and logistics capabilities.

The entitlement of "Capital Ship" definitely passed from the battleship—mainstay of W.W.I and W.W. II—to the aircraft carrier after the defeat of Japan. The big question after World War II, was how to operate fast jet aircraft from a floating platform. The first documented carrier landing by a jet was a British Vampire fighter, which landed on the *HMS Ocean* on December 3rd 1945. Seven months later America saw the first jet take off from the *USS Franklin D. Roosevelt*. With the innovations of more powerful jet engines, the angled deck, the catapult, the mirror landing device[6], and nuclear power, the U.S. Navy's Carrier Battle Group became a powerful force; a hybrid creation that enables the navy to conquer sea, air and land simultaneously.

The carrier is the Big Kahunna surrounded by its multitudinous support ships and platforms; but if the carrier is the big Kahunna, the Carrier Battle Group is really the big gorilla—King Kong's brother (or sister)—it is the one that really goes where ever it wants!

The Carrier Battle Group is an awesome array of men, ships, and weapons. And its goal in the society of the United States of America is to sustain world freedom and safekeep our national interests. It has been said to this author, that the U.S. is acting as the world's police force, that we are too involved in keeping world peace, we should withdraw and let the rest of the world solve its own problems. I see and hear more than once on television news commentators asking, "Why does the rest of the world hate the US so much?" I do not know that they do hate the US. I have been to 68 countries; most people I have met admire anything American, and many, many want to come here. You do not hear on the news about people trying to sneak into Russia, Cuba, Iraq, North Korea, or China—in fact it is the reverse. During the Korean War—a war, luckily I got into at the tail end—the South Koreans held 106,376 Chinese and North Korean prisoners; the communists were thought to be holding about 10,000 Americans and South Koreans. To the best of anyone's knowledge, virtually all of the Americans wanted to return home. But among the Chinese and North Korean prisoners, only around 31,000 indicated they wanted to be repatriated—less than a third of those held.

Recently someone one from the East—Pakistan or Iraq—published in a newspaper an offer of a reward to anyone who killed an American—any American.

---

[6] A mirror device which gave the pilot precise information about his perspective and height above the flight deck,

Someone wrote the following to let everyone know what an American is, so they would know when they found one. I think the definition is apropos:

"An American is English, or French, or Italian, German Spanish, Polish, Russian or Greek. An American may also be Canadian, Mexican, African, Indian, Chinese, Japanese, Korean, Australian, Iranian, Asian, or Arab, or Pakistani, or Afghan. An American may also be a Cherokee, Osage, Blackfoot, Navaho, Apache, Seminole or one of the many other tribes known as native Americans.

"An American is a Christian, or a Jew, or Buddhist, or Muslin. In fact, there are more Muslims in America than in Afghanistan. The only difference is that in America they are free to worship as each chooses. An American is also free to believe in no religion.

"An American is from the most prosperous land in the history of the world. The root of that prosperity can be found in the Declaration of Independence, which recognizes the right of each person, the pursuit of freedom.

"Americans are generous; Americans have helped out about very other nation in the world in their time of need and have a habit of rebuilding defeated nations, not attempting to enslave them.

"Americans welcome the best; the best products, the best books, music, food and the best athlete's. However, they also welcome the least.

"The national symbol of America, the Statue of Liberty, welcomes the tired, the poor, the wretched refuse of other countries. Some of them were working in the Twin Towers the morning of September 11, 2002, earning a better life for their families—at least 30 other countries, cultures, and languages, including those that aided and abetted the terrorists.

"So you can try to kill an American if you must. Hitler tried. So did the rulers of Japan, and Stalin, and Mao Tse-Tung. They did not have much success. However, in killing Americans, you are just killing everyone—perhaps your own people—because Americans are not a certain people from a certain place. Americans are the embodiment of the human spirit to be free, and everyone who holds to that spirit, everyone, everywhere, is an American."

In two hundred years, while the rest of the world squabbled among them selves, the fledging American colonies became, with the collapse of the Soviet Union, the world's only Superpower; and in today's world of fast delivery weapons, aggressiveness by dictators and erosion of personal freedom, isolation is impossible. We know from history that isolation breeds ignorance and weakness invites aggression. The preservation of freedom demands strength, will and realistic knowledge of friend and foe alike, goals that our people have paid for in the past and goals we must strive and pay for in the future. American can afford nothing less.

Saipan

It is said that, "Luck favors the prepared mind." I do not know about his mind, but Ed was going to be prepared. His preparation was a deck of cards. He wanted me to teach him how to play Blackjack, so he purchased a two-deck box of playing cards in Guam for $7.50, and gave a deck to a pilot who came around needing a deck the exact same day. Looking at the fresh unopened cellophane packing he uttered the famous words, " He owes me" referring to the pilot.

" Yippee Ti Yi Yo! " Why " Yippee Ti Yi Yo! "? Because Ed came in saying, "Ya wanna go to Saipan. Do some gambling?"

"Wha . . ."

"That Hummer pilot. He's making a run to Saipan. He says we can go! He owes me."

"No Shit!"

"When's he comin' back?" I asked.

"Today. Tonight."

"Shit."

Ed looked at me. "You gotta limited vocabulary. Whatta you think?"

"How far is it?"

" An hour."

"Who do we ask? Bob?"

"I'm thinkin' nobody" replied Ed. "We go, we come back. Five-six hours tops."

I had been in a cargo plane; the pilot had shown me about. It was not too unusual for a plane-driver to take a VIP out for a mail run; at Ford Island in Hawaii when I was there on the *USS Peleliu*, a pilot offered me a ride if I missed the sailing of the ship telling me "No problemmo!"

"You know what Shakespeare said?' Ed taught English, always correcting those long red ink-stained inane essays.

"What?"

"Discretion is the better part of valour."

"Nope. I didn't know Shakespeare said it. I know somebody said it—I think John Paul Jones or Gregory Peck—but I don't know what it means anyway!"

"It means 'we don't ask nobody, they can't say no Big Guy.'"

I noticed our use of the English language slipped into the vernacular when we were ragging Bob or planning something devious.

"They don't care anyway." He continued. "They got better things to do than worry about us. No classes today. No boss. Screw the ESO. He wont even know we are gone, an' he don't care anyway . . . I think."

"They can't court-martial us . . . can they?"

"They doen care; they wont know."

We went.

And came back.

Nobody said a thing.

Saipan is the capital of the Northern Mariana Islands and is located in the perpetually warm climate between Guam and the Tropic of Cancer. The Northern Marianas are a 300-miles-long archipelago consisting of 14 islands. The islands were first brought to European attention by their "discovery" in 1521 by Magellan and named the Ladrones (Thieves). "Thieves" as a name not fitting in with their religious philosophy, the Spanish Jesuits, in 1668, renamed the islands. Germany purchased them from Spain—without consulting the indignant population, as conquering bullies are apt to do—in 1899. In 1914 the islands were captured by Japan and were made a Japanese mandate by the League of Nations in 1920. After the war, in 1947, they became part of the U.S. trust territory. Voters approved separate status for the islands as a U.S. commonwealth in 1975. They became internally self-governing in 1978. Like the native peoples of Guam, the people of the Northern Marianas are predominantly of Chamorro cultural extraction.

Although there are 14 islands, the population is concentrated in three of them: Saipan, Rota, and Tinian, all names familiar to anyone knowledgeable about the War in the Pacific. In 1944 Newspapers headlined:

> "Saipan in the Marianas falls to U.S. troops July 9th after Yoshitsugo Saito and 31,000 troops have fought to the death in a 23-day battle that has cost 3,500 U.S. lives. Hundreds of Japanese civilians throw themselves and their children off cliffs at the

islands northern tip. 956 U.S. planes outmatch Japan's 473 carrier-based planes and 3 of Japan's 9 carriers are sunk. Losing more than 400 planes and nearly that many flyers effectively ends her viability as an air power.

Time Weekly Newsmagazine detailed the blows falling on the Empire of Japan that faithful time in Saipan's history:

"July 3rd, 1944. From the airfields in western China, United States planes began regular bombing runs against the home islands. U.S. soldiers and Marines attacked Saipan, only 1,500 miles from Japan. And in an air and naval battle that would become known as the "Marianas Turkey Shoot," United States carrier forces demonstrated their overwhelming air superiority by shooting down 227 of the attacking 326 Japanese planes in just a few hours, the biggest bag ever for one day.

"The U.S. assault on the key Jap bases in the Marianas had begun nine days before. For four days, a U.S. naval force had pounded Saipan. Bombers from U.S. carriers had delivered their loads of destruction. For two days U.S. battleships, cruisers, and destroyers unloaded their long, hot guns on the island. On the fifth day, transports made a rendezvous outside the coral reefs of the island, and the landing craft swarmed in towards the deadly beaches. American soldiers and Marines swarmed ashore at Agingan Point, while Japs who survived the naval bombardment bit into them with enfilading fire from pre-sighted automatic rifles and pounded then with mortar shells. The consensus was 'if we can land on Saipan, we can land anywhere there are Japanese.'

"Early reports indicated that the fight was going slowly against fanatical resistance. After establishing a beachhead, the U.S. amphibious—the Marines—had to give ground before fierce Jap counterattacks, but they hung as Marines do and by the third day, the Marines were pressing inland. The soldiers and Marines fought their bloody way across the lower end of the island, seized Aslito Airfield, showered Jap civilians and soldiers with leaflets with invitations to surrender."

The Japanese on Saipan did not surrender. The sons of Nippon—the Land of the Rising Sun—could not afford to let Saipan go because the next target was the big red ball on a white field—the flag of the Japanese people—the bull's eye of Japan's homeland.

Of course, there was a catch on our trip to Saipan.

We couldn't go off the military base. On all Navy ships I have departed in a foreign port, I have not had to go through customs. Arriving in Phuket, Thailand, Perth, Australia, and Guam, I just walked off with the sailors. It is the same when the *Carl Vinson* or the *Kitty Hawk* stops for a three-day R&R in Pattaya, Thailand where I live. The sailors come ashore, drink beer, shop, and fraternize with the locals, leave. Only an identity card is needed. I have left Tokyo, Japan, Aukland, New Zealand, and even Bahrain, the same way.

But not today.

No visa—and I did not yet have the new civilian/military card.

I believe the immigration clerk just did not understand the rules governing Ed and my situation; it did not matter—we could not go to the city. We stayed on base. While our pilot took care of his business, I had to make do with the commercial handout for my one and only visit to the World War II graveyard of the Pacific—Saipan.

Saipan was the site of one of the bloodiest battles in the Pacific Theater. Japanese civilians died at their own hand, casting their children off the cliffs into the sea to escape surrender. Over forty thousand dead. That was near half a century ago. Today I read of Saipan. Taking some liberty, I paraphrase the local Chamber of Commerce news handout.

Saipan has many entertaining opportunities for visitors, from its beautiful, clean beaches (washed in warriors blood) and splendid water sports (taking potshots at amphibious assault ships) to an exciting nightlife centered around the modern hotels (crouching in fox holes out of the glare of flares).

Today Saipan is far from remote; the island of 50,000 has thousands of tourists, some 75 percent of them from Japan. *Reinvading*? visiting in a continual flow. Nearly half of the population—22,000 people—are registered aliens—*what planet?*—finding employment in the busy tourism and entertainment businesses, where half of the island work force is employed, and in the garment and manufacturing industries. *More than number was killed in two weeks of fighting*. Island residents enjoy a per capita income of US $11,500 and a literacy rate of 97 percent. *Good! They can read about the stupid war!*

Saipan offers visitors a glimpse into the past, especially the remnants of WWII, concluded just over 50 years ago. *The war has only been concluded militarily; it still goes on today economically*. Saipan has not forgotten her Japanese heritage—*where she made the Chamoros second class citizens*—and has carefully tended the many relics for visitors to appreciate—*and pay for seeing.* You may even visit the remains of the Japanese Prison, where, many believe, famous aviatrix Amelia Earhart was held shortly before her disappearance—*$8 ticket, tip not included.*

There are also the remains of a much more ancient past to peer into. The famed Taga House on Tinian contains the tallest Latte stones yet found, dating back to pre-written history. While on Tinian, visitors may see the actual bomb pits used to load the atomic bombs in the U.S. Air Force bombers that carried them to Japan—*another 180,000 dead.* At one time, tiny Tinian had 300 huge B-29 bombers using six runways, each 1.5 miles long—*to pound Japan.*

People come to Saipan to enjoy the beauty of the islands—*didn't they already say that?* —and the surrounding seas. The Marianas Islands lie along the edge of the deepest part of the ocean to be found, the Marianas Trench. The water is approximately 36,000 feet deep—*about seven miles*—and it's said that a cannonball would take an hour to reach the bottom. *What about a torpedoed ship?*

The beautiful clear waters provide excellent deep-sea fishing for marlin, mahi-mahi—*the fish, not the rum drink*—and tuna—*Charlie-From-The-Sea*—scuba diving and snorkeling along the reefs, or just a perfect backdrop for sunbathing on the beach. *In Pattaya, the Japanese tourists, who travel in regimented groups, giggle en masse when they see a topless sunbather—the result of living in an imposed-conformity society.*

In addition, speaking of restaurants—*I wasn't*! There are many to choose from offering seafood, American, French, Chinese, Japanese, Korean, Italian, Mexican, and local specialties. Some hotels offer dinner shows with exotic—*naked*—entertainment, and there are several dinner cruise boats to choose from.

Use the guide to the best Saipan has to offer, and enjoy your visit to the historic Marianas!

Nowhere in the guide does it say the real reason visitors come to Saipan. It is the gambling Mecca of the South Seas, an island Las Vegas for the 75% of the visitors—all from Japan—to escape the rigorous winter and high prices of the homeland.

Do Madi Goto!

Chapter 12

"Since my last report
This officer has reached rock bottom,
And has started to dig."
Officer fitness report.

Notes from daily journal:

Sent postcard to a friend in Sacramento, a fellow I taught with many years. Jim Harlan is a big man, in heart as well as size. He has a lovely wife, Marie. He and I, along with Bill Solenberger, were the only male coaches at Joaquin Miller Junior High School in the sixties. Jim and Bill played the 9th champions in volleyball, twice each year, just the two of them against the 9th grade complete team. They had never lost a game; the two of them beating the championship team each time. The year I joined the coaching staff, they invited me to participate in the twice-yearly event. Surely three coaches of exceptional athletic ability should do much better than two. Well we did not! We lost! The first time the coaches had ever lost. *Ever!* For several weeks there were certain bad things said about my athletic ability and crude references to my ape-like ancestry.

That was many years ago. However, being in Guam jogged my rusty memory: Jim had been stationed in *GUAM*! He had been in the *Army!* I was an ex-Marine. Therefore, I did what any warm-hearted Marine would do for an old army friend; I decided to send my friend and military brother a post card knowing that his wife usually got the mail.

Dear Jem – You menber
Yer girl fren here in guam an yor
Son yu doen know. we cume yor home
now SaraymInto so yu meet yor son to
Live with ferever you.
i lub yu
Mitchiuu

As the man says, "Revenge is best served cold."

Item from ship's paper:

"Today starts three days of drills to assess the carrier's TSA (Total Survival Ability). Today more than half of the U.S. Navy is deployed around the world entailing the use of 29% of total ships (102). Approximately 50,000 sailors and marines are "Forward Deployed." Forward Deployed means the navy keeps a carrier based somewhere other the U. S., to project America's naval air power and protecting U.S. national interest around the world. As of this TSA action, the *USS Independence*. " Freedom's Flagship" has been on the cutting edge of forward deployment.

7 AM class canceled—drills.

10 AM class—two students—drills continue. Held class anyway.

Announced over the con at noon: "1,900 miles to Alaska—2,300 to Sydney, Australia."

Midnight. Awaken hot and sweaty. Crawled down from bunk stepping on Bob's arm eliciting a bear-like grunt. Made way to the brightly-lit head and shower. Soaked T-shirt in lukewarm water in sink and put on. Hair awry, staggered back to bunk. Forgot to go pee. Groaning, five minutes later crawled down from bunk. Staggered along the passageway back to the shower room wearing shorts and wet T-shirt—screw the rules. Frightened myself by reflection as passed mirror. Dribbled down my leg. Staggered back. Climbed up toward my bunk. A falsetto voice from Ed's bunk, "Thank you darling!"

"Would you fuckers shut up!"

"You jealous me, Bob?"

Another day:

Ed and I suggested to Bob "That when he was Admiral, he could ride his Harley Hog around the flight deck!"

Bob replied, "Screw you guys!"

Bob is not a spendthrift with words.

Crossed the Equator. Hot!

Half-day classes because of "Ratings"[1] testing.

Another day:
Lat. 6 degrees Long. 154 degrees. We are a few miles east of New Guinea. Can see nothing but rain squalls in the distance. Hot! Wished stupid rainsquall come this way.

Went to post office. Sailors lined up near the library entrance for urine test. Many were clutching water and/or soda bottles. Why? I don't know. Drugs I guess. Not interested enough to find out—besides, might have me in there trying to stick my dick down a test-tube.

Bob came in saying, "Captain on deck! Be a-lert!"
Ed replied, "Our country needs more lerts!"

Hot and humid. No islands in sight. The *Indy* has been steadily steaming south.

Today New Britain is on our starboard side, the Solomon Islands the port. New Britian is the largest island in the Bismarck Archipelago. Mostly volcanic it spewed out hot magma and lighting the sky as late as 1995. In 1943, there was a different kind of fireworks on New Britain. In the Pacific, General MacArthur's Australians and Americans were leapfrogging in slow motion along the north coast of New Guinea. The U.S. Marines began perfecting the island-hopping techniques that would make them so successful, bypassing Japanese soldiers on isolated islands who, without supplies, could do nothing but wait for the end. The Marines worked their way through "The Slot" of the Solomon's reaching for Rabaul: Rabaul the seemingly invincible Japanese base at Rabaul on the north end of New Britian.

Rabaul was important because the Japanese needed the huge south pacific base on New Britian, to send wave after wave of reinforcements to retake Guadalcanal—the key to control of the Pacific.

Rabaul took a place in history—as little out-of-the-way-places sometimes do—by another historical wartime event. U.S. intelligence intercepted and decoded a Japanese message about an inspection trip by the man most responsible for the success of one of the cheapest military triumphs on record, the sinking of the American Navy during

---

[1] Test to rise in rank.

the Japanese sneak attack against the American forces at Pearl Harbor, Hawaii, on December 7th, 1941. The man was Yamamoto.

Admiral Isoroku Yamamoto was the Commander in Chief of the Imperial Japanese Navy at the outbreak of World War II. Having had an illustrious career dating back to the victory of Japan over Russia in 1904, he was considered Japan's greatest military leader by both the civilian population and the armed forces of Japan. The naval genius entrusted by Japan with the vital task of smashing the U.S. Pacific fleet was a many-sided man. In contrast to most Japanese military leaders, Admiral Yamamoto was an poised world traveler who spoke fluent English, admired somewhat the United States, claiming many American friends. He argued against attacking the U.S., but a patriot, when ordered to fight, he waged war brilliantly.

In 1919, Commander Yamamoto was sent to Harvard University where he studied English, mastered bridge and poker. In 1934, Vice-Admiral Yamamoto served as Japan's chief delegate to the London Naval Conference, where he forced the termination by the end of 1936 the treaty that had kept Japan's fleet to a ratio of 5 to 3 in favor of Britain and America. Then, over opposition of Japan's old-line battleship admirals, he successfully lobbied for the construction of aircraft carriers. By 1943, Yamamoto was the heart and soul of the Japanese campaign of conquest in the Pacific.

"Three may keep a secret, if two of them are dead."
"U.S Intelligence breaks Japanese code."

By April 1943, the tide of war had begun to move ever so slowly against the Empire of Japan. Their fleet had been stopped at the Battle of Midway, and the U.S. Marines had taken the island of Guadalcanal from them. To bolster Japanese morale in the Pacific, Yamamoto decided to visit some of his island outposts. Having broken the Japanese military code, on April 14, 1943, US Intelligence intercepted a message about Yamamoto. The message read that Yamamoto would be flying from Rabaul to Bougainville on the 18th. It even specified that he would be in a Betty, a Mitsubishi twin-engine Naval Land-based Bomber that could cruise at 250 m.p.h. with a top speed of 325 m.p.h. and escorted by fighters originally called MitsubishiA6M5 "Zeke", but known to the American pilots that had to go against it as the Zero, one of the best standard carrier-borne fighter in the Japanese navy.

The message stated that the flight would arrive at 0800 hours and then Yamamoto would depart 0840 hours by boat.

Admiral Chester Nimitz with the backing of President Roosevelt, gave the order. "Get Yamamoto!"

A meeting was held on Guadalcanal where it was decided to give the job to Major John Mitchell of the U.S. Army 13th Air Force, 339th Squadron. The squadron flew P-38 fighter planes, the only planes that had the capability of flying the 425 miles to Bougainville and returning. The P-38 has twin engines, a twin fuselage, four 50-caliber machine guns, and a 20-millimeter cannon. At the time, it was the best plane for the job. The P-38's used in this strike also had 300 gallon auxiliary gas tanks fitted to augment the existing 165 gallons tanks with which they were normally equipped. They needed all the gasoline and ammunition they could carry because they estimated that at least 80 Japanese planes would rise form Bougainville as an escort when Yamamoto's plane drew near.

The P 38s flight was uneventful, and the long shot paid off, because no sooner had they reached Bougainville when the Japanese flight was spotted. A thousand to one shot had come home! Instead of one Betty however, there were two, so both were downed, one exploding into the ocean, the other into the jungle. One American and his plane were lost.

The Americans kept the operation secret until after the war so the Japanese would not know their code had been broken. The men in the operation were also taken out of the area for fear they might fall into Japanese hands and reveal the mission. As for the Japanese, they waited awhile before announcing that Yamamoto had been killed in action. They released no details.

In 1984, the leader of the Japanese rescue team searching out Yamamoto's plane crash was interviewed. He stated that the body of Yomamoto was onboard the bomber down in the jungle.

*****

Ed: "Jim! Is it true Bob wears his military ribbons on his skivvy shorts?"

Jim: "I wouldn't take it for a three-dimensional fact, but that's what his queer petty officer buddies told me!"

"When you yard birds open your mouths, It's evident that you both are depriving some villages of an idiot."

New Guinea is out there. We can smell it. Can't see it, but the rotted smell of vegetables hang heavy in the humid air.

Bougainville, Guadalcanal, Tarawa: Off to the port side. The Marines were there during WWII. Many still are.

Discussed World War II rationing of goods with a few of my class members on the fantail—all young guys born in the seventies.

" 1942 . . . nationwide gasoline rationing is ordered to reduce rubber consumption. Rationing begun in May on the East Coast, where U-boat sinkings have reduced tanker shipments. All U.S. motorists are assigned A, B, or C stickers as of December 1. Those with A stickers are allowed four gallons of gasoline per week. Later it was reduced to three. Pleasure driving is banned and a 35-mile-per-hour speed limit is imposed."

" . . . cheese is rationed at the rate of four pounds per week, but requires red stamps that may also be used for meat. . . "

Most of my students (sailors) on the *Indy* had never heard of rationing nor of rationing cards or stamps. I mentioned a little ditty that we kids sang in the mid-forties:

"An' when I die, please bury me
Beneath a ton of sugar, by a rubber tree;
Lay me to rest in an auto machine
And water my grave with gasoline."

They thought it and I were weird.
Now that I read it fifty years later, I agree with them.

1500: While four of us were amiably chatting on the flight deck, a Tomcat swung in over the carrier, passing overhead as quick as a thought, the noise from its passing blasting us to the deck. Whipping into a climbing turn the Turkey released four sputtering glaring flares, then flipped back plowing the ocean with its machine guns. We didn't hear it coming, didn't even know it was lurking about. Fantastic! We'd of been chopped hamburger if the pilot so wanted. I guess the Captain thought we needed a little entertainment to take our minds off the heat. Didn't work. Just left us awe-stricken with a little putty roll in our knickers. It was still hot—the weather and the plane.

Another day:

934 sailors took advancement exams for E-4 and E-5 ratings on the mess decks. The Navy is big on testing. Upon entering the Navy, each recruit is given an Armed Services Vocational Aptitude Battery (ASVAB). The ASVAB is used to measure basic aptitudes just as it says; in other words, it attempts to find out what the recruit learned in school other than looking down Ms. English Teacher's neckline while she is correcting papers. It is concerned with how much the recruit can *learn*, rather than how much he *knows*. ASVAB is a fancy name for an IQ test.

Two other tests are administered upon entering the Navy: The Nuclear Field Qualification Test (NFQT) and the Defense Language Aptitude Battery (DLAB). These tests are used to screen recruits for advanced specialized training and the eligibility to take these tests depends on the recruit's ASVAB scores. The Navy wants the best they can get.

A rating is a Navy job—a duty for certain skills and aptitudes. A rate is a paygrade within a rating. Therefore, an engineman for example, calls for persons who are good with their hands and are mechanically inclined. Thus, an engineman third class (EN3) would have a rating of engineman, and a rate of third-class petty officer. The higher the rating, the more the pay and responsibility.

I ironed another shirt—use two to three per day because of sweating. Drank over a gallon of water, urinated dribbles; the rest came out through my back. Ed asked me if I wanted to iron his shirt. I asked him, "Ed, you know what they call that zit you got on your butt?" He looked back over his shoulder. "No . . . what?"

"A brain tumor."

Bob grunted in appreciation. It was too hot to laugh.

"Does that mean you ain't gonna iron it?"

Not too interested in eating.

Another day:

Something whitely whirled across top of the radar mast, than danced down to the deck. Clouds of it. *Snow*! *It was snowing!* Someone yelled out the words. "SNOW! SNOW!" I went to investigate. *Snow*! *Here*? Damn! I am sweating like a hard-hearted sinner at a camp meetin' an' here it's *snowing!* I started to pick some up. It smeared on my hands. It was not snow. Momentarily confused I looked closely. It was ash. Grey-white ashes. Lasted about two minutes. *Volcanic? Where in the hell did it come from?* We never did find out.

Fine spring days went by—somewhere. Summer rains freshened the air—somewhere. Somewhere was not here. We sweated, transudated, perspired—we sweltered. We wished that we were somewhere else. A guy, an old time lumber worker whose wife didn't come home anymore, told me once that he was leaving the mill, leaving Placerville, my home town. Being a young, naive pre-teenager, I asked, "Where you going?" He chewed on some Days Work in his cheek, squinting his tired eyes into the sun replying, "Somewhere." I looked at him and said, "I've never been there. Like to go someday. It sounds like an interesting place." Now I have been there. Lots of times.

Must stop teasing the kid—seaman apprentice—who comes in to clean the deck in our cabin and mop the passageway. He's supposed to make our bunks, empty the waste can, and generally clean up. We are too democratic for that; we do it ourselves, but we give him a joking hard time. I climbed out of my bunk after a sweaty nap, pulled the door inward to go to the head to discover he had put wide masking tape in a web pattern all across the doorway. Had to cut my way out with scissors. *Little bastard.* Probably from Texas. Swear to get even. I wadded the mess of tape up and stuck it under Ed's mattress. Like to keep the place neat.

Another day:

Ed: *"What did you do?"*

Jim: " . . . well, so I got on my knees beside the couch an' . . ."

Bob: "Don't you bozos talk about anything except pussy? Talk 'bout somethin' else like the ship or somethin' to eat!"

Jim: "What makes you think we ain't talkin' 'bout somethin' to eat?"

Ship's newspaper reports that 850 men and women discharged for homosexuality in the past year! 18% more than in 1995 and 42% more than in 1994.

"Hard to believe" I said. "More homosexuality."

"Aw! . . . I don't think so," said Ed. "Just more people coming out."

"Yeah! I think that you're right."

"I doen like queer guys" said Jorgenson, one of the chief petty officers. We were having cokes in the 7/11. "Like queer gals though. Specially they goin' down on each other."

Goes without saying.

Ed says he has always been a lesbian.

Ed wants to play blackjack—vingt-et-un—as the French call it: Twenty-one. That is why he bought the cards to practice for the defunct trip to Saipan. I am a fairly decent blackjack player: by that, I mean that I've played hundreds and hundreds of games on my computer. Also, I have played the game in Macaw, Nepal, Las Vegas, Reno, Australia, New Zealand, Costa Rica and on an English ship on the North Sea. The best place to play blackjack for the odds: Las Vegas. Over the years, I am about even, which, if you know anything about speculating in such places of speculation, means that I'm tolerably proficient. So, ol' Ed, listening to my "always split eight's and aces" and "don't hit twelve to sixteen if the dealer has a six up (showing), wanted to play. Ed has the least card discipline in any human alive. An orangutan could play cards more sensibly. I would tell him to *never* double his bet when he was losing and, immediately he doubled, "as a way to get my money back faster." All doubling does is accelerate the losing program. He lost everything—his money, clothed, future paychecks and, at one desperation point, he was betting his mother's house and car. He lost! I was in stitches, laughing hysterically as he acted out being in a casino, waving his arms, shouting 'HIT ME! HIT ME AGAIN! *OH, MOMMA!* Then he play-acted being subdued by casino guards and hauled out of the place while yelling over his shoulder *"BET IT ALL! BET IT ALL!"*

Another day:

South to the Coral Sea.
To
The Battle of Midway

The Coral Sea is often described as an arm of the southwest Pacific Ocean bounded by the New Hebrides, northeast Australia, and southeast New Guinea. The *USS Independence* steaming approximately 1200 miles from my final destination of Sydney, Australia was smack dab in the middle of the Coral Sea Island Territories. We were right at the area where the Battle of the Coral Sea took place so many years ago in 1942.

As chronicled earlier, the American Navy had one great secret weapon: its code breakers could read Japanese naval messages. From those, Pacific Fleet commander Chester Nimitz knew that the Japanese planned to seize the eastern approaches to Australia by attacking Port Moresby on the west side of New Guinea. In the first week in May, 1942, Nimitz stripped bare Pearl Harbor's defenses to mount an all-out attack on the Japanese invaders as they entered the Coral Sea. The Battle of the Coral Sea was the first naval battle in history in which the rival fleets never saw each other. The two carrier forces maneuvered between 100 and 200 miles apart while their planes attacked. The action included some absurd errors. Several Japanese planes tried unsuccessfully to land on the deck of the *Yorktown*; several American pilots tried unsuccessfully to bomb the cruiser *Australia*.

In the first U.S. attack on a major Japanese warship, though, bombers from the *Lexington* and the *Yorktown* trapped and sank the 12,000-ton light carrier *Shoho*; nearly 700 of her 900 crewmen went down with her. The Americans drew first blood.

A lieutenant Commander Robert Dixon triumphantly radioed, "Dixon to carrier, scratch one flattop."

The second day of the battle, both fleets sent off their planes again. The *Yorktown's* bombers started a fuel fire on the *Shokaku*, but were chased away by Zero fighters. Though the *Lexington* and the *Yorktown* similarly fought off Japanese bombers, a mysterious explosion in the generator room crippled the 42,000-ton *"Lay Lex."* The crew ran up a banner on the mainmast that signaled:

THIS SHIP NEEDS HELP

In late afternoon, the captain gave the order to abandon the *Lexington*.

Both sides claimed victory in the Battle of the Coral Sea. The U.S. had lost the *Lexington* plus a destroyer and a tanker; the Japanese had lost the carrier *Shoho*, plus a tanker and a destroyer. The Japanese lost a few more planes—77 vs. 66—as well as more men—1,074 vs. 543. However, in strategic terms, the essential fact was that the Japanese troop transports bound for Port Moresby had to turn back.

The Japanese Empire had reached its outer limits.

Before his death, the imperial navy's Admiral Isoroku Yamamoto was still determined to do what he had failed to do at Pearl Harbor: draw the U.S. Pacific Fleet into a high-seas confrontation where he could destroy it. His strategy, which he hoped would win the war for Japan or at least open the way to California, was to seize the two tiny islands collectively known as Midway. A lonely outpost 1,100 miles northwest of Pearl Harbor, this was the westernmost U.S. base now that Guam, Wake, and the Philippines were lost. The U.S. Navy would have to defend Midway, Yamamoto figured, and then he would attack it with the most powerful fleet ever assembled: 11 battleships, 8 carriers, 23 cruisers, 65 destroyers—190 ships in all, plus more than 200 planes on the strike-force carriers.

Yamamoto, who had stayed in Japan during the Pearl Harbor attack, took personal command of this huge armada. His flagship was the largest battleship in creation, the 64,000-ton *Yamato*, whose 18.1-in. guns had a range of more than 25 miles. His carrier chief was Vice Admiral Chuichi Nagumo, the Pearl Harbor commander who had gone on to wreak havoc on the British fleet. With virtually no losses, Nagumo's planes had bombed British bases at Darwin, Australia, and Colombo, Ceylon; sunk the carrier *Hermes* and two cruisers; and driven the Royal Navy all the way across the Indian Ocean.

Again, cautious staff admirals in Tokyo opposed Yamamoto's strategy as too risky. Again, he threatened to resign if he did not get his way. Again, the admirals gave in.

America had zero battleships vs. Japan's 11; 3 carriers to Japan's 8 (and one was the Yorktown, barely patched together at Pearl Harbor after its mauling in the Coral Sea). Although he had only 76 ships against Yamamoto's 190 (some historical writers list Yamamoto's fleet at 162) Nimitz had "Magic" the now official name of the Japanese code-breaking ability possessed by the Intelligence department of the U.S. government. "Magic", headed by Lieutenant-Commander Joseph Rochefort's code-breaking team in Pearl Harbor, told Nimitz that Midway was Yamamoto's main target, that there would be a secondary attack against the Aleutians as a diversion, and that the strike at Midway was set for June 4.

The fates that had condemned the U.S. to blind complacency at Pearl Harbor now visited the same kismet on Japan. As Roselle Montgomery once wrote:

"The fates are not quite obdurate;
They have a grim, sardonic way
Of granting them who supplicate
The thing they wanted yesterday."[2]

Nagumo talked smugly as he neared his launching point: "The enemy is not aware of our plans."

The Japanese blindness and "Magic" enabled the outnumbered Americans to plan an ambush as decisive as that of the Concord Minutemen of 1775, when they fired their "shot heard round the world." In the new style of naval warfare, which admirals around the world were just beginning to learn, aircraft carriers were supreme. They could destroy anything but were highly vulnerable, so the key was to find and attack the enemy's carriers—first.

Keeping his enormous "main fleet" in reserve for the future battle that would never materialize, Yamamoto sent Nagumo ahead with four of the six carriers from the task force that had devastated Pearl Harbor. Before dawn on June 4, Nagumo launched 108 planes, half his force, to pulverize Midway's defenses. But his scout planes failed to spot two U.S. carriers, the *Enterprise* and the *Hornet*, lying in wait less than 200 miles to the northeast under the command Rear Admiral Raymond Spruance. Taking an immense risk, Spruance committed virtually all his planes—67 Dauntless dive-bombers, 29 Devastator torpedo bombers, and 20 Wildcat fighters—to a desperate counterattack. By some combination of inspired calculations and pure luck, Spruance's planes reached Nagumo's fleet just as the carriers were taking in their returning bombers and reloading for a second strike at Midway. To exploit that moment of supreme vulnerability, the Devastator torpedo bombers roared in. Despite the Americans' advantage of surprise, they too encountered a shock: the overwhelming superiority of the Zero fighters defending the Japanese carriers. As each torpedo bomber lumbered toward a carrier, it was shot to pieces. Fifteen torpedo bombers left the *Hornet*; the only survivor was Ensign George Gay, who was shot down and wounded in the arm and leg but managed to float until rescuers found him the next day.

Eight times the American planes attacked Nagumo's carriers, and

---

[2] Roselle Mercier Montgomery (1974-1933) U.S. writer. The Fates.

eight times they were beaten off. When the last torpedo bomber was shot down at about 10:25 a.m., it looked as though Nagumo had won the Battle of Midway. However, the Zeros embroiled in low-level combat against the torpedo bombers didn't see what was happening high overhead. At 15,000 ft. above the carrier *Kaga*, Lieutenant-Commander Clarence Wade McClusky, nearly out of gas from searching for his quarry, nosed his Dauntless dive-bomber into a screaming plunge. Behind him, 25 of his pilots did the same. At 1,800 feet, McClusky pulled the bomb release. He later remembered the image of the *Kaga's* clean, empty hardwood deck, then the tremendous explosion. Bleeding from five bullet wounds, McClusky barely got back to the *Enterprise*, with less than 5 gallons of aviation fuel in his tank.

Lieutenant Richard Best took on the next carrier, which he did not realize was the *Akagi*, Nagumo's flagship. "Don't let this carrier escape," he shouted over his radio to the four remaining bombers as he started his dive. His bomb landed next to Nagumo's bridge, starting a huge fire. At almost that very moment, the dive-bombers received reinforcements from a third carrier, the patched-up *Yorktown*. Lieutenant-Commander Maxwell Leslie led 17 more bombers from the *Yorktown* in a dive that smashed and crippled a third carrier, the *Soryu*.

In less than 10 minutes, Nagumo had seen three of his four carriers transformed into blazing hulks. In addition, he had been transformed from the commander of all he surveyed into a desperate survivor who had to clamber out a window to escape from his burning flagship to a nearby cruiser.

It was not being a good day for the Japanese Empire's Navy. In six minutes, Naguma had lost three carriers.

Nagumo still had one carrier left, the *Hiryu*, and one carrier could still sting, and sting fatally.

"Bogeys, 32 miles, closing!" cried the *Yorktown's* radar officer. A dozen fighters from the *Yorktown* were circling overhead, and more than twice as many antiaircraft guns were firing, when the *Hiryu's* dive bombers and torpedo bombers struck. As the *Yorktown's* guns demolished one attacking bomber, its bomb exploded with a huge orange flash behind the carrier's bridge. Then another two bombs penetrated deep below decks, and the carrier's whole bow went up in flames. The *Yorktown* was doomed. Nearly all the 2,270 men—nearly all the crew—were rescued.

No sooner had the *Hiryu's* torpedo bombers returned to their ship than they were ordered out again. Few were in shape to go—five dive-bombers and four torpedo planes—and their crews were so exhausted that the commander ordered a break before the next take-offs. The rice balls were just being served when the alarm sounded: "Enemy dive bombers directly overhead." Swooping down, planes from the *Enterprise* and the dying *Yorktown* started the fires that would destroy the *Hiryu*.

Admiral Nagumo discreetly refrained for hours from reporting the full extent of the disaster to Yamamoto. Only in late afternoon did he finally tell him that the *Hiryu*, the last of his carriers, was burning out of control. With that, Nagumo decided to withdraw the remnants of his fleet from the battlefield. Yamamoto sank into a chair and sat staring into space. He had a right to be stunned: For the first time in 350 years Japan had suffered a naval defeat!

Finally stirring, Yamamoto sent a message of MacArthurian unreality:

"The enemy fleet, which has practically been destroyed, is retiring to the east . . . Immediately contact and destroy the enemy."

As a further measure, he also relieved Nagumo of his command.

Imperial headquarters in Japan reported that a great triumph had been achieved, bringing "supreme power in the Pacific." They neglected to say to whom.

What the outnumbered Americans had accomplished at the Coral Sea and Midway was even greater than they at first realized. Describing "this memorable American victory," Churchill wrote:

"At one stroke, the dominant position of Japan in the Pacific was reversed . . . The annals of war at sea present no more intense, heart-shaking shock than these two battles, in which the qualities of the United States Navy and Air Force and of the American race shone forth in splendor."

What had the "Outnumbered Americans" accomplished? In a single day's fighting, all the advantages gained by the Japanese at Pearl Harbor were canceled out. Equality in carrier power between America and Japan was restored six to six. The spreading tentacles of the Japanese Empire were checked and . . . never on the defense again, the Americans were now free to go on the offense.

Before General Douglas MacArthur finally received the Japanese surrender in Tokyo Bay September 2, 1945, though, would come three grinding years of "island hopping," the slow and painful campaign across the South Pacific from the fetid jungles of New Guinea to the barricaded caves of Okinawa. The first of these battles, and one of the worst, occurred at the southern tip of the Solomon Islands, where the U.S. Marines made their first landing of the war early in the morning of Aug. 7, 1942.

The natives sometimes called the island by it capital's name, Honiara.

The Japanese, who would fight more than six months to hold that desolate island, gave it another name:

They called it *Gadarukanaru.*

It entered American history under the name of Guadalcanal.

The United States Marines called it Hell.

Chapter 13

"This must be heaven I know
For I've served my time in hell!
Guadalcanal Marine

Guadalcanal

"Why didn't I think of that?"

Sometimes a solution or and idea sounds so simple when proposed that the automatic response is:

"Why didn't I think of that?"

The words were not uttered, but they were there, pasted on the faces of the dumb-founded Admirals and Generals sitting around a conference table in Australia as they planned the campaign to take back the islands of the Solomon Islands. In his book, *The Wars of America*, Robert Lechie stated the fact that for 30 years the United States military maintained that a war in the Pacific would be an island war, that although the islands were fortified and heavy defended, they would have to be seized. The cost would be high in men and materials. Attacking from the sea against fortified beaches would take a terrible toll in man and equipment. The British had learned this hard lesson at Gallipoli when the lost thousands of soldiers attacking dug in Turkish forces from the sea. They retreated. The cost was too high. Any commander realizes that to attack is to lose more men than the defenders. Napoleon lost over 400,000 Frenchmen attacking Russia in the winter. He finally retreated. The cost was too high. Nazi Germany made the same mistake as Napoleon when it attacked Russia in the winter losing an army. Germany retreated. The cost was too high.

The American Admirals and Generals knew the cost to retake the Solomon Islands would be costly, but they believed that it could be done. The Marines maintained that they could do it; that landings could be made across open beaches, even beaches protected by underwater obstacle, barbed wire, and entrenched artillery. The Marines had developed the tactics of amphibious warfare to a high degree. Using Close Air Support—a tactic where Marine pilots would shot, fire rockets, and drop bombs against enemy targets sometimes only yards from friendly forces—combined with continuous air and naval bombardment of coastal defenses and use of special vehicles—such as landing craft that could disembark tanks and infantry in shallow water—the Marines could take any military objective. However, the cost was always high.

While the Admirals and Generals were lamentably calculating the cost of not only lives and equipment to take island after island, but the possible political fallout, an unprecedented voice from one the junior officers spoke out:

"Pardon me Sir. Why do we have to take each island?"

The Admirals and Generals looked at the upstart. It was suggested he explain. He explained that:

"Since the Battle of the Coral Sea and Midway . . . we have control of the air and most of the sea; we can stop supplies from reaching most of the islands. Just by-pass them. Let them sit there. We can come back and get them later."

The Admirals and Generals sat in their hard straight-backed chairs, quiet . . . pondering. This tactic was not in the military history books; no strategy professor at Annapolis or the Naval Academy had lectured on it; no war in history had been an island war where the islands were scattered across the sea like a handful of tossed pebbles..

What would the Isolated Japanese do? Use their radios. So what? No rescuers will be able to come and liberate them. If they do, we will ambush them. Use launches and take to the sea. Thousand of troops and a few launches! Not likely! If they try, so what? We can run airplane patrols. Blast them out of the sea. They have food and water. They can hold out for weeks. So what? They will eventually run out. After that, they can eat each other.

"Why didn't we think of that?"

Actually, early in the Pacific war Admiral Nimitz and General MacArthur concluded that it would be a costly mistake to attempt to take all or most of the island forts with which the Japanese proposed to defend her Pacific Empire. The Japanese were known for not surrendering; they were expected to fight to the last soldier killing as many of the invading Americans as possible. (President Truman partly based the use of the dropping of the atom bomb on mainland Japan for the same reasons.) Nimitz and MacArthur decided to seize the most important islands bypassing the others, leaving them to whiter on the vine. Without supplies, the Japanese would run out of food, medicine, and ordinance. Should any be a menace, they would be attacked by carrier and land-based aircraft.

So, the concept of "Island-Hopping" was introduced into military jargon. Island hopping speeded up the retaking of the islands and, history tells us, was one of the main reasons for the defeat of Japan.

As the *Indy* sailed through the Louisiade Archipelago rounding the tip of Papua New Guinea to starboard, I knew that to port, about 300 miles, Guadalcanal lay festering, hot and humid in the boiling sun. An inferno of heat, bugs, disease, and enemy troops, Guadalcanal was not one of the islands that could afford to be island-hopped. Its geographical location made it an unacceptable threat to the important supply line from the United States to Australia. After the Battle of the Coral Sea and McArthur's American and Australian defense of Port Moresby in New Guinea against a Japanese assault, the U.S. began its offense against the Solomon Islands. The new offensive started with Guadalcanal.

Dante's *Inferno* recounts an imaginary journey through Hell, Purgatory, and Paradise (Inferno, Purgatorio, Paradiso) and the beginning includes the line "Abandon hope, all ye who enter here." The Japanese could not afford to give up Guadalcanal. As expected, they were instructed by their superiors to fight to the last man. The Marines had been advised what to expect when they hit the beaches at Guadalcanal. The American generals planned on heavy losses and were prepared for marines to die—marines from majors down in rank—it is an axiom that colonels and generals direct a war, but not to die for it. But, whatever the projected outcome, the blow was struck. The Marines were told to abandoned hope, to stop thinking about going home, to concentrate instead on their main objective—to kill Japs.

Stiff resistance was encountered, but it was nowhere near as formidable as expected. To the generals' surprise—contrary to all intelligence—the Japanese had not been expecting the attack; they were not ready. When the Marines stormed ashore on what was soon to be called "The Canal" or just "The Island," they encountered a relatively small opposing force; they took the island in three days of spirited fighting. The U.S. did lose a cruiser and another was damaged along with two destroyers and a troop transport barge, but this loss was a smaller price than the Americans expected to pay. The Marines had landed and the situation was well in hand.

For awhile.

A few days of respite.

Then the real inferno began.

The Admirals and Generals knew that after the opening round, the Japanese would counter-attack: the only question was: "how quick and how powerful?"

Then, in Marine parlance . . . "the excreta collided with the rapidly revolving blades of the electro-mechanical cooling device", or, in plain English "*the shit hit the fan!*"

North of Guadalcanal, on the island of truk—renamed Chuuk after World War II—using 1,200 Nauarans from the island of Nauru, just south of the Equator, as slave labors, the Japanese built a large naval base. Down from this base on Truk, swept a great Japanese armada of battleships, carriers, cruisers, and transports plus elements of the Japanese Air Force and Army attacking Guadalcanal. Before the fighting was over, the 7th Marines would reinforce the attack and all three infantry regiments of the 2nd Marine Division would see action, as would thousands of American soldiers. Robert Leckie describes the fighting:

> "It was a most savage battle. Neither side gave or asked quarter. Japanese laborers and native Melanesians as well as the Marines, soldiers, sailors, and flyers of both nations fought each other from every imaginable type of vehicle, ship or air-craft, wielding every kind of gun or knife, striking with spears and axes, clubs and fists and stones, even, and often continuing the fight within the water where shipwrecked sailors or downed airmen clawed at each other with bare hands until, sometimes, sharks brought the battle to a horrible end. And while they fought, both sides were scourged with malaria, racked by dysentery, emaciated by hunger, and scorched or drenched by turns in the blistering sun and torrential rains that made their battleground a stinking, steaming, festering slime."[1]

---

[1] Robert Lechie. *The Wars of America*. Castle Books, 1968, pg. 750.

The Inferno of Guadalcanal was a firestorm of hurricane proportions consuming dozens of ships, hundreds of planes, and over 15,000 lives.

"Their sighs, lamentations, and loud wailings resounded through the starless air, so that at first it made me weep; strange tongues, horrible language, words of pain, tones of anger, voices loud and hoarse, and with these the sounds of hands, made a tumult which is whirling through the air forever dark, and sand eddies in a whirlwind."

(Dante)

Dante was not the only poet of anguish, misery, of suffering. Some Marines had their say:

"When this bloody war is over,
Oh, how happy I will be;
Just to be a plain civilian,
No more soldiering for me.
No more dress parade on Sunday,
No more asking for a pass;
You can tell the Sergeant Major,
Stick the Marine Corps up his ass.
Anonymous

And:

"This must be heaven I know
For I've served my time in hell!
I was there when my buddies died,
There . . . there on Guadalcanal."
Guadalcanal Marine

*****

Bob came into the cabin with a harsh set to his face, his tail dragging. It was easy to see that he was weary, dead tired. He rarely enjoyed a full night of uninterrupted rest: as Chief Bo'sun he had multiple duties, someone constantly needed his advice, expertise, or permission to do something. The Tandem Thrust exercise had him working eighteen to twenty hours a day; his sleep was constantly being interrupted to solve yet another pressing problem; as Chief Boatswain of the ship, his responsibilities seemed endless. While Bob's work increased, mine became lighter; the busier the men on the ship became the less time they had for class. While anthropology may be a course important for world understanding and survival, on a warship it becomes a luxury. Yet my increased free time was not put to much use. I could only feel powerless, there was nothing I could do to help; I know a lot about cultures, genetics and DNA, but not much about running a three and a half billion dollar boat. My foremost contribution was just to stay out of the way.

Earlier in the morning some lieutenant "read off" one of Bob's men. "He read me off from asshole to appetite"—for being seen in work clothes by VIP visitors to the ship—some civilians officials who were wasting taxpayer's money roaming around the ocean. It was a wrong call by the lieutenant for two reason: he had no connection with the work party; out of courtesy he should have come to Bob, and he did it in front of the working party; a good officer *never* reads off another man in front of the men. The Navy as well as the Marine corps is well versed in the principle "Praise in public, criticize in private."

Lieutenants are young; they have not been in the service long, so they are expected to do dumb things! Bob has been in this man's Navy over twenty years, the Shitbird[2] lieutenant probably less than one. (Lieutenants are usually called ninety-day wonders for that is how long it takes boot camp to change a college puke into an Officer and a Gentleman.)

Bob, irritated at the young officer's remarks to his men—for he thinks that his men are the real VIP's aboard; they are the experts and do the work and Bob has a hell of lot more status (and power) than a mere lieutenant—in turn, made a few remarks to the lieutenant. The Chief Bo'sun was then accused of not being a "Team Player" by the XO (Bob doesn't get along with the XO anyway, however the XO does have a lot of rank), but it rankled Bob to be chastised. It was a case of too many chiefs butting into the Indian's work, powwowing into places they should not. Bob can retire in four years—I think that he is ready now!

Ed took some of the electricity out of the air with his unbriled levity.

"Hey Bob! Don't ya know the military organization on this ship is like a tree full of monkeys!"

---

[2] Shitbird: a Feather Merchant, a nothing person, a recruit.

I knew that Bob was not in a mood for repartee, so I jumped in. "Whatta ya mean?"

"Weelll . . . " drawled Ed. " This tree is full of monkey's see (as I said, Ed's English always suffers when he got into one of his narratives). "An' these monkeys see . . . they're all on different limbs at different levels see, some climbin' up the tree, an' some climbin' down and some just idlin', fartin' around, not doin' nuthin' just like in any big office.

"Weelll . . . the monkeys at the top look *down* and what do they see? They see a tree full of smilin' faces shining up at 'em, all bushy-tailed an' bright-eyed. The monkeys on the bottom *look* up an' what do they see? *They see nuthin' but a bunch assholes!"*

Ed has a style of clarification of the complex in simplistic terms.

Bob, bent over his bunk, smiled. I knew that he was thinking of the lieutenant and the XO.

Another day of inching across the map of the Coral Sea; I pencil in another dot on my map. Longitude 150,50 E, latitude 20.27 S. We are nothing but a graphite mark on a tan paper background. For you landlubber's *longitude* is the angular distance on the earth's surface measured along the equator east or west of the prime meridian, which is at 0 degrees. *Latitude* is the angular distance from the equator of any point on the surface. Yeah! I know. So what? Well just look at it this way: *Longitude* is those little lines that go up and down, and *latitude* lines go right and left on the globe as you learned in Miss High Heel's 6th grade Science class at East Egghead Elementary PS #4. I knew what longitude, latitude, and land are, but what about *lubbers as* in landlubbers? I didn't know. I looked it up. A lubber is defined as an "unrefined person, a klutz, a country bumpkin." Sorry. I am guilty of calling someone a term I did not know and did not know what I was talking about. I'll use land-*dwellers* next time. Or maybe *personlubbers*. On the other hand, *landpersons* might work. Who knows what is politically correct anymore? *I understand from an impeachable source—Ed—that there is serious debate about eliminating the missionary position as it violates the Equal Rights people's idea of Equal Opportunity and Fairness.*

The map of Australia and the South-West Pacific is profusely illustrated with islands, straits, and archipelagos. The *Indy* is now near the Marion Reef. We do not see the reef. We do not even see Marion.

We see nothing but sea and sky. The railings on the *Indy* are free of bird guano; not even they come out here in the heat. They stay over on New Guinea where it is cooler, only about a hundred and five or so—practically give you a chill.

Out of bed at 0400. Kris, one of the messmen, makes me a fresh pot of coffee each morning when I totter in, still sleepy, but not able to sleep. While I wait for the coffee to bubble and giggle to its finish, I gnaw on a roll, scribble in the journal, and read the Declaration, the ship's daily newspaper.

Tips on Children and Deployment

Here are some tips that can be used to help your children adjust to the absence of their daddy on a six-month deployment.

1. Reassure the children that daddy misses them very much and doesn't like to be away from them.
2. Take pictures of their daddy doing ordinary things about the house. Put the pictures where the children can see them.
3. Time chains are really neat and they really help. You can do it for every day the parent is gone or every week. It is exciting to watch the chain shrink as it gets closer to the homecoming.
4. Send cassette back and forth to each other. This way the children can hear daddy's voice, plus it helps the spouse out to!
5. Keep the letters coming. Send the children's schoolwork, drawings, and have daddy write the children back.
6. Most of all, TALK about daddy a lot.

Reading these tips saddened me some; I read the *Tips on Children and Dependents* from the view of an ex-teacher having taught from sixth grade through college and as an anthropologist who has taught many chapters on *Sex, Marriage, and the Family*. Simplistic and redundant, the *Tips* offer little assistance. The national divorce rate in the U. S. is somewhere around 50%. In the Navy the divorce rate tops 70%. *Tips* does not address a wife and mother having to move the household by herself, fixing the broken washing machine, having the car repaired, paying bills from a low military salary, and the loneliness of a young housewife and mother left alone for probably the first time in her life, often in a strange environment—a strange town with no family backup. Drinking becomes a temporary escape, transitory affairs happen. Navy life is spurts of happiness interspersed with months of getting-by. 70%. Only three marriages out of ten make it. Not a good statistic.

Page 3 of the *Declaration*:

"Commander Jeff Cathey made his 1,000th carrier landing yesterday." Amazing.

After coffee, I took a look at the sea as slate-gray dawn lightened the sky, then headed fir the cabin to work on lecture notes. I have decided to reduce the amount of material for lectures. It is impossible to cover all the material outlined in the course summary—too many interruptions, not enough class time—so will stress the main points.

Encountered a couple of my 3rd period class students on the fantail who said a chaplain told them Darwin recanted his Theory of Evolution on his deathbed. I answered, "Yes. I have heard that allegory before. Do not put too much trust in its validity." I was nice. I did not say that I had heard that bullshit before.

I then asked them, "So what? Does that mean the theory is not viable?"

"I don't believe it's a fact," one said.

"No one says it is" I replied. "It's a theory—scientists work as if it *were* a fact, but they will assure you it is a theory. What's a theory?" I went on.

" A hypothesis?"

"No. A hypothesis is an idea to be investigated. An' from that you formulate a theory. Once you get a workable theory, you try to see if it will stand up long enough to become a fact."

"What's a theory?"

"We talked about that in class. Maybe you weren't there. Anyway, there's a definition in your book. A theory is an explanation of a phenomena or assumptions generally accepted until proven false—in other words it seems to hold true over time and in light of new theory. The Theory of Evolution states that humans evolved or changed over a period of time."

"But the bible says it ain't true."

"I don't think so. Who told you that? I asked. He didn't know.

"I think what the bible says is that mankind—Homo Sapiens—was created a certain way and the Theory of Evolution doesn't agree with that."

"But they can't prove the Theory of Evolution" one of them said.

"Well . . . The Theory has undergone modification over time since Darwin worked it out, but it still rests on essentially the same basis he emphasized and is supported by research in genetics, anatomy, embryology, geography, paleontology and biochemistry. It is used by every reputable school I know about."

"What about comin' from apes?"

"Who said that?" I asked.

"The Theory of Evolution says that."

"That's not true," I said. "No anthropologist, no scientist who understands the Theory of Evolution says that mankind came from apes. I believe the Creationists say that . . . not anthropologists. What the Theory says is that apes are man's cousin way back—not that humans came from apes, but that humans and other primates—including apes—came from a common ancestor way, way back."

I looked at the two faces before me. Like many I have talked to, old and well as young, they want to understand the scientific face of humans, they just do not want to offend or give up their religious beliefs—even when they do not practice them.

"By the way . . . " I said. The creation theory cannot be proven either."

"But the bible says its true!"

"Are you sure, or are you just getting somebody's interpretation?"

"The Chaplain said something about it."

"Who wrote the bible?"

"Umm . . . I not sure."

"Maybe you should find out," I said. "You might be surprised to find it is a bunch of stories by a lot of people."

"But . . . All that aside" I said. "A wise person regulates his life by the theories of both religion and science—but do not regard these theories as ultimate fact—do not force them on others—and you must admit, if you have read any history, that peoples, in the name of religion, have done some fairly awful things. Try to understand, not condemn."

They went off to their jobs. Do not believe I convinced them.

I wish that I had given them some for instances. I could have quoted Mark Twain:

"I was afraid of a unified church; it makes a mighty power, the mightiest can crumble, and then when it by and by gets into selfish hands, as it always bound to do, it means death to human liberty and paralysis to human thought,"

Or his from "Puddin'head Wilson:

"Faith is believing what you know ain't so."

Or Blackman's:

"The principal business of good Christians is, beyond all controversy, to fight with one another." [3]

I did not think of it at the time. I will the save the quotes and use them for part of a lecture. Should piss a lot of creationists off. As for understanding anything about the origin of mankind and origin of the universe, we are like an ant crawling around inside a jet engine: the ant doesn't know where it is and does not have enough information or brain power to figure it out. In order to keep from going insane, the ant makes up things about its origin, its home, and the world of the shiny jet engine—just as we do about the earth, the solar system, and the Universe.

Talked to Ed at breakfast later. Ed refused the draft. He was called up during the Vietnam horror. He told them "No!" Officials called him in and talked to him, he listened, nodded a couple of times, then went home. Nothing ever came of it he told me. He was investigated later while teaching on the ships. Somebody wrote a report. Nothing ever came of it either. Strange. Lucky. Fortunate.

Another Day:

A message came out over the speaker. We were stepping up involvement in Tandem Thrust because a hurricane was heading for us.

---

[3] R.D. Blackman. Lorna Doone, p. 3.

Chapter 14

"Alone, alone, all, all, alone:
Alone on a wide, wide sea."
The Rime of the Ancient Mariner

Tandem Thrust

February 26 began with isolated rainsqualls, a welcome relief after the scorching hot days of the past week that baked us dry. The high today was predicted at 82 degrees, just three degrees higher than last nights muggy 79. Three degrees difference. Not too refreshing. 82 is not hot, but the humidity drags at you. Went searching for fresh air. The *Indy* was knocking off 25-30 knots creating a nice breeze at the elevator bay, not too bad for the old lady.

Stopped off in the wardroom for coffee. Talked to friendly mess men about IRA saving accounts and annuities. Gave a morning class in physical anthropology on genetics. It went well. Genetics is a popular subject; the students are always interested in it. Today I threw out this little tidbit from one of our more arcane actors—Mr. Marlon Brando—for the class to write a pro or con half-page essay on:

"I don't think I was constructed to be monogamous. I don't think it's the nature of any man to be monogamous . . . Men are propelled by genetically ordained impulses over which they have no control to distribute their seed into as many females as possible."[1] I always get many good arguments in a regular college class when I present this chauvinistic quotation—especially form the female students. However, in this all-male class, strangely, there were few dissidents.

Walked through brightly lit empty passageways to the stern of the hanger deck into the engine testing room—all deserted—on outside to the fantail. The morning gazers were there, usually four or five people who like the daybreak as I do, enjoying the invigorating dawn air, staring, almost transfixed, at the ever-changing colors of the sea. This morning nature splashed the swells with copious amounts of deep co-

---

[1] **Marlon Brando** (b. 1924). U.S. actor. *Brando: Songs My Mother Taught Me*, Random House 1994.

balt blue, bleaching the sky a washed out pale blue that the rising sun's rays were brightening further, while scattered cotton clouds sailed through the ocean sky still sprinkled with pinpoints of starlight. A full moon was saying goodbye to the ascending sun as it cut a burnt-apricot path across the still-darkened sea. Myriads of little rainbows flashed as the sunbeams touched frowning rainsqualls in the distance. A truly beautiful morning.

Bob came to stand by me. He was dressed in a Class-A uniform even though so early in the day. Probably had been to see the Admiral or the Captain. He hit the sack last night at 2200; his telephone rang at 2300 with a problem. He muttered a solution to some workingman's question from the bowels of the ship, then to sleep until 0300 when the telephone called him again. His bunk was empty when I made a head call at 0400. With all the meetings, running the deck crews, and supervising taking on fuel from an oiler ship, Bob is sleeping in snatches. We talked quietly of his retirement in four and a half years. He was ready. Wanted to spend more time with his wife in their home in Hawaii, work on his antique motorcycles and take another cross-country trip. He and his wife once rode a large part of the U.S, on motorcycles. They want to some more of that kind of traveling.

Stopped off at the wardroom for coffee winding up in a discussion on the cloning in England of a sheep. Since I had just finished a chapter on genetics where we had discussed this very thing in some detail, my input was listened to with adequate respect. Talking about respect reminded me of the time when my wife did a paper for a college class on Samuel Johnson. She asked me to proof read for her; in doing so, I learned considerable about Mr. Johnston heretofore not knowing one iota about the man. The very next morning—the coincidence was amazing—as I walked into the college administration office to check my mail box, an every morning task, one of the secretaries said, "I bet Mr. Gunn knows!" There were several professors and clerks in the office at the time.

Sorting mail and papers on the counter I said, without looking up, "Know what?"

"Who Samuel Johnston was . . .."

Still sorting I threw out display of knowledge pomposity without looking up; "Samuel Johnston was an English author who at 46 became responsible for the *Dictionary of the English Language*. He was one of the leading literary figures in the second half of the 18th century.

He took a trip with Boswell (I had no idea who Boswell was) to the Hebrides (I had no idea where the Hebrides were) and . . . "

Pedantically I went on to describe the man's wife, when he was born and died, what his children did and how many times a day he took a shit. Still without looking up, I gathered my papers and busily walked out, basking in awe. *One smart son-of-a-bitch!*

Finishing the discourse on genetics in the wardroom, I took my leave with Chaplain Ross's "So Long Professor" ringing in my ears. *Ah! To be so appreciated!*

Arrived on the flight deck just a few minutes prior to 1000 to watch a scheduled missile launch. Four or five hundred personnel gathered on the flight deck to watch today's show. It started on time with a booming overhead crescendo as an F-14A Tomcat superfighter thundered overhead with all the finesse of a ballerina and the noise of half a dozen steam locomotives bearing down on you. Climbing into a weave pattern, the silver Defender of the Fleet spread its variable swing wings giving it more low-speed maneuverability, as it did a barrel roll, coming out at about 3,000 feet popping out a shimmering flare as it did another barrel roll tucking its bullet-shaped nose down, heading for the wave tops with astonishing speed and agility fast becoming a dot in the far distance. As the flare, a shimmering Fourth-of-July sparkler the size of a dime from this distance of about five miles, began its swinging descent, a voice echoed over the con: "MISSILE DEPARTING STARBOARD REAR!"

I turned to the left to hear a loud FIZZZ-PLOP! A slender telephone pole burst out of a rectangular rocket launcher leaving a wobbly trail of dirty-white smoke as it began its acceleration a few feet above the flight deck. At first, the missile seemed to dawdle along, loafing, clearly visible. Its nose seemed to be wagging—like a hound dog sniffing a trail—until suddenly, it steadied, increased speed tremendously, covering the five miles to the target in as little time as it took it to cross the yards of flight deck. *WOW!* It arched up in a curving slight turn to the left and was on the flare faster than a duck on a June bug, exploding in a soundless cumulus cloud with a blackened-red flower center. A few seconds later the sound of the explosion, muffled, drifted thunder-like across the sea.

Talking to a deck-handler I learned the missile was a General Dynamics Surface-to-air RIM-6 type. It is about a foot in diameter and twenty-six feet long. The size of a slender telephone pole, but a tad more costly—around a $150,000 per pole more costly. Propelled by a solid-propellant booster motor the missile could speed to Mach 2.5 (1,855 m.p.h.) and track as far as 52 miles to a height of 80,000 feet. As a pilot, I would not want one of those telephone poles flying up my tailpipe on a quiet Sunday morning. It could mess up the rest of an afternoon.

In the cabin, I looked up the definition of Mach. I knew it was the speed of sound, however, I was not sure of the speed at sea level. Webster's states that Mach 1 is the speed of sound—1,088 feet per second—at sea level with a temperature of 32 degrees Fahrenheit. 1,088 times 60 equals 65,280 feet per minute or 3,916,800 feet per hour or 742 miles per hour rounded-off . . . I think. Therefore, if the RIM-6 was knocking off Mach 2.5 it was moving out at over 1,800 miles per hour. *Zowie! Puttin' the peddle to the ol' metal-missile.* No way a plane is going to outrun one of those telephone poles.

The Defender of the Fleet—the F-14A Tomcat—can go 1,584 miles per hour at 40,000 feet. Lower down—slower speed because of denser air resistance. 1,855 to 1,584. Not good odds if you are the Radar Officer sitting in the back seat of the F-14 looking over your shoulder and glimpse one of those Robin Hood twenty-six foot long arrows whizzing toward your backside. Make you want to start kicking the back of the pilot's seat telling him that perhaps he might want to get the lead out, and *GIT OUT*! Otherwise gonna have a telephone pole sticking up the old gazoo! That could cause a serious case of acid reflux.

The *USS Independence* was leaving the Coral Sea edging into the Tasman Sea, an arm of the South Pacific Ocean, between Australia and New Zealand, named after the Dutch explorer Abel Tasman. Brisbane, some four hundreds mile above Sydney, Australia, lay a hundred miles off starboard. Our next landfall—and my last on the *Indy*—is Sydney, Australia. Approaching the territorial waters of the "Land Down Under," the crew is occupied with "Tandem Thrust".

Mentioned previously, Tandem Thrust is a series of exercises involving all four branches of the United States Armed Forces and the Australian Defense Force. Approximately 22,000 U.S. and 5,500 Australian Defense Force personnel will be involved in this three weeks exercise conducted at the Shoalwater Bay Training Area off the coast of Queensland, Australia. This operation has been designed to bring the U.S. and Australians together as a combined task force. The exercise involves combined military operations at sea, in the air, and ashore. Independence and Carrier Air Wing FIVE aircraft will be heavily involved with training over three airfields in addition to sea operations.

I thought, "This is a neat idea. The Australians and Americans training together." I was not aware at the time that our military presence was not altogether welcome by all Australians.

Following "Tandem Thrust" and my departure from the *Indy*, the *USS Independence Battle Group* will continue on to Operation "Cobra Gold", an exercise between the United States, Thai and Singaporean armed forces in the Andaman Sea and the Gulf of Thailand. Strange how things often turn out. I had never heard of Cobra Gold until after the *Indy* left Guam and the ship became preoccupied with Tandem Thrust. Months later, I would be aboard the *USS Peleliu* departing the ship at Phuket, Thailand for a month's visit. Again, some months later, I would visit Thailand at the invitation of the Dr.Promote Nakornthabto to teach a semester at First Global College in Nongkhai, northeastern Thailand, near the Thai-Laos border. One thing led to another—see my book *Sawasdee*—and I wound up living in Pattaya, Thailand, the partner/owner with Ms. Wilai Wongsa of a couple of business's in that resort town. Unbeknown to me was anything connected to Cobra Gold until I looked out my window one morning to see a huge aircraft carrier four miles out in the bay. It was my first ship, the first nuclear carrier I was on, the *USS Carl Vinson CVN-70.* It seems Cobra Gold always started in Pattaya and since that first sighting, I have seen the *USS Kitty Hawk* grace our shores twice, several U.S. destroyers, frigates, cruisers, and the *Carl Vinson* twice through three Cobra Gold operations. Each time Cobra Gold happens, some 5,000 sailors swamp the resort town of Pattaya with about $6,000,000. This makes Ms. Wongsa very happy; when Ms. Wongsa is happy, Mr. Jim Gunn is very happy. He likes Ms. Wongsa to be happy.

In general, the Cobra Gold exercises are held after Songkran—the rain festival—and on into May, thereby giving Pattaya as well as the naval town of Sattahip and U-Tapao up the coast a much needed economic boost. The armed forces of Thailand and the United States have been conducting military exercises together since the Vietnam War. Thailand has been a staunch ally of the United States ever since Abraham Lincoln was president during the dark days of the Civil War. Back then, King Mongkut (Rama IV) offered a herd of war elephants to the embattled US president, an offer he politely declined. Thailand followed America into the First World War. Not wanting to be enslaved by the Japanese in World War II, Thailand, after an agreement with the U.S., the Thai's sided with the Japanese until they began to retreat then the Thai's began to pick them off. Thailand contributed forces to the Korean War and the Vietnam War, as well as permitting the United States to build military basis in Thailand during the conflict.

I try to be in Pattaya during the Cobra Gold exercises and have done so two out of the last three years. I walk to the beach that has a curving walkway approximately two miles long, eye balling the European women in their three ounces of wispy bikini's—seldom do you see a Thai females in a swimming attire—on the beach; Thai women swim in trousers and a shirt. If you do see a Thai female in a swimming suit, she is usually young or at a tourist hotel. I walk to the pier where sailors from the battle group are launched in from the ships. Pattaya Bay is too shallow for even a destroyed to approach within a mile of the shore. There I show my military card, establish my status as a PACE instructor, and gossip with some of the sailors, giving a little advice on the blessings and pitfalls of this raucous resort town. In addition, I like to be in Thailand during the Sonkgran Festival that is held about the same time of the year as the Cobra Gold exercises.

The Sonkgran Festival—the equivalent of the our New Year—is probably the most well known of all the Thai holidays and is one of only a few that are celebrated on a fixed date (April 12-14) rather than being subject to the lunar calendar. It actually becomes a four-day national public holiday and the Thais will try to travel home to their families for the many parades and other activities. The Songkran Festival is commonly known as the Water Festival, it is actually one of the two water festivals held each year. Songkran is a time to pray for good rains for the crops, the other festival is Loi Krathong where small decorated rafts are launched in the rivers to find a new romance and to say thank you for the rains. Both these festivals are held on slightly different dates and under other names in many countries of Asia.

Songkran is much the same as many western Spring festivals with prayers for a good harvest, people in new clothes and cleaning the house in preparation for the New Year. In addition to the people, the Buddha images in the temples are also bathed and robed in new clothing to mark the coming of spring. In its original form, the festival was one of ritual bathing, with the young pouring scented water into the hands of family members and elders in a sign of respect. Over the years, the amount of water used has increased and the ceremony has moved from the homes to the streets. In many urban centers, especially Chiang Mai, Bangkok, and Pattaya, there is now an annual parade of gigantic proportions and walking the streets without getting wet is impossible—even if you are wearing a suit. Kids will shot you with a water gun and little old shopkeeper ladies will dash you with a bucket of water as you walk down the sidewalk. Once, in Nongkhai, I was in the third day of being wet and was a bit tired of the festivities—it is difficult to prepare for college classes with wet clothes and wet papers. At the end of the fourth day, looking forward to having dry clothing once again as the festivities were winding down, I bussed across Friendship Bridge from Nongkhai to Laos to renew my visa. When departing the bus, I received a bucket of water in my face while three miniature Laotian kids' shot me with water guns. Laos was just beginning their version of Songkran!

The ship's newspaper, *The Declaration*, came out with a few articles on Tandem Thrust:

Okinawa Marines ready
To go to Tandem Thrust

by
Patrick Buffett
Stripes Okinawa Bureau

WHITE BEACH-About 350 Okinawa-based Marines flaunted their flight-deck skills during training off Okinawa this week. Pilots, crew men, aircraft maintenance specialists and commanders from the 31st Marine Expeditionary Unit, Camp Hansen, conducted takeoff and landing operations in CH_46 personnel and AH-1W attack helicopters during a three-day certification exercise off Okinawa's east coast.

The amphibious assault ships USS Dubuque, USS Fort McHenry and USS Germantown took part in the training. Normally berthed at Sasebo Naval Base, Japan, the vessels came to White Beach to transport a 2,100 member Marine task force to Australia for Tandem Thrust's joint training.

That deployment began Friday

"Tandem Thrust is one of the reasons why this certification training is so important," said Capt. Mark MeClelland, the 31st's spokesman. "It gives our Marines a chance to reacquaint themselves with flight deck operations before diving in to a major exercise.

MeClelland said the unit is required to regularly complete certification training. During a mission, Marine expeditionary units are often the first to use amphibious assault vehicles or helicopters.

Pilot and crew safety is, by far, the biggest consideration in conducting helicopter certification training. MeClelland said.

"It's during these events that we learn what works and what doesn't," he said

US MARINES BRIEF
10-22 March 1997
Shoalwater Bay,
Central Queensland, Australia

Marine forces will conduct amphibious Landings, air operations and ground maneuvers. During amphibious operations units will not maneuver on beaches or dunes. Only established roads will used for off beach movement of vehicles and equipment. (Issued by the Directorate of Public Relations, Dept. of Defense, Canberra, Australia.)

***

Australian ***DEMOCRATS***
Senator Meg Lees
Spokesperson
Australian Democrat Deputy Leader and Environment

ANOTHER TANDEM THRUST BUNGLE
Now it's smoke grenades-what next?

THE loss of a carton of 50 smoke grenades dropped in the sea off Townsville during the unloading of US Navy vessel *Kilauea* was further proof of the folly of Tandem Thrust, the Australian Democrats say.

Spokesperson Senator Meg Lees said two pre-exercise fiascoes which had been revealed in recent days-the refueling with its risks to the Great Barrier Reef and dropped grenades-showed there were too many risks associated with operation Tandem Thrust.

Senator Lees was appalled by reports that the US Navy had "fully intended" to refuel the *Kiluea* on the edge of the reef, saying the region was too precious to put in jeopardy. "Is Operation Tandem Thrust an exercise in incompetence? These major mistakes should not have had a chance to happen.

Senator Lees also hit back at Defense Minister Ian McLachan, who today accused the Democrats of scaremongering.

"I challenge the Defense minister to tell the Australian people we have no right to be asking questions about the Great Barrier Reef and about military exercises on our shores. This is not scaremongering-it is demanding the best for our environment."

***

Whales on the net
Queensland, Australia
JOINT MILITARY OPERATIONS QUESTIONED

BRISBANE, AAP-Conservationist have questioned the need for the joint US-Australian military operation Tandem Thrust to be held off the north Queensland coast following the revelation today smoke grenades were lost overboard from a US supply ship. The Queensland Conservation coordinator Imogen Zethoven said, "It should not be happening in the Shoalwater Bay area, a part of the Great Barrier Reef Marine Park. Dugongs[2] are already under threat in the area and with 17,000 US troops and 5,000 Australian troops moving into the area as well as a nuclear-powered submarine, the threat to the environment is tremendous." She demanded to know why tens of millions of dollars are being spent on this operation. "Why are we doing it? Who are our enemies that we have to have this sort of operation?"

Queensland Commercial Fisherman's Organization president Ted Loveday said the grenades could be a problem if they were in an area used by trawlers. "We would hope that the navy contact the local fishermen and advise them," Mr. Loveday said that following World War II, a lot of ammunition has been dumped at sea off Queensland coast.

"Throughout the years we've trawled up bombs and things but the fishermen are usually very careful and stay right away from them," he said.

***

On our little spot far out in the Pacific—with limited access to up-to-date broadcasts or publications—we were not aware of any controversy about Tandem Thrust even though we were right in the mist of it; we did not know there *was* a controversy until the operation was over.

At this time, I was preoccupied with the fact that we were in the middle of the deepest part of the Pacific Ocean—*the very deepest hole:* the Marianas Trench area. The Marianas Trench is so deep and the water pressure so great that—as mentioned in Chapter 11—it would take a cannonball an hour to sink to the bottom. Passing beneath the keel of the *Indy* were 38,198 feet of water: cold, dark, salty seawater. Mt. Everest is sticking 29,057 feet into the bright skies of the Himalayas; I stood at its base staring upwards at its great height once, however, its apex, the summit, its top, would still be about *one and*

---

[2] **The Dugong** also known as the Halicore, is the best known of the sirenians. It has a large torpedo-like body with a short neck, a small rounded head, no external ears, and a truncated muzzle. A full-grown bull dugong will measure 9 feet in length, the smaller female measures about 7 or 8 feet. The animal's skin is hairless and blue-gray in color. Its eyes are small and sunken in the head. The upper lip is cleft in the middle and supports stiff bristles. The nostrils are valve-like, opening when the dugong takes in fresh air and closing when it submerges. The forelimbs are modified paddles and the broad, flat tail is crescent-shaped like the flukes of a whale. The lower jaw is bent downward and supports a pair of tusklike incisor teeth of the upper jaw. These tusklike teeth, which grow continuously throughout the animal's life, have sharp cutting edges.

three-quarters miles below the surface of the waters we are now sailing upon.

Seven and a quarter miles down there are valleys, plains, mountains, and mud; in addition, some territories we do not even know about! Imagine flying at the usual 35,000 feet in a modern commercial 747 and looking down; that's what we were doing, *looking down that far from sea level!* As Superboy says, "HO-LY MO-LY!" Scattered in those deep, dark valleys, on those sodden plains, along the slopes of subterraneous mountains, sunken into cold, slimy mud are the remains of modern man; ships, planes, trucks, food, men, women. In fact, everything that is needed for numerous villages, towns or, perhaps, cities is down there; the litter of war; the casualties of the Battle for the Pacific during World War II, victims of the Red Horseman.[3]

My interest in the ocean abyss was interrupted the next day when the carrier started smashing through ten-foot waves. Preparing to hit the sack: laying out clothes, putting shoes on top of my locker out of the way, making sure my glasses were within reach by the shoes, finding a paper back not yet read, I noticed that it was a lot less hot. The cooler air accompanying the ocean rollers was welcome though we were suspicious of what waves might be the forerunner of—what was coming. Bob and Ed clambered in just as I was scaling up to my perch three bunks elevated amid a tangle of pipes and electrical wiring. Checked for my nautical spider. Yep! He was still there, all buttoned up, waiting for the storm. Eerie up there sometimes with only an arachnid as a bunkmate—but, . . . come to think of it—I've had spookier bedmates—a redhead named Arlene from Los Angeles who drove a Porsche Spyder and was into spanking and Mazola Oil comes to mind. Our relationship was like a fairy tale—Grimm. A guy told me once that he wanted to wrestle an alligator—I told him to go to bed with Arlene.

Ed, as usual, was talking as he and Bob came in:

"So, she ask' me, she says, *'Ed Darrlliiinng*. Why don't you ever call out my name when we are making love?'" An' I tol' her. I said, "Well Mabel Darling. Ah didn' wan'to wake you!"

---

[3] **Four Horsemen of the Apocalypse**. Allegorical figures in Revelations in the Bible. One interpretation of the rider on the rider on the white horse is that he represents Jesus. The rider on the red horse is war; on the black horse, famine; and on the pale horse, death.

Laughing, Bob looked up at me and said, "You might want to lash in up there Jimbo."

I cocked my head, raising my eyebrows.

"We're headed for a hurricane."

For the next two weeks the *USS Independence* and most of her battle group skirted cyclone[4] JUSTIN.

The Australians call them cyclones; we call them hurricanes[5], but it did not matter what Justin was called; he was on time to the job and he did his work with unsurpassed zeal. Justin roamed around wreaking havoc over the whole of the South Pacific. To miss the greater part of the hazard, our captain altered course. Lives were lost on land and at sea south of Papua New Guinea as JUSTIN swept across *Indy's* two days old wake. Poseidon smiled on us, just allowing the edge of his maelstrom to play with our toy vessel tossing it around a bit. Severe property and tree damage occurred over Papua New Guinea and about 25 lives were lost with several people swept away. We took the God of the Sea's warning, sidestepped to the south, cranked up to thirty-five knots and avoided the worst of the tropical tempest.

The *Indy*, hardly rocking in the 10 and 12 foot whitecaps, used helicopters to bring on board fifteen crewmen from Australian ships closed to the vortex of the turmoil, personnel injured in the storm, one with a broken shoulder. On the *Indy* Bob, Ed, and I did not even have to tie ourselves in our bunks. I checked out the spider; he was okay, not even wearing a life jacket.

A message received by the ship's radio and printed in the daily news told of at least six of twenty-two crewmembers died in a collision between two Panamanian registered vessels at the edge of the storm. The message said the *M/V Las Sierras* and *M/V Halo Cygnus* were apparently on their way to Australia when they collided, impacting bow

---

[4] **Cyclone.** An atmospheric system characterized by the rapid, inward circulation of air masses about a low-pressure center, usually accompanied by stormy, often destructive, weather. Cyclones circulate counterclockwise in the Northern Hemisphere and clockwise in the Southern Hemisphere.

[5] **Hurricane.** A severe tropical cyclone originating in the equatorial regions of the Atlantic Ocean or Caribbean Sea, traveling north, northwest, or northeast from its point of origin, and usually involving heavy rains.

on bow. Four perished as a result of the initial impact and two died trying to control the flooding.

Bob came in as I was correcting essays; he was again in a hurry. Bob was only busy during departure, underway, and when we made port—which is—all the time. This time it was a serious emergency. The *USS New Orleans LPH-11*—part of our battle group—is an Iwo Jima Class Assault carrier, more commonly known as a helicopter carrier. The *New Orleans* was in trouble. Built in 1968, she is the third Navy ship to bear the name. A third shorter than the big carriers such as the *Independence,* the *New Orleans* looks stubby in comparison. Its main job, like the *USS Peleliu* on which I later served, is to carry helicopters assisting Marines in Amphibious landings.

Was there a relationship between the damage sustained during the cyclone and the decommissioning of the ship? I never found out. However, later that year, in December of 1997, the *USS New Orleans* was laid in reserve at Suisun Bay pending preservation at Long Beach. Later, I read the ship was scheduled for "disposal" the fall of 1998.

The *USS New Orleans* enjoyed some unique media highlight during its career. In 1971, the popular Mike Douglas TV Show was once filmed onboard. In addition she was in all the space program recoveries of capsules and several portions of the Oscar winning movie *"Apollo 13"* were shot onboard. The New Orleans Hollywood career ended in May 1997, after the crew participated in the filming of the TV movie tentatively titled *"A Thousand Men and a Baby."* The movie is based on a true story about a U.S. Navy ship that recovered and cared for an infant during the Korean War. (The Navy likes movie publicity.)

Tandem Thrust and Hurricane Justin's turbulent affair with the U.S. Navy was over. There was some damage, some deaths from the storm. At least thirty died from hurricane JUSTIN, thirty that we heard about. "We are as near to heaven by sea as by land," said Sir Humphrey Gilbert during a storm on his last, fatal voyage back from Newfoundland.[6] Divorced from us, Tandem Thrust and JUSTIN departed their separate ways; we once again, after cleaning up, settled into ho-humness. Each day came and departed much as the day before. Af-

---

[6] Sir Humphrey Gilbert. 1573?-1583, English soldier, navigator, explorer. Quoted in: Richard Halduyt, The Principal Navigations, voyages, Traffics and Discoveries of the English Nation. Vol.3 (1600)

ter the violent storm, the tropic heat came back with renewed vengeance while its brother, humidity, clothed us with lethargy. We talked of the hurricane, the Aussie sailor's daily rum or beer rations; we could not remember what is was they got to drink—American ships are dry of alcoholic beverages—and not a bad idea as far as I am concerned. When people are handling volatile jet fuel, hazardous ammunition, not to mention nuclear stuff, and flying around in airplanes, I do not want them to be nursing a hangover, needing an Alka-Seltzer milkshake, when pushing around a cart with a Sidewinder on it while their stomach is doing a nautical version of the Delirium Tremens Tango.

We slept. We snoozed surrounded by perpetual noise. Chow and classes was my prominent part of the day. Bob and the sailors make up for sleep lost the previous week. The Navy understands. When you have done your work, lying around on the bunk is okay. Sleep is good. Refreshes the body, fights depression. In the Marines, you want to sleep? No problem! Lie down on the floor, deck, grass, rocks—anywhere—except the bunk! If god had wanted Marines to sleep on beds, he would not have made the ground.

One afternoon the spider was gone! I remade my bunk—well! . . . it needed it anyway—but there was no sign of the little critter. I searched the overhead pipes doing a little dusting in the process. No Itsy-Bitsy spider. I know that a pretty little collection of weaknesses and a terror of spiders are an indispensable stock-in-trade of all men—I read that somewhere. And that nine out of ten men are superstitious, nineteen out of twenty believe in bad luck of black cats, and ninety-eight out of a hundred are afraid of spiders. I am not afraid of spiders, I just didn't want to accidentally sit on him with his little fangs sticking' in my butt. The next morning HE WAS BACK! Sitting in the middle of the web, quiet and motionless. Where'd he go? I don't KNOW. Took a vacation. *Visited his girlfriend?*

We trooped to watch the sun come up every morning—golden and rose saffron and pink, the morning sun smoked away the misty night and the fantail was crowded at night when the sun went to bed. Tropical sunrises and sunsets are to be seen to be believed—colorful, spectacular—beats television all to hell. Small things gain importance on the ship. Mail, when it arrived, is one; popcorn is a festive occasion in the wardroom at the start of the Saturday movie. The predictable days were even more conspicuous in that despite the boredom, everyone stayed even-tempered—manners exaggerated. It was "Good

Day!" and "Hello Shipmate!" and "May I join you?" When you spoke, people listened attentively. People were just damn polite! The Captain spoke over the speaker each night with kudos to individuals, calling them by name, departments were praised for doing their jobs well, such as keeping a head or passageway especially clean, and mechanics, store-keepers, students taking classes, and even the old professor received vocal commendations. Ordinary acts—positive ordinary acts—were magnified out of proportion; we were praised, as a mother would exalt a five year-old for tying shoes. Kudos were thrown to everyone and—it worked! If the Captain had pasted a gold star on my forehead, I would have worn it proudly. (Bob and I attempted to paste one on Ed, but he awoke before we could get it all spitted up.) It was silly stuff, but—it worked.

We left JUSTIN behind. Or, maybe Justine left us. We really did not know. News is hard to come by out in the ocean. The big ocean. The BIG Pacific Ocean.

The Pacific Ocean is the world's largest ocean. It occupies about 70,000,000 square miles covering a third of the earth's surface between the west coasts of North and South America and the east coasts of Australia and Asia. It has a maximum length of 9,000 miles, a maximum width of 11,000 miles, and a maximum depth of about 7 miles. A series of volcanoes, the so-called Ring of Fire, rims the mighty ocean. Map makers speak of the Pacific Ocean, the Atlantic, the Indian. In reality, there are not several oceans on he earth separated by landmasses. If one looks at the earth from space one sees that there is only one great salt-water ocean with landmasses floating about. Life came from the Great Ocean; it determines our weather and has forged our history. This one Great Ocean covers more than 140,000,000 square miles, about three-fourths of the surface of the planet, an ocean twice the surface area of the planet Mars and nine times the surface area of the moon. 70% of the Earth's surface is water; 24% is desert, ice, and mountains. 6% is left for humans to live, squabble about, and to die on.

"Wide sea, that one continuous murmur breeds
Along the pebbled shore of memory!"
John Keets

Frigate

It is not always hot in the tropics.

Chapter 15

"The worst enemy of every sailor
Was not his opponent,
But inactivity and boredom."
Military saying

I asked Bob and Ed:

"Hey guys. What if I found this beautiful blonde gal built like a brick shithouse . . ."

Ed, as usual was correcting a seemingly endless pile of scrawling, ink-splattered English papers; Bob, flat on his back in his bunk, was reading a shiny magazine with curvaceous blonde, wearing three ounces of bikini, astride a big red and black Harley motorcycle on the cover—the same one he has been perusing for a month. Mail delivery of motorcycle magazines is slow in the south pacific.

Always a theoretical thinker, I wanted to get the unbiased, sophisticated male view of important, modern-day problems between the sexes.

" . . . this beautiful blonde gal built like a brick shithouse . . . wearin' a filmy gauze wisp of silk over her luscious smooth-skinned body, an' you could see two rosy nipples proudly standing out on two heavenly breasts an' . . ." I paused, waiting.

Ed still held his red pen, poised over squiggles, his brow wrinkled with imagination. Bob was looking at his magazine, but he wasn't reading.

I waited a bit longer . . .

"Well?" said Ed.

"Come on dummy! You rotten Gunn. You always doin' this. Now I can't concentrate. What's the rest of it?" said Bob.

"Oh! I didn't want to interrupt your reading, Chief Bo'sun. But since you ask . . . Well . . . supposin' I took this luscious blonde, you know, she's about five seven, blue eyes, little dimples in her cute little knees, sweet luscious red-lipped smile . . . supposin' I took this sweet thing, gave her a bubble bath, wiped down that tawny skin, then . . ." my mind stared into space, dreaming.

"Come on, Come on!"

" . . . an' I drenched her in some expensive perfume, rubbed her down with a touch of that good-smellin' baby powder . . .well! Here's my question, an' I'm quoting from this woman's magazine . . . these women editors seem a little confused; they don't know what a man thinks . . ."

"He's thinkin' 'bout sex," said Bob.

"Yep!" echoed Ed. "Women think 'How they go about sex; men jist think 'When!'"

"Here's the question the magazine asks: 'Would either of you go down on her?'"

"Huh!" Ed said, turning back to his papers. "Forget the bath and perfume 'cause I don't want to waste no time. Just get her ass in here!"

Bob: "Hell! I don't care she's been working out in the gym an' she ain't takin' a bath inna week. Just tell her to come in and drop her skivvies," he said, going back to his reading.

These intimate relation's questions between men and women seem to be a perplexing concern to women magazine writers. Ed and Bob have the unique, innate ability to cut right to the heart of the problem.

Email is wonderful.[1] Today I received one from my son.

"Hello 'Semper Fi' dad. How's everything going" No word yet on the flight plans to Australia. Everything is going well here. Applied for a new job at the hospital. It's working with telemedicine. Evaluating patient medical information over distance through the use of digital imaging/audio. It sounds interesting. A colleague of mine is heading-up the project and wanted me to apply. Send me an email if you get a chance. The last one I sent was not confirmed, so I don't know if you received it. The mail system aboard ship may not have this feature. Take care..."

He used to ride on my shoulders; now he is the head of a division at University California Medial Center in Sacramento. What happened to the time?

---

[1] One Navy publication stated that, on the average, each sailor at sea sends one email per day.

Notice received today from Chief of Naval Operations to the ship's crew:

As of Today:

1. More than half of the Navy is deployed.
2. 29% of ships are deployed (102).
3. Approximately 50,000 sailors and marines are forward deployed.

Forward Presence Essential
To American Interests
By
Admiral jay L. Johnson
Chief of Naval Operations, and
General Charles C. Krulak,
Commandant of the Marine Corps

WASHINGTON—Keys are turning in front doors of thousands of American business offices "forward deployed" all over the world. American companies invest in overseas presence because being there is clearly the best way to do business.

Also this morning, United States Navy amphibious assault ships carrying 4,400 combat-ready American Marines are forward deployed in the waters of the Mediterranean Sea and the Persian Gulf. And at sea in the Mediterranean and in the Persian Gulf are aircraft battle groups with 16,000 Sailors and 2 air wings of combat ready aircraft. And finally, in the Far East, the United States has permanently deployed a third aircraft carrier battle group and a third amphibious ready group. The vigilant "forward presence" of these forces is vital, but not always as visible to Americans as it is to the rest of the world. Their routine daily headlines don't always make the headlines, but they are vitally important to world peace and stability.

Some argue that the forward presence these forces represent is no longer necessary. They argue that forces reacting from the United States are enough to maintain stability. They further maintain that "brush fires" or outbreaks of regional instability are insignificant or incidental at best. And they argue that America can no longer afford the forward presence of these forces on what amounts to a near continuous basis.

We would argue just the opposite. Forward deployed U.S. forces, primarily naval expeditionary forces—the Navy-Marine Corps team—are vital to regional stability and to keeping these crises from escalating into full-scale wars. To those who argue that the United States can't afford to have this degree of vigilance anymore, we say: The United States can't afford not to.

These brush fires, whether the result of long-standing ethnic tensions or resurgent nationalism in the wake of the Cold War will only continue. The Cold War was anomaly.

Never again will we live in a bipolar world whose nuclear shadow suppressed nationalism and ethnic tensions. We have in some respects reverted back to the world our ancestors knew: a world in disorder. Somalia, Bosia, Liberia, Haiti, Rwanda, Iraq, and the Taiwan Straits are merely examples of the types of continuing crises we now face. Some might call this period an age of chaos.

The United States and the world cannot afford to allow any crises to escalate into threats to the United States and the world's vital interests. And while the skies are not dark with smoke from these brush fires, today's world demands a new approach. The concept of choice must be selective and committed engagement, unencumbered global operations, and prompt crises resolution. There is no better way to maintain and enforce these concepts than with the forward presence of the U.S. Navy-Marine Corps team.

There are four basic tenets to international security in today's world: prevention, deterrence, crisis resolution, and war termination. The underlying assumption of these tenets is that the U.S. and its allies should not be forced into winning a war in an overwhelming (and expensive) fashion. Instead, it is much better—and cheaper—to resolve a crisis before it burns out of control.

PREVENT: The key to prevention is continuous presence in a region. This lets our friends know we have an interest and lets potential foes know that we're there to check any move. Although hard to measure, the psychological impact of naval expeditionary forces is undeniable. This regional presence underwrites political and economic stability.

This is forward presence.

Deter: Presence does not prevent every crisis. Some rogues are going to be tempted to strike no matter what the odds, and will require active measures to be deterred. Naval expeditionary forces can quickly take on the role of the very visible fist. Friends and potential enemies recognize naval expeditionary forces as capable of defending or destroying. This visible fist forms the bedrock of regional deterrence. For example, the mere presence of naval expeditionary forces deterred Chinese attempts to derail the democratic process in Taiwan and countered Iraq saber-rattling toward Jordan. It's hard to quantify the cost savings of deterring a crisis before it requires our intervention. But the savings are real—in dollars, and often in blood and human misery.

This is forward presence.

Resolve: If a crisis can be neither prevented nor deterred, then prompt and decisive crisis resolution in imperative before the crisis threatens vital interests. U.S. naval expeditionary forces simultaneously and unilaterally deployed to Liberia and to the Central African Republic to protect U.S. and International citizens. They also launched measured retaliatory Tomahawk strikes to constrain unacceptable Iraqi behavior and conducted naval air and Tomahawk strikes which brought the warring parties in Bosnia to the negotiating table.

This is forward presence.

Terminate: Each of the above tenets is worthy of the United States paying an annual peace insurance premium. Otherwise, we and our allies risk paying the emotional, physical, and financial costs of a full-blown conflagration that began as just another brush fire. If there is a war, naval expeditionary forces will be first to fight. They are inherently capable of enabling the follow-on forces from the United States for as long as it takes.

This is forward presence.

The Iraqis, Central Africas, Somalias and Bosnias inevitably destabilize and erode world order and respect for the rule of law. A failure to respond to them encourages future—more serious—crisis.

The United States must foster stability around the world, today and tomorrow. The peace insurance premium is a small price and is the cost of leadership. Who else is capable of this type of forward presence on a global basis? For the United States, maintaining a steady commitment to stability will be a challenge. But maintain it we must, or the price, literally and figuratively, will be much greater down the road.

America's Navy-Marine corps team is underway, ready and on-scene at trouble spots around the world. Forward presence makes it—and will keep it—the right force, tailor-made for those uncertain and sometimes fiery times.

*****

Notes at sea.

I ate dinner with five officers not previously met. They were attentive to me upon finding out I knew a bit about real estate and construction and that I had been in the Korean War. I now have a fresh role in life: a wise senior citizen dispensing knowledge and advice.

I am amazed at what is thrown over the fantail. This morning I saw hundreds of heads of blackened, spoiled lettuce go into the briny. That is not so disturbing—except for cost—but hundreds of used aluminum soda cans and dozens of ketchup bottle with lids on bothered me. Glass will last down there for a thousand years as will plastic! Also broken chairs, one typewriter, metal parts, and tons of paper and cardboard went over the side . . . actually, over the stern.

Today I wrote the shortest poem about Crabs.

Ed was scratching his butt and Bob said, "What . . .You got cooties?"

"Prob'ly has a lousy louse!" I said.

"What's the difference between a louse and a lice?" Bob asked.

"I think lice is plural for louse." I told him. "Is that right Ed?"

"I think so. An' a nit is a little-bitty-baby-lousy lice.

"Yeah!" I said. "An' those little-bitty bites on your ass are prob'ly a pedicular bite."

"You mean 'particular?'"

"No. 'ped-ic-u-lar'"

"Oh! Shit! Here we go again. The Pree-fess-whore" Said Bob. "What's ped-i-dy-k-laer?"

"It s a bite by licesses."

"You guys is as full of it as a Christmas turkey!"

"Gee Bob!" Ed said wrinkling his brow. I don't eat *that*. We stuff our turkey with bread crumbs."

"What do you stuff your turkey with Bob?" I asked.

"I dunno. The wife does it."

"'Probably stuff it with pineapple there in Hawa-ya," said Ed. "Or eat pork."

"We used to use bread crumbs, tangerines and sometimes peas," I said.

"Peas?"

"Yeah. Peas. You wanna hear my Thanksgiving prayer?" I looked at Ed, then Bob.

"No!" Said Ed.

"Not particularly," said Bob, going back to his paperwork.

"Well . . . It goes like this. I quoted:

"Yes ma'am, no ma'am,
Thank you ma'am, please.
Open up the turkey's butt
And fork out the peas."

Bob looked at me, squinting his eyes, puzzlement on his face. "Just how long *did* you live up there in that lumber camp, Gunn? Did you have long winters where you just sat around whittling a piece of wood? Did the family sit around an' drool a lot?"

"I think his mother married her cousin," said Ed.

"Huh" I said. "Don't pick on me. Put you two guys brains together, you'd end up with half-wit."

"Listen Gunn." went on Bob. "Did you have a grandmother, or where you just cloned?"

"I'll have you know my grandmother was in a class of her own. As a matter of fact, that how she was in school, 'in a class of her *own*.' She was too dangerous to let any other kids near. But . . . she could really run fast!"

Hell! I doen doubt that!" said Ed. "She probably had four legs!"

"I gotta a lot of good stuff like that!

"Like what?"

"Like turkeys . . . cows . . . lice . . . songs . . . poems."

"Well' . . .write a song about it!"

"How's-about a poem about lice?" I asked.

They agreed I could write a poem about the sucking louse that generally infests the pubic region causing itching—crabs. "Just don't make it too long or boring," was the only restraint.

I wrote:

The Louse
by
James Gunn

"Adam had 'em."
The End

They said that it was a tad long, but otherwise agreed it was a good poem.

Everyone is talking about going ashore in Australia; they talk about women, beer, and Sydney. The enlistment posters say "Join the

Navy and see the World." Sailors do get to go a lot of places, however, I think what most sailors see is a port, a few bars, and a poorly represented part of the population. Many of the younger sailors are dejected and lonely, especially those with wives and young children and those with girl friends. For the others, there is little chance of them meeting quality females in the areas they generally visit when ashore.

Many of the younger, inexperienced sailors work at unrewarding jobs in sometimes very dangerous situations. Standing a lonely night watch in wretched weather thinking about Mary Jane Hot pants back home can wreck a good day—and there have not been a lot of good days lately. Sailors bunk areas are crowded—there are few places to be alone—and for the last two weeks, hot! As I have repeated the *USS Independence* is not nuclear which means it has limited power to run air conditioners, desalinate seawater, and produce electricity. The ship is old; it flies the flag "*Don't Tread On Me!*" a pennant flown only by the oldest active naval ship. The *Indy* is rusty, noisy, and difficult to keep clean. Sailors constantly chip rust and repaint. I noticed metal fasteners holding lifeboat pods broken and the steel grating on some of the catwalks rusted away—not enough to be dangerous, but unsightly. The ship is scheduled to be decommissioned the coming year. Sadly, it is time.

Today we sailed inside the Great Barrier Reef. Labeled one of the Seven Natural Wonders of the World, the Great Barrier Reef is the largest known deposit of coral in the world. Around 1,250 miles long and is separated from the mainland by a shallow lagoon up to a 100 miles wide affording excellent protection to disturbances in the Coral Sea. Actually the reef is composed of hundreds of individual reefs and has many islets, coral gardens, and spectacular marine life not the least being the Great White shark.

Another morning.

I awoke at 0200, could not get back to sleep on the narrow, thin-padded mattress. The *Indy* was commissioned January 10, 1959, so the accommodation's are Spartan compared to the new guys, the *Vinson* and the *Lincoln*. The *Indy* is due to be decommissioned in 1998 or go into inactive reserve in the Naval Inactive Ship Maintenance Facility (NISMF), at Bremerton, Washington. (I received an invitation to her decommissioning.) There was another *Independence CV-22* commissioned in 1943. It was sunk as a target in 1951. Ignoble way to end. When I am decommissioned, I hope that it is not in that manner.

Toddled off to the wardroom for coffee and paper work on my classes. The anthropology classes are going well—students are interested in the subject, more so than my regular stateside 18 to 20 year-olds. Not liking too much government regimentation and nosing into citizen's affairs, I tentatively venture to say it would not be a terribly bad idea for students out of high school to spend a couple of years in the service to make the break under another pseudo-parent—to get away from Mom and Daddy—to grow up, acquire self-discipline, then go to college.

I left the wardroom at 0400, showered and went back to sleep until 0530.

Up again, and Bob and I breakfasted together. Bob ate SOS[2]–forgoing his usual yogurt mess—congratulating the messmen with a "Good job, fellows! Outstanding!" Nothing is "good" in navy jargon when evaluating; it is always "Outstanding!"

I shipped unpurchased textbooks back to San Diego. Mail is delivered and picked up once a week by helicopter or at least it is attempted when near land; out in deep ocean people make do with email. We are closing on Australia and the end of my sojourn with the *Indy*. Ed and I were at chow this day when an officer asked me what a wild group of gorillas was called. "You know!" he said. "Like a 'bunch of geese is called a gaggle.'"

I told him it would be called a "band."

Ed then wanted to know "If a bunch of gorillas is a "*band*," then are four gorillas a "Quartet?" (Ed has been at sea too long!)

Today we had a visit by the Chief of Naval Operations, Admiral Jay L. Johnson. A tall, spare, well-set-up man. I took photographs of his coming aboard. Officers of the *Independence* dressed in impeccable Whites formed a welcoming line across the flight deck. Impressive. I did not have a close-up view of him today, but a year or so later I was on the *USS John Young* standing near the brow when we docked in Fremantle, the port for Perth, Australia. I was a yard or so away as he came aboard wearing summer class A uniform with short sleeves and I saw that his arms seemed severely scarred as if from fire. Knowing he

---

2 Shit-on-a-shingle.

is a pilot, I wondered what the source of the wounds. He gave a short talk today:

"This Navy, our Navy and the Marine Corps; the strength that we give our country, and the strength that we give to the world is anchored in something we call forward presence, That's why we are here!"

Today, At 0700, the Captain announced that we would be docking in Sydney one day early; cheers resounded down the passageway. 658 miles to Australia. A few days previous, I was told we were 400 miles from Australia but that was up near Brisbane. Sydney is a bit further south.

Wrote a letter to the Captain:

Sir:

I wish to express my appreciation of the professionalism of The Educational Service Officer, Lieutenant Ray Copuz and PN3 Pierson for the help they gave me in performing my duties as a PACE instructor aboard the *USS Independence*.

Supplies, books, and other materials were made readily available and office personnel were helpful throughout the course. It was a pleasure to work with such dedicated people.

Cordially,

J.A. Gunn
Anthropology instructor

*****

Wrote a letter to Adar Bray—a fellow teacher for many years, now an author and big game hunter.

"Dear Ol' Bawanna Adar,

*♭"Once a jolly swagman
Sat beside the Bilabong,
Under the shade of
A Kullba tree . . ."♭*

A'e mate! . . .C'me on 'nd 'ave a bit o' toff now want ye?" I have been practicing my Australian lingo.

A few days and I will be off this sauna bath and on the beach in Sydney. The carrier is part of a task force participating with Australian armed forces in an exercise called "Tandem Thrust"—53 ships and 28,000 Marines and sailors. Things began a bit out of wrack when we ran into a different kind of enemy called Justine—a typhoon slightly south of New Guinea. For a week we skirted the edge of the storm at Lat. 15, Long. 157 in the Coral Sea. The carrier rides the swells fairly well, but a Marine Helicopter Attack Carrier took a roll and 14 Marines were transferred from it. They also lost a couple of helicopters over the side.

For the last few weeks, I have changed clothes often because of the heat and humidity although we have been in a storm. Not a lot of rain, but a lot of tossing around. The Typhoon just sits there, not moving as a normal storm is supposed to—probably did not get the word—like those students we used to have. Since we are living in a steel box, the cold water taps runneth with hot water, so all showers are hot showers on a hot ship on a hot day. It is hot.

Regarding your hunting of cats in Botswana: I suggest that you might want to make it sporting, forget the reloading of the 390's; just do as the Masaii; go for the "Big Cats" with a slender spear—I'll be happy to be your backup; way back in the Land Rover with the windows up and the doors locked.

Your letter took 21 days to get here and we land in Australia in a few days so if you write again I probably will not receive it until I return as I will be driving in the "Outback." I will also try to see New Zealand and will drop you a line from there.

We stooped over in Guam for four days. I took a hotel, rented a car, and took a drive around the island—stopped off at a seaside village where there was a little carnival day going on, enjoyed it—so returned the following day. Downtown Guam is nothing as I had expected; it is a little Las Vegas without the gambling; a Planet Hollywood, big Hawaii type hotels, massage parlors, and strip joints—the joints and fast-food places catering to the military, the rest of the overpriced everything to the Japanese tourist. I visited the war memorials thinking the Japanese lost Guam by force during WW II, now they are taking it back by the dollar. Prices are at least 50% more than in the U.S.

Will send you a card later.

As the Captain says every night over the speaker:

"See you on deck!"

Lord Jim"

*****

Up this morning at 0500. I breakfasted on French toast, coffee, pineapple juice, and a bagel. Bob had his usual papaya, yogurt, toast, and coffee—god-awful mess—then left to prepare for a supply lift by helicopter and I for my last week of classes. Beautiful soft-sunny day viewed from the elevator bay—five ships visible at one time. Classroom so noisy from jets taking off had to cancel, and reschedule—I think that one could become ill from the noise. Noticed my calves are bulging from climbing so many stairwells daily.

Later in early evening, I climbed up to the flight deck to watch a fuel transfer, the first transfer done at night while I have been aboard. No ships were in sight when I arrived on the catwalk above the flight deck. A misty rain cooled the early evening air, a welcome comfort from the hot and humidedness of the past weeks. It was the 20th of March—the first day of spring at home, but here, in the Coral Sea, the first day of fall. This morning the sun arose at 0523 (5:23), and set at 1723 (5:23).

Awaiting the oil transfer, a few sailors of the fuel detail stood on the flight deck in a carpet of waist-high fog left over from the little shower we ran through earlier in the day. We have seen other squalls dotting the sea, bright sunshine surrounding them as they sail darkly across the ocean, rain slanting down from their black bellies. I have never seen the phenomenon on land; the rainsqualls looked like a bunch of spread-out jellyfish trailing tentacles, chasing one another across the sky, their bodies black with moisture, their tentacles slanting rain.

Solitary figures moved about the flight deck, making no sound as they checked lashing on the planes, each person's job identifiable by the low powered, colored flashlight carried in hand or attached to a

Velcro strap on the vest. I walked softly among the slender fighter jets in perfect lines, perched forward on their landing gear; tense gray birds of prey laden with terrible power, ready to screech and pounce. The F-14s multiple tail fins stuck up in the shadowy darkness and mist like ashen tombstones in a foggy graveyard. With hands stuffed into my windbreaker I looked at the silent jets, at the under-carriage, the intakes, the exhausts, and climbing up one repair ladder, I looked into the confined cockpits with is myriad gauges, dials, switches, and handles. Up close, the jets are not so sleek; there are metal joints riveted, dark streaks of burned oil along the intakes and flaking paint. I am an alien here; as a civilian non-pilot, I do not belong among these intricate war machines. I do not have the ability to fly one of these deadly performers, now just inert bundles of metal, plastic, and rubber, but when fired up, a frightful killing machine.

Coming down the repair ladder, a light flickered at the corner of my right eye. Far on the horizon, to the right rear of the *Indy,* something out of the ordinary blinked. Something moved. I looked directly at it, nothing there. Spooky. Scanning the dark sea intently, I caught a dim red glow out of the corner of my eye. I repeated the action. If I looked directly at it, I could not see it. The rods in my eyes—the ones that saw black and white were working in the dim light, the cones for color were not—then as my eyes adjusted, two faint whites dots were visible. Then they disappeared again. I could only see them with my rods out of the corner of my sight; when I stared directly at them, they were not there. Then the lights steadied and, I sensed them; two bodyguards—destroyers—and the supply ship were coming up on us astern: vague phantasmal outlines, ominously alien here in the cold dark as I stood alone, the antagonistic wind clutching at my clothing. A wee bit spooky. One of the white lights moved on an oblique course, a mile out to the right flank, while the other remained dogging our wake, an iffy safety net in case someone fell overboard. The red light—the middle one—came up fast on our stern.

The red light grew brighter materializing into the supply ship. No name on the bow. A large board on the superstructure reads *USNS Guadelupe*. The *Guadelupe* came barreling in, white foam high at her bow, edging closer along side, paralleling us no more than 60 yards away. A millrace of white, turbulent rushing sea developed, compressed between the two racing hulls—not a place one would ever want to fall into. Each sailor must wear a life jacket to which is attached a light that will automatically start flashing upon contact with water. A life-buoy watch is stationed well aft of the engaged side of the ship with a hand-held walkie-talkie and, in addition to the lifeguard ship in our wake; a rescue helicopter is whopping up overhead.

The *Guadeloupe* suddenly turned on all her multicolored deck lights; a magic trick that lit up the darkness with a flourish—a Christmas tree rushing through the black night. *Boy!* She must be a sight from the other ships. Sent a tingle up my spine. She came out of pitch darkness; then lit up like a space ship form *Close Encounters of the Third Kind*. Fantastic!

Bob came on deck in his "space suit." He had on a bulky white outfit—much like a bundled up six-year old would wear in the snow—arms sticking out from his side like an over-developed body builder and atop his safety helmet a blinking light was attached. The flashing safety light served two purposes: it allowed the personnel on the *Guadelupe* to see him as director of operations and was a locator if he fell overboard. The body suit was to keep him afloat and to insulate against the cold. He looked comical, but no one laughed; it was a night of danger; it was raining now, the sea was choppier, the wind gusting—today it had been summer; now it was winter. I gathered the hood of my windbreaker over my head, trying to keep the rain off my glasses as gusts of wind pushed me about. Holding tightly to railings, I made way to a better view of the complicated procedure going on below. (Here I was again being stupid: no one is supposed to be alone at night unless on watch—but they couldn't do anything to me so . . . anyway, the going-on's were too engrossing to miss!)

The USNS Guadeloupe (T-A) 200) was to become a familiar welcome sight to us and I was to see her again from another vessel, the *USS John Young* in another ocean, at another time. The *Guadelupe* is an "Underway Replenishment Oiler" Thirteen ships similar to the Guadeloupe are operated by MSC[3] providing underway supplies of fuel to non-nuclear ships and jet fuel for aircraft assigned to carriers. The supply ships actually look like small refineries with varied-colored pipes intricately festooned about the deck and telescoping towers handling several six-inch fuel lines. The T-AOs are good-sized: 678 feet long, about two-thirds the length of the carrier. They carry approximately 180,000 barrels of fuel oil or jet fuel and have a speed of around 20 knots.

---

[3] Military Sealift Command.

During World War II, when a ship ran low on fuel, supplies, or ammunition, it had to return to port, or the fleet had to lie to while it was replenished by small boats; a fleet lying to for replenishment was vulnerable to attack. Underway Replenishment (UNREP) refers to any method of transferring fuel, munitions, supplies, and personnel from one ship to another at sea. With the modern-day methods of UNREP, an entire fleet can be resupplied, rearmed, and refueled within hours, while it is moving, proceeding on its mission.

Bob motioned the two-man line-throwing crew forward from the shadows to a circle of brightly-lit deck area. The men wore red helmets and highly visible red jackets over dungarees for identification. A loose coil of light rope was handy at their feet in a bucket. When the *Guadelupe* inched into the proper position, both ships loud speakers blasted forth at just about the same instance. "STAND BY FOR SHOT LINE! STAND BY FOR SHOT LINE! ALL HANDS TAKE COVER! ALL HANDS TAKE COVER!" Bob sounded a blast on a mouth whistle, everyone took cover, and the rifleman fired his piece—a modified M-1 Garand firing blanks.[4] The light line arched snake-like across the yards of rushing sea, curving down to land mid-deck on the supply ship—a perfect shot. It would be tied to a heavy hawser that would be hauled aboard by hand and tied off. The hawser would support the heavy fuel line.

When the transfer is completed—an hour to an hour and a half—the refueling crew from the *Indy* attaches a gift of cookies or some such to the line as a "Thank you!" then the line is pulled back to the supply ship. As the ships disengage, a voice crashes over the loudspeaker from the carrier "*THANKS FOR A JOB WELL DONE GUADELUPE!*" The *Indy* peels off to the left, the *Guadelupe* to the right, while resounding jazzy music blares across the ocean and goose pimples run down my spine.

The next morning I climbed out of the sack dressing quietly as Bob was still flaked out; he came in very late from the UNREP. He came to breakfast at 0600, walking with an exhaustive gait. After eating two plates of rice and hash, he finally admitted that he was physically and mentally exhausted—I didn't wonder—about all he does on this iron lady is work.

---

[4] 'Piece". Military term for a rifle.

After the morning class was over, I took the usual route through the hanger deck past the plane elevators and there, sliding past the opening was a gray slab of steel, another ship was moving along side. I took a closer look. Nine escort ships were moving into position around the *USS Independence*. I quickly ran to the cabin for a camera, then up to the roost for photographs. What the heck was going on? *Are we coming into Sydney? Nobody never tells me nuthin'!*

COMMANDING OFFICER
UNITED STATES SHIP INDEPENDENCE

15 May 1997

Dear Dr. Gunn,

Sir, it was an absolute pleasure having you teach Anthropology Classes aboard Freedom's Flagship during our transit from Yokosuka, Japan to Sydney, Australia. The men were happy to have the opportunity to have you onboard. I certainly hope you had a memorable and enjoyable time while aboard. You are welcome onboard INDEPENDENCE anytime.

I would like to also thank you for your observation and kind words concerning my ship and crew. I am very proud of them.

I hope to have an opportunity to work with you again in the future, if not in Yokosuka, perhaps back in the states. All the best to you and your family.

Sincerely,

T. S. FELLIN
Captain, United States Navy

Dr. James A. Gunn
1731 Howe Avenue Suite 122
Sacramento, CA 95825

Chapter 16

"I was born in Australia
Because my mother
Wanted me to be near her."
Outback saying

Australia

Standing on vulture's roost, camera in hand, I was momentarily transfixed by all the ships steaming alongside the *Indy* plus the scene developing below on the flight deck. Stretching out over 200 feet across the flight deck and 100 feet wide (I could tell the distances because of markings on the flight deck) 662 crewmembers were assembled to create a blue, yellow, black, green, and red Olympic rings. On the opposite side of the flight deck, across from the island, an additional 480 sailors all in Dress Whites, spelled out Sydney 2000—in honor of the Olympic Games to be held there in that year. To my left, behind the island, six airplanes were precisely lined up, their tails sticking out over the ocean. At the stern eight delta-wing F-14 Tomcats were evenly spaced; and at the bow seventeen Tomcats, wings swept out, were evenly spaced, poised to take flight. What a sight to stir the old patriotic heart.

I learned from the Public Affairs Officer, Lt. Cmdr. Terry Sutherland, that his team began last night laying out the positions of each man with spray paint and ropes. This morning the call came for everyone to assemble for the photomontage for the HS-14 helicopter hovering overhead.

"This is our way of showing our support to the host country we'll be visiting," Sutherland told me. He went on to say that mostly the spell out was *USS Independence's* way of displaying her thanks to Australia and wish them well in the 2000 Olympics. Sutherland said he came up with the Olympic Rings idea to keep *Independence* alive in the memory of Australia long after she has departed.

Saying "Good morning" to Captain Kircher (first name 'Hardy', but I would not dare call him that), I remarked on the presentation.

"It went very well," he said. "They did an outstanding job pulling this off. Everyone was coordinated and organized which is a heck of a challenge with this many people."

Soon, we will be steaming into Sydney harbor. Today was the last day at sea; tomorrow my contract is finished and I will depart the ship—if I wish. It was surreptitious implied—and I'll mentioned no names—by one of my bunkmates who had a lot of command over the whole ship, *AND* by higher-ups in the educational hierarchy, *AND* by a figure who occupies the same position on the *USS Independence* as Ahab did on the *Pequod*, that should I so desire, I could stay onboard for the trip around the "Down-under continent" for the time that it would take to arrive at the next port of call: Perth on the other side of the continent. Whipping out a ruler and a map of the South-West Pacific I calculated it was 10 inches through the Bass straight between Australia and Tasmania—about 4,000 plus miles. It would take over a week. I had already made plans to drive awhile touring Australia and then go to New Zealand, so let the offer slide. The ESO officer asked me if I could return; he said that I was the best instructor he had had aboard. I always knew he was a very intelligent fellow—extremely astute!

Independence the Floating City

By
Denver Mottau
Sydney News

The timing was immaculate as the US Navy slid into Sydney on a seven-day goodwill visit. The crew of the aircraft carrier *USS INDEPENDENCE* lined up in formation on the ship's deck, saluting the Olympic city, displaying the Olympic rings and the words Sydney 2000. This was the ship's first visit to Sydney in five years.

It was an opportunity for Sydneysiders to view one of the world's largest warship and her escort missile frigate *CURTS*. Both ships were open for public inspection over the Easter weekend at the RAN Fleet Base in Woolloomooloo last Wednesday. Thousands of people queued up to inspect the working interior of this "floating city" with a crew of more than 5,000 officers and sailors on board.

Over 6,000 sailors keen to enjoy a bit of R&R toured the sights and enticements of Sydney spending millions of tourist dollars over a period of seven days. Trucks carrying thousands of dollars worth of Australian dairy products, meat, fruit, and vegetables were seen loading up the ships before they sail to Perth. Based in Yokosuka, Japan, *INDEPENDENCE*, and her escorting ships guided missile cruiser *MOBILE BAY*, destroyer *CURTIS WILBUR* and frigate *CURTS* were here to participate in an exercise off the coast of Queensland.

It is US policy not to carry nuclear weapons on any ship, aircraft, or submarine operating in these waters.

*****

As with every landing, activity on the ship heightens. People are excited, eager to go ashore my self included. When I came aboard the *Indy*, I noticed that when I climbed the dozens or so stairwells each day, my legs were rubbery and my wind was spent. Now, I can go up and down the flights like a rabbit, albeit, an older Br'er Rabbit. I gave final tests, collected folders, and spent a couple of days correcting and evaluating. As I told the classes at the beginning, my goal was for them to enjoy the subject, and to develop a further interest in anthropology, during readings on their own. Because of the teaching situation and introductory quality of the subject, I graded easy. I am not so hot on grades anyway—perhaps if this were medical school it would be a different story. In addition, I made sure each member of the class received their grade before leaving the ship; I do this for several reasons. I do not want them to suffer any anguish from waiting for grades to be mailed to them. Some instructors do this saying they need the time to make of the grades—this simply means that they are inefficient or that they do not want to be around to argue grades. Also, I may make a mistake in name or grade, so I wish to be available to the student to correct this situation. I posted final grades on the classroom door using a code for the name. Each student had a number that only he knew; only he would know his grade. I waited a couple of days. A couple of guys congraduated me on the class, thanked me for "giving" them a good grade. Each time I would explain that no grades were "given"; they were earned.

No one came to complain. *What a great teacher!*

There were no further messages from my son about his coming to meet me in Australia. I really did not expect him to come. It was a long way and it would be expensive for him.

So, I prepared for Australia. I had $2,000 in cash, and a credit card—that may or may not be honored—AND there is gambling in the land of "*Tie Me Kangaroo Down Boy*!" I might pick up a few Australian kangaroo skins playing blackjack. In Costa Rica (1996) I took 'em for $655—paid for the air ticket. (Went back in 2002 and lost $336.

Damn!) Anyway, if I become destitute, I have a free ticket home thanks to the Navy.

This day I awakened at 0200 for a head call. I stood at the urinal sighing with relief. My uncombed hair stuck out in all directions, my eyes were half-open, and I wore nothing but hiking shorts and shower thongs. I turned from the urinal zipping up when the zipper stuck. I started jerking it up and down trying to get a piece of cloth out of the zipper teeth, bent over, my hair sticking out, face sleep-swollen, when an enlisted man walked in obviously startled at the aberration in the head in the middle of the night. He quickly did about face and hurried out. I wondered what he related to his buddies. At that point, I was glad I was leaving the ship.

At breakfast, I met with Eric Klinker, a young guy, a civilian computer expert from Arlington, Virginia who also was leaving the ship in Sydney. We have been discussing renting an automobile and taking a driving trip around southern Australia. Today we firmed up our plans. While there, he handed me a newsletter from the ship's security department.

Underway, South Pacific
USS Independence Security Department

The *Indy* Legal Department and Security Division's "62nd Precinct" brings this newsletter to you. It is our intent to "get the word to the I-5 Team" on security related issues and provide other legal and security information that is published in the base newspaper and other Navy publications.

Protest Activity

Anti-nuclear protests against USN ships visiting Australian ports used to occur on a regular basis. Recent visits have been demonstration free.

Stay clear of areas where demonstrations appear to be forming. Do not "catcall" or make comments to demonstrators. Avoid provocation of or physical contact with demonstrators.

Alcoholic beverages cannot be brought into Australia without paying full customs duty. *I thought this somewhat redundant since no drinking booze is allowed on US navy ships anyway.*

No currency in excess of $4,000 US can be taken ashore.

No problemo.

No weapons of any type can be taken ashore including firearms, knives, or box cutters.

Crime Prevention

Do not carry or "flash" large amounts of money in public places.
It is required to use the BUDDY SYSEM.
Remain sober and alert. *HAH*
Do carry your armed forces identification card (AFID) while on liberty.
Do not be drunk in public. Personnel observed to be drunk or disorderly will be returned to the ship.
And they ain't kiddin'
Do not wear bandannas. They can be considered gang affiliation.
You gotta be kiddin'!

R & R Overview

Australia has been host to hundreds of thousands of USN and USMC personnel since the frequency of port visits began to increase in 1980. The mild climate, modern facilities, and friendly Australian people have made Australian ports some of the most popular in the navy.

NOTE: Personnel found in violation of these restrictions are subject to disciplinary action in accordance with the Uniform Code of Military Justice (UCMJ).

Do have a good time.
Honestly, I did not add this last sentence. It was on the original newsletter.

*****

Actually, I thought the liberty call instructions were fairly lenient, especially in light of what I had head the Colonel say to the Marines when I was in Guam on the *USS Peleliu.* I guessed the *Independence* was more understanding about the needs of sailors ashore. It wasn't.

Trying not to act like a reporter, although I was a correspondent for the SacraMetro News, a weekly paper in Sacramento, I went to the ship's newspaper office and was able to talk to the assistant editor of the Declaration, SN Martin Moore. He gave me a brief outline of the next front page of the Declaration.

USS Independence pulling into Sydney . . . Soon.

"Liberty call, liberty call." Soon you will be hearing it announced over the 1MC. But do you know the liberty policies and local laws to keep you out of trouble?

Before you ever see the sights, expect to have a haircut inspection on your way off the after brow. If you have short hair on the sides and long hair on top that is slicked back, you will not be allowed to leave the ship.

Unlike Guam, Sydney's port visit requires a collared shirt because this is not a tropical environment. *Could have fooled me!* Unless you are on the beach, do not let the shore patrol catch you without a collard shirt.

All #-3 and below must be back on board by midnight. The only way personnel E-3 and below can have overnight liberty is with an approved chit from the Commanding Officer to visit a direct family member. Even with this chit, you must be in your hotel room or family's home by midnight. *Tough*!

Many sailors will likely end up in the club and bar district of Kings Cross. Be cautious to dark areas, as muggings are prevalent in this area. (I went to Kings Cross and on the second night, about eleven PM, I saw three young men stop their car in a well lighted area, license plate clearly visible. One dashed out to a man lying asleep on a bus bench, shoved him over, and took his wallet dashing back to the car. The streets were well-crowded, but no policemen in sight.)

Be aware that the average beer in Australia has double the alcohol content of American beer. In addition, Australians are very strict towards drunk driving. Police hold roadside alcohol breath tests by pulling over cars randomly and you must breathe into a bag. If your breath is more than .05, you will be charged and arrested.

*****

About 1300, there was an emergency announcement of an oil or gas leak and everyone had to evacuate quarters to gather on the hanger deck or flight deck. Ed, usually the easiest going guy, became irritated when one of the Fire-Control team yelled "YOU TWO! THIS WAY!" We were held on deck for one and one-half hours. I did not mind; if the ship was on fire, I wanted to be on deck. I kept looking for the best route to land and another ship thinking how do you abandon ship with over five thousand souls on board. At the end of the emergency, Ed and I were lingering along, waiting for the crowd to disperse when we saw a deck crew using fork lifts push and drop over 200 wooden pallets over the side along with wire strapping and refrigerator-size cardboard boxes leaving a floating trail of debris miles long. I don't know why, but a helicopter dogged the trail for over an hour perhaps waiting to see what happened to the junk. I do not know for sure that is what he was doing. Seemed strange, the whole thing.

I wrote to my son:

Dear Jamie,

I sent you an email about four days ago, however I do not know if you received it. We are arriving a day early in Sydney—on the 26th. Along with some of the officers, I have arranged a tour for the 28th and 29th. If I do not hear from you before departing the ship, I will write you from Sydney. My classes are finished so do not have much to do aboard except eat and watch the sea. Let me know what your plans are.

Take care.

Love.

Dad

Received an email in return:

Author: Jim Gunn at smtp-gate
Date: 3/21/97 9:52 AM
Priority: Normal
Receipt: Requested
BCC: ADJONES54 at INDY-ADP
TO: "ADJONES54_at_INDY-ADP@smpt-gw.cv62.navy.mil" at smpt-gate
Subject: James A. Gunn – Australia.

Dear Dad. .
I don't think I can make it down under. I have that San Diego conference in the middle of April. If I depart before the conference, I won't have enough time down under to do everything I want. If I leave after the conference, you won't be there. I've been offered that telemedicine job. I have not made a decision to take it, yet. If I take it, I can probably get out of my conference. If that happens, I'll check on a flight to Sydney. When do you expect to return home? I sndormf#4!d.....Interrrppppttt...

Well . . . Sometimes, I love email.

Another night of not sleeping more than two hours at a stretch. Bob and I were about at 0630—new time—although our bodies told us it was 0530—because we set clocks ahead one hour last night. Ed mumbled from his bunk on the floor, something about bring him back a girl from morning chow. Slipping on his tan Class A Eisenhower-cut jacket, Bob said to Ed:

"Ed . . . I want you to know ol' shipmate . . . he that lies with dogs, riseth with fleas" kicking the edge of Ed's bunk for emphasis.

"I didn't say a dog, I said a girl . . . you know. As in *FEE-MALE*!"

"What if there ain't nothing up there but pigs?" I threw in.

"That's okay!"

"Ed! You wrestle with pigs—you only get dirty and the pig has all the fun."

"I tol' you . . . I didn't say dogs or pigs—I said A WO-MAN!"

"What about SHE have the fleas?"

"That's okay."

"What if she ain't one hundred percent female?"

"That's okay."

"Fastidious bastard, aren't ya?"

We went on out the hatchway leaving Ed to his late-morning rising—in several ways. Habitually, he lay abed later than Bob and I.

"Particular about his women ain't he?" said Bob as we made way down the passageway.

"Picky, picky " I replied. " A regular connoisseur about what he eats."

Bob—evidently off his yogurt goop for an interim, ate two huge plates of rice with scrambled eggs—but the way he works, he will burn it off fast. A flight surgeon, a good-looking guy about 32, trim and neat, ate with us. He was transferring to San Diego and happy to be doing so.

I continued finishing up, getting ready to leave the *USS Independence*. I like the ship and I like the people. I packed some class records, attendance lists, grades, expense sheets, lectures; a bunch of papers that was just in the way now, something to carry around, but would be important to the administration and the students later. Threw away some stuff. Packed a box of my clothes and miscellaneous items to send home by mail. Struggling with all this crap, I made way down stairwells to the hanger deck labyrinth of jets, heading for the post office. Saw a big, big oil tanker, as big as the *Indy*, slide by in the opposite direction. Huffing and puffing up the final stairway, I found the post office closed. I rechecked the schedule; it was supposed to be open. *Guy took off already*. One of my students—he has earned over eighty credits while in the Navy—was on knees waxing the passageway. Discovering my plight, he opened the post office and checked my stuff in. Nice Guy.

Moped around the pilot's mess looking for ice cream. Messmate said they had three kinds: vanilla, chocolate, and strawberry. Original. Told him I would have all three. He must have misunderstood for he brought me out three bowls with three colors in each. We laughed. He said, "No problem. I will take two back." I looked at him aghast saying, "Well . . . no need to go to all that trouble and since it is here . . ." I ate 'em all.

Speakers blasted out with there will be a demonstration of CSAR in twenty minutes. I did not know what SEE-SAR was; but headed for the flight deck anyway, disappointed that I did not get seconds on the ice cream—I only had nine dips . . . Well . . . plus the gook that went on top with the nuts and M & M's. Low Fat, no doubt.

Coming out of the island onto the flight deck I ran into a maelstrom: Three helicopters, their combined six blades blasting down, were about thirty yards above the stern deck rappelling—the rope under one thigh and over the opposite shoulder—fully-combat loaded Marines down to the deck, firing as they descended. I do not how in the hell they do it; when I did it many, many ice creams ago, I needed three hands just to keep from slipping down the rope too fast. While the rappelling is going on, some body let off half a dozen blindingly-bright flares at about 3,000 feet that were immediately blasted by a three-plane-flight of Grumman A-6 Intruders firing what I think were AIM-9 Sidewinder Heat-seeking missiles banking around in a weave pattern. *Sheeiiittt!*

I did not know much about Navy planes at the time I sailed on the USS Independence. I was to learn a lot more on the *USS John Young*, the *USS Abraham Lincoln*, the *USS Pelel*iu, and the *USS Carl Vinson*. I did know that the A-6 Intruder proved itself over North Vietnam. Pilot Captain Kenneth L. Coskey, USN (Retired), states, "It was the best Navy plane I flew. The A-6 not only carried twice the load of the much smaller A-7 Corsair ii, a Navy light bomber, but was also faster. Power came from two large Pratt and Whitney turbojets, which provided a top speed of 685 mph."[1]

Gattling guns, firing thousands of round per minute, churned the ocean into a froth as a "Aluminum Cloud"—a nick-name for the F-14 Tomcat because of its large size—screamed around the bow of the carrier to our port side. The F-14 is sometimes called the "Turkey" because—some pilots say—the movements of the control surfaces makes it look like a turkey flapping its wings.

Impressive. Everytime I see a demonstration such as the one today, I am impressed to the point of amazement at the skill and the power our navy has it its call. It is truly "Outstanding."

While we were finishing morning chow, the purser and his help came in with a couple of aluminum suitcase-sized boxes and began

---

[1] Captain Kenneth L. Caskey. *Postwar Carrier Pilot.*

setting up a bank in the wardroom in order to change money for the officers. After eating, I changed $500 American to Australian dollars. As I was coming out of the wardroom someone shouted to me:

"Mr. Gunn—against the bulkhead please!"

What? Were they going to arrest me? I looked at the money clutched in my hand. Nothing wrong there!

The voice was from one of my students. He was striding down the passageway, back-bone straight, wearing a sidearm while escorting two comely ladies, Australian females—wearing dresses, stockings, high heels, and as they passed by *they smelled good*—the girls, not the dresses, stockings, and shoes, but I bet they smelled okay too—each *dragging* a money sack across the deck. Ed came by and suggested we offer to help with the money bags; I suggested we help with the young ladies—*damn!* Two good-looking women with money! So much dinero they couldn't carry it! *Wonder if their dad owned a bar.* As the trio continued toward the wardroom, we gazed alternately at the moneybags and the ladies undulating buttocks. *Damn. That is what it's all about: Economics and Interfacing (sex).*

Ed wanted to know about the money exchange rate. I told him it was $1.21 Australian for $1 American. He had already found out the rate was $1.24 at the commercial exchanges on the wharf, and $1.25 at the banks in town. Later, while Ed scarfed down a trio of hamburgers at lunch, salad and ice cream—I had a bowl of chili—the laundry officer told us the ladies brought $1,000,000 aboard during the day (The gals, women, girls, ladies, wenches—I do not know what term to use anymore after the feminists got hold of me once—were accompanied by only one guard on the ship, but a whole shit-pot full of uniformed-armed protectors waited on the wharf). He also told us that the ship would make a profit of approximately $40,000 Australian dollars today in exchange rates. Puzzled, I asked him for an explanation. Borrowing Eric's calculator, he tapped in a million bucks. "Now" he said. "The ship dispenses let's say $1,000,000 US today at a rate of 1.21. When they bought the money at the bank, they got a rate, let's say . . . 1.25. They got $1,250,000 Australian dollars for $1,000,000 USD. Right? Then when they sell it to the sailors they sell it at $1.21 or $1,210,000 Australian dollars. 1,210,000 from 1,250,000 leaves 40,000 . . . $40,000 Australian dollars. Therefore, they made a profit of .04 Australian on the dollar. Four Australian cents, which comes to $40,000 Australian dollars divided by the bank rate of 1.25; the ship made $32,000 US."

Damn! I thought. *I'm in the wrong business.*

I knew from the newspaper that the sailors would contribute approximately $6,000,000 to the economy while in port four days. All the American dollars would eventually have to be converted wouldn't it? Potential for a lot of profit there just on currency changing. *Damn!*

Ate dinner with Bob, Chaplain Ross, and Eric. Three students came by to shake hands, to say goodbye. Heard someone at another table say, "There's Indiana Jones." I had only known these guys and the ship seven weeks; I was already maudlin at the thought of leaving.

Chapter 17

"In the weltering heat of the Mooroorooplain
The Yatala Wangary withers and dies,
And the Worrow Wanilla, demented with pain,
To the Woolgoolga woodlands
Despairingly flies."
Mark Twain
Australian place names

Sydney

The *Indy* boldly steamed into Sydney harbor this morning at 1000. Great beautiful harbor. Clean water, clean-looking city, and clean green hills. Sydney harbor rivals San Francisco in its symmetrical dazzling brilliance. A flock of news helicopters swirled overhead like semi-demented delighted fans at the Oscars, each maneuvering for a position to photograph the **SYDNEY 2000** and the intertwined Olympic Rings spelled out on the flight deck by over a thousand sailors dressed in gleaming colors. The old *Indy* tooled on in as menacing looking as a black bull in a china shop then, calming down, slamming on her brakes and letting the tugs swing her 89,000 tons of steel around, backing slowly into a parking spot *right down town!* (I calculated that 413 tons of that 89,000 tons of the *Indy's* weight is people) I wondered that so many tons of the leviathan ship could be handled so deftly. The anchorage is very close to houses stacked up the hill side just across a street and is practically downtown, so there is a feeling of intimacy. Thousands of people lining the wharf, in balconies on buildings, and streets very vocally began welcoming us to their city. Automobile horns honked, people yelled and waved.

Ed and I were in no hurry to get off the ship as we were in Guam. I had a second breakfast with Chaplain Ross, Eric, and a couple of officers, their class-A khaki's so stiff with starch they crackled when the men sat. No other branches of the service have such neat dressing officers as the Navy, not even the Marines. You say "What about the

Marines Dress Blues?" Despite what the television adds show in Marine recruiting where a six foot tall handsome Marine stands with his shinning sword held vertically while he is wearing tailored Dress Blues, most foot-slogging Marines hold the formal uniform in disdain. Dress Blues, when I was in the marines, were worn only by the band, color guard, and a few backwater kids from the South when they went home to Whistle Stop, USA. We called Dress Blues the "Monkey Suit."

Latter in the morning, shouldering my camera bag, I made way to the brow and out the base gate. ATT had set up telephone banks inside the base just as they had done in Guam, and there were a few souvenir stands just outside in the parking lot. Several wives from stateside were being welcomed by a Captain; they flew over to be with their husbands—officer's wives—delicious looking!

Following the white clad navy horde, all spiffied out in my Indiana Jones duds, I studied a map one of the girls at the gate was passing out with free drink chits from various cafes and bars, fishing for customers, angling for some of the six million American dollars that would be flowing from vaults in the U.S. to the pockets of sailors via the purser to the bars, souvenir stands, and "ladies" of Kings Cross. Most *were* for Kings Cross, an area just up the hill from the *Indy*, the bars-girls-souvenir area pandering over-priced "goods" to the military. Ed caught up with me on the sidewalk and we spent an hour or so checking out hotels for him in the Kings Cross-neighborhood. The cheapest he could find was $50 A$. About 40 US$. King Cross may be the tawdry disreputable part of Sydney, but it possessed a magnificent view. From the hilltop area, all of Sydney lay at one's feet. In one gaze, I could see the famous "Bird-Cage" or "Toothpick" Harbour Bridge, the ultra-modern Sydney Opera House, and the Centerpoint Tower. It is a beautiful city in a beautiful setting.

Ed found a place right on the main drag of Kings Cross, up a staircase, right off the sidewalk over a bar-restaurant. Staying there, he could have his women, food, and booze sent up at the same time. Save a trip. Leaving Ed to his own ramifications—Ed liked to socialize on the ship, however on land he was strictly a lone wolf—I looked unabashedly around, checking tour prices, seeing how far it was to Perth, Alice Springs, Adelaide, and point's south. Ran into several groups of guys from the *Indy*, all looking totally different in civvies.

I stopped at an outdoor restaurant mainly because a female about 25 was sitting at a side walk table in a blouse cut so low her breastworks were exposed to the elements. I could not figure it: all these guys walking about ignoring this poor young delectable female sitting alone, probably chilled because she could not afford to by sufficient clothing to cover her upper works. Nautical wise, she was a clipper ship: beautiful long, well-kept dark hair, arching eyebrows, full lips, blood-red fingernail polish, black high heels. She had a book a hand, next to a cup of dark liquid, most likely tea. *Probably a librarian. She looked right at me, into my eyes!*

♫ *"She was a nice girl,*
A proper girl,
But, one of the roving kind!" ♫♪

Why are guys so fascinated by a bountiful pair of mammary glands? I don't KNOW! Maybe it is because we were breast-fed as babies, and are still hungry. Every male that I know is preoccupied with breasts, tits, titties, jugs, knockers, paps, bosoms, busts, boobs, and on and on . . .Even the Hebrew bible gets into the act in the Song of Solomon 4:5, "Thy two breasts are like two young roes that are twins, which feed among the lilies." *I never did understand the analogy of a roe deer with breasts eating flowers, but I am not about to argue with the Hebrew bible.* Some people seen to not be happy with breasts. Mainly women, not men. Germaine Greer writes that a full bosom is actually a millstone around a woman's neck . . . men want to make a mammet of her . . .men don't see her . . . just her bosom . . . her breasts are not part of her person but lures—decoys for attracting animals—slung around her neck, to be kneaded and twisted like magic putty, or mumbled and mouthed like lolly ices.[1] Well . . . although I do not know what "mammet" means, I do know that "lolly" is hard candy of some type . . . so I rather have to agree with Ms. Greer—. When men meet a well-endowed lady, they cannot tell you later the color of her eyes; they do like to attempt to sculpture something already well-formed; and they do like to suck on hard candy! Most men think that breasts are like money; only too much is enough. *Animals!*

I looked for a table, while deliberately standing by hers—*come on lady, help this rube out!* With a nod and a slight wave of a delicate manicured hand—a white dove in flight—she indicated that I could share hers, and, just as I sat down managing to look down her ample

[1] Germaine Greer (b. 1939), Australian feminist writer. *The Female Eunuch*, "Curves" (1970)

cleavage, her girlfriend showed. Introductions were made, we discoursed a bit, laughed gaily—ha! ha!—and a couple of tee hee's—until unfortunately, our ménage came to a time-clock end, as they had to go to their jobs in a lady's clothing store. However, she did give me her card—*the old fox still has it!*—taking it out of a slim, dark purse as she arose, jiggling nicely. *Women must have different sets of shock absorbers built in their bodies than men do.* I still have the card right here, pasted in the old tattered journal. Name of Toni Bennett; lives on Rushcutters Bay. If you read this Toni, I would still like to be welcomed into the bosom of your family . . . well . . . yours anyway. If a husband happens to read this, forget the whole thing.

"Uncorseted, her friendly bust,
Gives promise of pneumatic bliss."

Nice little poem. Wish that I had written it. T.S. Eliot beat me to it.

Talked to another member of the opposite sex pushing a red-haired baby in a stroller. Cute lady, homely kid. As the Marines delicately put it, she was built like a brick shithouse. The woman, not the child. They are so friendly—so pretty. Australian women. Short skirts. Skirts so short that, as the Chinese say, *"You feel that you are right at the celestial gate."* Lovely legs. Long, . . . lovely legs. *Sigh.* Lovely. Reminds me of the time when Three-Ski-Jackets-With-The-Sales-Tags-Still-On Joyce was reclining on the deck of a bachelor's pad ChrisCraft 20-footer I once owned, named the Blue Bayou II.

"James . . ." Mellow voice. "Do you consider my legs long? . . ." she asked, stretching out her barely bikini-clad, James-lotion-oiled thighs with little dimpled knees, and little pink-painted pinkie phalanges while at the same time pointing with her impressive breasts barely contained within the wisp of red see-through fabric.

"Yep!" I said, trailing my nomadic brown eyes from boobs to crotch. "Whenever possible." [2]

I strolled through Sydney constantly checking my map, ambling along a curving sidewalk, through an upscale neighborhood of two-

---

[2] **Note to young bachelors.** There are three things that will get a lady to take her blouse off on the spot, faster than you can shuck an ear of corn—toute a l'heure. They are a 21-foot boat, a hot tub, or a bottle of good booze. The booze is the cheapest.

story, ivy covered well-kept homes, down the hill toward the harbor landing and the ship. Visited the botanical gardens—had a "cuppa"—hot tea liberally laced with milk and sugar, a nice pick-me-up when walking, and visited the art museum.

Although the term "Outstanding" is a tad over used in the military, I did see something that was truly remarkable, truly "outstanding." While strolling about gawking at the sights, I walked over the famous bridge that crossed the bay looking down on the casino. Nearby is a maritime museum with a couple of sailing ships, a Russian submarine, and—what caught my eye—was a PBY Catalina Flying Boat, a Consolated Vultee PBY-5A Catalina Amphibian, what I consider one of the most beautiful airplanes ever built. It is said that life began in the ocean, and so did commercial aviation. According to Ian Marshall,[3] aircraft that operated on water included two broad categories: flying boats, which lack wheels and can land only on water—like the Alaskan bush pilot's float planes—and amphibians, which have wheels and can set down on either water or land. With more than 70 percent of the Earth's surface covered by water, such aircraft were necessary the fledging days of airport poor America.

The Catalina made its first flights in 1935 and has been in continuous service in the US Navy since 1936. The Catalina's primary role was as a patrol bomber, but it has been used a torpedo carrier, as a convoy protection, as an anti-submarine weapon and as had performed air/sea rescue duties. Many a downed pilot has looked up to see the welcome sight of a long-range "Cat" blinking its rescue lights, coming in for a mid-ocean landing.

Along with the Catalinas was the development of the China Clippers. In the 1930's, there were few airports, but there were lots of rivers, reservoirs, and oceans. Pam Am's built refueling bases and passenger accommodations on Midway, Wake, and Guam, the stepping stones that allowed flights from San Francisco to Hawaii to the Philippines in five days. The San Francisco to Hawaii flight took about 18 hours, a modern commercial jet takes 5 hours. The British used the giant flying boats on their British Empire Middle East routes to India landing in the Nile River near Cairo.

One flying boat, the Pacific Clipper, was moored in Auckland, New Zealand during the attack on Pearl Harbor. Not able to cross the Pacific because of Japanese domination of the sky with fighter planes,

---

[3] Ian Marshall. Flying Boats: The J-Class Yachts of Aviation. Howell Press, 2002.

it was forced to head west seeking out friendlies for land and fuel, flying 31,500 miles to arrive at the Marine Air Terminal in New York a month later.

Truly beautiful airplanes.

Checked back into the base meeting Eric who was headed out. He invited me to spend the night at the Hilton—$130 a night for which his company was picking up the tab—where he had a double, so I said okay. He gave me directions; it was on the other side of the harbor, in the new part of the city. I would hike over there after I finished some more paperwork aboard.

Packed my traveling clothes, grabbed the old camera bag I have lugged all over the world and left the ship for the night. I actually had no further authorization to be aboard the *USS Independence*, but no one seemed to mind. On the way to the new part of Sydney, across the bridge I—who do not particularly care for beer—sucked down a couple of Melbourne Bitters while eye-balling the local architecture—physical buildings as well as physical females, then continued strolling back through the botanical gardens toward the business district and the Hilton. The sky was darkening, I was tiring, the bags were getting heavier, but the scenery was good, the evening air bracing. I finally staggered up the last hill broken-winded, arriving at the Hilton; Eric had not.

"Sorry, Ocker, the hotel is choka," explained the skinny male clerk at the Hilton reservation desk, looking down at the reservation book, his long, unkempt hair hanging down. *Guy needs to wash his locks.* I was not impressed by the décor of the Hilton; it was fancy on the outside, but not much better than a Bakersfield Highway 50 Motel 6 in the foyer. *Sorry, Focker, the hotel is WHAT. Whatta this guy call me?*

"I beg your pardon?" I said.

He stared at me not answering.

"Are you speaking English?"

"Yes. Of course. Oh, sorry mate," said the clerk, coming back into the world. "I didn't realize you were from O.S.

"I'm not. I'm from California."

"Yes. That's O.S., —Overseas."

"What did you say? Sounded like 'The hotel's soccer.'"

The clerk chuckled. Condescendingly, he explained, "Mate, what I said was, 'Sorry Ocker, the hotel is choka'. That means 'Sorry, friend, the hotel is full.'" *I will get back to this "friend" definition later.*

I was getting a speck disconcerted with this clown. Some people are like Slinkies, not really good for anything, but you still cannot help but smile when they tumble down the stairs.

I explained that I did not need a room, that I was checking to see if Mr. . . . Uh . . . The Admiral . . . If Admiral Klinker had checked in. I stood a little straighter and looked stern. That I was his aide-de-camp from the big canoe across the harbor.

"Aye Mate. He checked in not a half-ago. " 'ere's a note." He read the note. Then he said, "You the Gun?" *Kinda snotty! Have to pull a Ed & Jim on him.*

"Uh! . . . Yeah. I'm . . . ah, . . . in charge of the transaxle of the 5-inch, dual-purpose 20-millimeter Top Gun. I don't handle nuclear though. Top secret that"

He stared at me with wonderment—it may have been befuddlement. *Bastard oughta learn English.*

"The big Carrier, ay'? 'at's silvertail, mate. Saw it comes in, I did. Goodo!"

Comes in? Ats? Goodo! I had no idea what the hell this guy was talking about.

"Uh . . . Where can I wait for the admiral?"

"She'll be apples, Mate. Jist ave' a middy or a schooner inna bar if ye like!" He indicated the way to a double-door opening into a brightly-lit room full of mirrors and stacked liquor bottles. The blasted place was lit up like a ice cream parlor.

I like my bars dark.

Professor Higgins said he would watch my bags, so I sauntered over to the opening where over the door, spelled out in bamboo script, Kangaroo Bar. I half expected to see a couple kangaroos in the place, but there was only the bartender wearing a tuxedo shirt—a bit o' class—and a lone male customer perched on a high bamboo stool. I believe I knew what a schooner was but . . . "I'll have a middy" I threw out, climbing on a stool. The bartender nodded a welcome—well, he nodded—turned, and drew off a urine-colored ten-ounce glass of tap beer setting it before me after he took a swipe at the bar with a cloth the size of a beach towel. Well, now I know what a middy is. In Australia anyway. A middy in the navy is a loose-fitting blouse with a small collar. How did a beer get to be a middy? Australians have a strange grasp of the English language. I once had lunch in the school cafeteria in Sacramento where we had a lovely redheaded lady originally from England working, serving the faculty. She and I often discussed her paintings of English bungalows; she was very good. One day I thanked her as she handed me my food, and she replied as I was turning to go to a table, "You're welcome. Keep your pecker up!" I about dropped my hot dog. You know over there they say things like *bonnet* for the hood of an automobile and *boot* for the trunk; why don't they learn to speak English.

Drank my middy perched next to the other customer, an engineer so he told me, who greeted me with something like "Ga'd Day!" His parents farm 400 acres "o' to Quanda, Y've know? P'ace cost a nine-tied thousand Y've know? Up good for re-vation home!"

I nodded like I understood a damn thing he was saying.

Maybe that was why the bartender nodded. He didn't understand half what these guys were saying.

I asked the barkeep if he knew where there was more than one casino in the city. He said that there was only the one; that it was just below the south end of the bridge spanning the neck of the harbor, the one I just crossed. I knew where it one was.

I took a sip of the foul-smelling beer thinking, *My gawd! What horse pissed in this?*

"Whew!" I exclaimed to the guy behind the bar. "WHAT'S in this?"

"Ye wanted a middy did y'u?"

"Uh . . . yeah!"

"Its spruce beer." The guy next to me said. I looked it up later. Spruce beer is made from twigs, leaves, and shit like that, boiled with molasses and sugar and yeast. *My gawd. Just go out in the woods and scoop up a bunch of trash. They never heard a' hops!*

As we sipped at the powerful potent—after half the glass, I was acquiring a taste for this warm buffalo piss; horse piss was too mild a term—a slim out-back looking guy—wearing washed-out jeans, beaten brown boots, a checkered shirt, and a cracked and stained leather broad-brimmed hat, much like his face—perched on a stool on the other side of the engineer. Quickly he got into the act. He heard the engineer and me talking about the casino.

"Ye ga-amble di ye? I'a ma jackeroo bein o'r Bot' way taken jum-buck off to sale, ye 'now.'

"Umm! . . . I nodded." I learned "understanding nodding" from the bartender. If you do not understand somebody, just nod. It works well; makes people think that you know what the hell they are talking about. Works best if the person is half-snozzled. Of course, nodding *could* get you into trouble. You might wind up engaged, but that is a chance you take.

"What ye play?"

"I play only Blackjack."

"I'a ma say ye off thingo sheep, the Indopendeunc?"

Am I off the ship?

"Umm! . . . I nodded."

I think "sheep" was ship, but I was not positive. I had heard they do other things to sheep down here other then make 'em into lamb chops. Reminded me of the old joke. A new guy comes to the sheep ranch. After a few weeks sans interconnecting with members of the opposite sex, he asks the boss what did they do for sex. The boss says we just grab one of the ewes and go to it. The new guy rejects that idea, but after another few weeks he changes his mind seeing the other hands with their girl-friend sheep, and asks the boss how he goes about it. The boss says just go out to the corral and grab one. The new guy does so, and as he is going about his business, the rest of the hands come out and start laughing hilariously at him.

"Why you laughing at me? He says. "You do the same thing."

"Yeah! But you picked the ugliest one in the bunch!"

Same story in Bahrain. A new guy comes to the desert oil fields. Horny, he asks the boss what he should do for sex. The boss says to go ahead and take one of the camels. The new guy, disgusted, waits a few weeks, but finally, giving in, he climbs on a box behind one of the camels and proceeds. Everyone, including the boss, begins to laugh at him.

"What ya laughing at?" he says to the boss. "You said ta take one of the camels!"

"Yeah!" replied the boss. "But I meant to town!"

Slim, the jackaroo, still wanted to talk.

"Travelin' do ye? Done a tifbit me-own, ye no, inna Nav once—me bruders too. Much too been all over the world . . . speking seven landgages I do."

Speaks seven languages? I should have nodded, but I asked, "Is one of them English?"

The engineer gulped and about spit up his beer.

"Huh?" said the jackeroo.

Not wanting to go to Fist City with this fellow, I said, "I said, your brudders, . . . is one o' them heinglish? . . an' canna I buy ye a middy now?" *How could his brother be English if he's Australian. Well, it was all I could think of at the time!*

"Aye, I think ye. No-em me bruders a stockman, rais broombies out inna Never, Never, anna thank ye the beer, mate, I'll br 'avin a tinny—MB."

Jesus H. Christ!

I was furtively looking over my shoulder for Admiral Klinker before we three "trousers" (Dudes) began to "Shout" (Buy a round of drinks as in "it's your shout".) and I know where that leads. Giving the engineer—I never find out what kind—and the Jackaroo a "Ta" (Thank you) I cut out.

A few days later I ran across a pamphlet titled *"AUSSIE LINGO" Learning English Down Under.* Seems the hotel clerk was not quite "ripper" with me when he explained that "Sorry, Ocker, the hotel is choka" meant "Sorry, friend, the hotel is full." He said that "ocker" meant friend, but my little pamphlet defined ocker as a "bumpkin" or "loudmouth." I also deciphered our conversation from the pamphlet. A Jackeroo is a male ranch hand, a broombie is a sheep, a tinny a can of beer, a MB is a Melbourne Bitter, and *Ta* means thank you. In *My Fair Lady*, professor Higgins enlightens us that the Americans haven't spoken English in years. He should go listen to the Aussies.

I escaped the Kangaroo Bar for the Hilton Gatehouse Grill where I ordered the "Stockman Special" wondering what I would receive. Was not too bad. Cold ham AND corned beef (strange combination), inoffensive green salad, pickles, apple tart and custard, and bun with New Zealand butter. Why New Zealand butter? I haven't a "premmie."

"Ohio Cozaimus" I said to the last one out. *Whew*! A lovely Japanese waitress wrote "Ohio Cozaimus" on a napkin in the dining room of the Hilton because innumerable Japanese tourists kept walking by my table, each one bowing and saying "Glood Evveningg" stopping to jabber away. Like the Australian's, I couldn't understand half of what they were saying. I couldn't get any food down there were so many. They must have thought I *was* Indiana Jones. Gotta stop wearing this leather jacket and 1943 tan fedora. I asked the waitress where *she* learned English. She replied somewhat haughtily, "Hotel School." The Japanese are something else. They have perfected good manners making them indistinguishable from rudeness.

Eric found me in the dinning room asking about this "admiral stuff." I told him I thought—even though he is a civilian—he deserved a promotion.

"I mean Eric. You are the only person in the world who can do what you do" I said.

He looked at me curiously. Knowing Ed and me, he did not know if that was a compliment or not. We checked out the room, tried to watch a rugby match on television but got to laughing each time the announcer said of the one of the players, " . . . he has lovely hands!" For the next two weeks Eric and I would see someone, a bartender, gas attendant, or whatever, and one of us would say "He has lovely hands" going into paroxysms of laughter.

Eric is the quietest sleeper in the world—I mean, he does not even breathe. About the same age as my son. The telephone rang at 2 AM—it was room service wanting to know if we ordered cheese and crackers. Half-awake, fighting aching sleepingness, a bit pissed, I said, "Sorry, Frocker, me Chucker's Ocker!" That'll hold 'em. I rolled over sleeping soundly until six.

Thursday, my second day in the land down under, the dawn came early tinting a cloudless sky the palest shade of pink. Blessed or cursed with the inability to sleep in, I watched the dawn from the picture window of the hotel after ordering room-service coffee—$1.40 A$ and worth the price—served nicely with pot, cups, utensils, sugar, milk, and napkins. In most countries that I have been in, especially Asian tourist areas, the service is fancier than in the States, and, of course, terribly cheaper. Here, in one of the most modern cities in the world, I heard roosters crowing before first light—even the Australian chickens were crazy bastards not knowing they were citified; that they were not down on the farm. City chickens. Leaving Eric a note, I headed out, enjoying the early morning walk. The harbor is surrounded by the city most of which sprawls across the hills. The ship and old town lay below, still dark with shadows, however, by the time I reached the botanical gardens, the sun had reached Kings Cross and light was descending toward the *Indy*. The air was pleasant, fresh, invigorating; coffee shops were opening, and well-dressed people were going to work. Morning has to be the best time of the day. (For walking, making love, and eating, but not other things like working.)

In half an hour I was through the naval base gate with no problem, up the brow—receiving a nice salute—and breakfasting on bagels slathered with jam washed down with the first navy cup of sunup coffee Whoo-Aw. I worked on roster sheets from eight until twelve-thirty, breaking to go to the ESO office in response to a call form Ray Corpus. Ray showed me an email that he was going to send to Dr. Bays in Administration at Central Texas College in San Diego, stating that I did an "outstanding job on Board." Nice guy. I need to send a copy of this email to a friend in Sacramento by the name of Terry Francino. A year after I taught at First Global College in Nongkhai, Thailand, Terry taught there having several of my students in his class. They told him I was "Most Beloved Teacher." When he left he said they told him that he was "Most Beloved Teacher." I think he is lying. This email will prove that I am now "Most Beloved Teacher" in the navy.

Talked to Bob. He had had no liberty yet. Too much to do. He was still putting in an eighteen-hour day.

Left the ship to walk a short distance up the hill that began across the street from the naval base to the Kings Cross-neighborhood. The roadway was so step, cars went to low gear grinding up it. The day before Eric booked a room at the Chateau Sydney hotel at 14 Macleay Street, at a part of the area called Potts Point—a very fancy hotel. I do not know why he did booked the Hilton, then the Chateau Sydney—perhaps his office booked the Hilton ahead of time. I did not know what company Eric worked for, but his expense account was first class. A fifteen-minute walk and I found the hotel near where Ed and I were walking the previous day. Eric the Admiral had not yet checked in yet, so, hoping he brought my bag with him, I strolled on the busy main drag. As I said, Kings Cross is on top of a ridge with views of Sydney Harbor, the Old Town, and the new city across the harbor, as well as spectacular views of the Pacific Ocean. There are many up-scale shops here, and talk about view property—a house must cost a fortune here.

My feet took me to the same outdoor café where I talked to the lady with the baby stroller and visually stormed the 25 year-old's breastworks. I ordered a coke to go with a sandwich I brought from the *Indy* sharing my table with a couple of guys from the ship. At 2 PM, I returned to the Chateau Sydney (145 US$ daily) to find Eric all checked in having brought my bag from the Hilton. Our room, #315, faced the Pacific and the harbor entrance—Eric planned and asked for the room so we could watch the *Indy* depart. Smart fellow. Plans ahead. That is why I promoted him to Admiral! *Come to think of it;*

with his brains, youth, and dedication, he probably could become an Admiral.

I napped from 2:30 until 4:00—dead asleep. Happily, no one telephoned about cheese and crackers.

Awakening, I telephoned the Australian Consulate, inquiring what do I do about a visa since I came in on a military ship but was leaving the country by commercial carrier. I did not want to go through that process again like Thailand where, being ignorant, I left the USS Peleliu at Phuket, visited Thailand for a few weeks, not realizing I had not checked into the country. When I went through customs a uniformed guard pulled me aside and sent for his superior. He looked at my passport and the contract with the Navy, and sent for *his* superior. The Superior-Superior listened to my explanation about getting off the military ship *Peleliu* replying, "You are too old!" Finally, I convinced him—I had a new military card giving me full U.S. military rights—then the problem became "What could he stamp on my passport?" He finally just wrote in the bow number of the ship and scribbled something in Thai. No charge. He was gladdened to be rid of me. Thai immigration is about the most accommodating in the world.

The Australian consulate clerk told me that it is no problem as the Australian government had an agreement with the American government concerning this type of situation; all I was to do to depart the Commonwealth was to present my passport along with the military contract at immigration. In Cambodia, I most likely would have been locked up—again! I was locked up there once for two hours because, running out of room, I pasted two additional pages in my passport. The Thai's did not care; they went ahead and stamped right on one of the new pages—their stamp takes up one-fourth of a page, as most do. The Cambodians came unglued. They did not know whether to shit or go blind. The first official asked why I pasted the pages in. I told him because I ran out of pages. He made me wait while he got his boss. His boss reminded me of the North Koreans in the movies, the ones who, wearing brown uniforms with red piping interrogate prisoners of war. I told him the same sad tale. He asked why I did not go to the embassy. I explained that the embassy was 300 miles away. He had me wait until he got his boss—more ribbons on his chest, nicer uniform. Same scenario. "Why you not go embassy?" 300 miles. "You wait."

I waited.

I waited some more thinking *these guys have the mentality of a chicken strangler.*

Wilai was waiting for me on the other side of the border at a jungle flea market. There, in about 800 stalls, you could buy anything—from an AKA-47rifle to clothing, jewelry, to a kid, a real kid, not a goat. Peculiarly, I was not too worried about these assholes. Every communist country that I have been in the bureaucrats are like this: suspicious, inefficient, and slightly rude—they think you are going to steal something although they have nothing worth stealing. Finally, the first honcho who questioned me, said that I would have to pay a fine of 200 baht ($4.65. I had already paid 1,100 baht for the visa fee, about $25.58.) Even then, they would not stamp the new pages. The clerk erased some other immigration stamps, four of them, as the Cambodian stamp—about the size of a playing card—took a whole page and stamped there. The second honcho came back, motioning me over, asking how long I was staying. I said that I am leaving now. He said not to ever come back. *I've been back three times since*. There was one more hurdle to get out of the La-La land of Cambodia. A male clerk sat at a table putting the final stamp in the passport. I was third in line. I had been sweating like a pig for two hours in a little concrete room, not knowing what was going to happen, worrying about Wilai waiting on the other side of the border. The clerk kept letting Cambodians and Japanese tour guides ahead of me. The Japanese tour guides each clutched a pile of passports that had to be processed that took some time. To go from third to first took a good twenty-five minutes. I noticed that the Cambodians would partially show a 100 baht bill from their left pocket, obviously to bribe the clerk, but stealthy so no one else could see. Hell, everybody in the place knew what they were doing. There was a red line on the floor just past the clerk. Once I was across that line I was done with these Jackaroos! Finally, deciding to get into the role, I exposed a 500 baht bill so the squinty-eyed clerk got a good look at it. Not speaking, his rimless eyeglasses sparkling, he motioned me forward, finally, reaching out his hand for my passport; I pulled the 500 Baht note further out, he stamped the passport, wrote something with a ball point pen, looked at my passport photograph, and handed my passport to me with his right hand, sliding his left to the edge of the table, ready to pick off my 500 Baht. Saying "Sawasdee Krop"—I don't know why I was speaking Thai to a Cambodian—I pulled the note out a bit further smiling a chicken-shit grin, while stepping across the line shoving the money back into my pocket. I did not look back, but the nape of my neck was expecting a bullet any minute. Assholes! Mess with kid, will you! *Ugly American; I hope so!*

Believe it or not, I had the temerity to ask the Australian consulate clerk if the casino was open—I'd hard it might not be—and she replied that it was and proceeded to give me directions how to get there. I said," That'll be apples! Goodo. *Ta!*"

I thought that the taxi driver was ripping me off when he charged me 13$ Australian for the trip to the "Rocks" where the casino was located; the hotel clerk said the fare should be around $A 6. Gambled a little Blackjack. Won $102 US. Secret of winning at Blackjack: know when to hit, know how to split, when to double down, and how much to vary the bet, *AND*, the most important part *AND* the hardest part *AND* the only way to win—*quit when you are ahead!*

Winnings this year at Blackjack—here called twenty-one—is $94.50 at Laughlin, Nevada, $665 at San Jose, Costa Rica, and $102 at Sydney. I am not a big winner, but I have discovered it is better to be a small winner than a big loser. My brother says, "Make a bet everyday, otherwise you might walk around lucky and never know it."

At 7:30, I took a taxi back to the Chateau Sydney to find Eric and a sailor buddy from the *Indy* —married to a Japanese lady in Yokosuka with two children—watching "The Making of Starwars. They reminded me of my son in their enthusiasm for anything to do with Starwars.

After the program was over, Eric's friend left for the ship—he had to be a board before midnight. Eric left to get addresses off the ship's computer; I went to bed at 10:30. At 11:30 I got up, dressed, and took a walk to King Cross and the Fountain restaurant. The streets, brightly lit, were alive with women, men, and cars. Good looking women everywhere! And—I must admit—a few not so good. On this walk I saw the three guys pull up in a car and rob a drunk sleeping on a bus bench; rolled him right over taking his wallet driving off laughing. Hit the sack at 12:30. Slept fitfully all night because one; I wasn't too sleepy, two; Mozzies—Aussie for mosquitoes—buzzed about chewing on me, and three; the couch-bed was not comfortable. Gave it up at 4:30. Dressed. Left a note for Eric. Headed for the ship.

I was in the wardroom by 0500. At 0530 made way to the stateroom (dungeon) to find Bob just getting up. Ed was ashore. I did a final pack-up, double-checking safe, desk, and locker. Bob went to work; I went to meet Eric on the quarter-deck. He was a no show. Climbed up to the flight deck to look down on about 400 sailors in formation on the wharf. Chaplain Derek Ross came over, then Paul, one of the officers from the Chaplain Department. Still no Eric. When I left the Chateau Sydney, I left a wake-up call for him at the front desk. Naturally, they had not called him; hurriedly he came down the hill—late. He was to catch a sightseeing bus at 0600. The bus, naturally, left forty-five minutes late, so all turned out. "She'll be apples" I told Eric. *Talk Aussie like a ocker I do.*

Not much was going on at the *Indy*. Hiked back to the top of the hill and to the hotel.

Jane and Linda are two diminutive Japanese girls who clean our room at the Chateau Sydney. I had a hell of time explaining a drawing I did of a bearded caveman holding a burning stick relating the drawing to Moses and the burning bush. I discovered that Buddhists know little about Moses and the crowd that he ran around with. Perhaps it would have been more fruitful if I understood Japanese or they would have understood English. Jane and Linda—Japanese? I told them my name was Jim so naturally they called me *Gim*. Their real names were ♑♍ (ling Zhang) and ♑♒☾ (Ya Yum) or something like that. The door was open as they were cleaning and another Japanese lady hearing the laughter popped in. She was a tad taller, about 5'4". She joined in spattering out a gaggle of Japanese while Ling and Ya spattered back. Her name ws Hou Ye-lin bastardized into Sherry.

So, I'm lying there on Eric's bed, hands behind my head, totally relaxed. Sherry is sitting in an easy chair telling me about the future of cybernetical theory—at least I think that is what the topic was—since I couldn't understand a word she was saying I wasn't quite sure; it may have been about her mother's antique quilt. I kept nodding understanding, so she kept jabbering. Linda was polishing the already gleaming dresser, and Jane was fixing me an iced coke from the dinky little refrigerator, when Admiral Eric walked in the open doorway.

His eyes bugged out.

I said, "Ladies! This is the Admiral!"

Immediately they grabbed their gear running out giggling.

I looked at Eric shaking my head and sighing.

He said, "How come I never get any girls in here?"

I said, "Prob'ly my animal magnetism, some of us got it; some don't!"

In the Navy, as in the Marines, friends are made in short period; friendships that often lasts for years. For example, I still communicate with Mike Kanocz and Gary Cole whom I met on outpost Nina in Korea in 1954. Something develops among men of good will and lightheartedness, a rapport that lasts, endures. Why? I do not know. Maybe it is sharing an adventure, or a hardship. I left some good friends on the *Indy*. Bob Yoder, Ed Morris, Chaplain Derek Ross, Eric Klinker: One I would see again, some years later at a book signing for a book I wrote on Egypt. He drove 160 miles to visit for a short hour. The others I talk to by email and telephone occasionally, when I can find them. What is a friend? There hundreds of definitions.

William Sherman said, "Grant stood by me when I was crazy, and I stood by him when he was drunk, and now we stand by each other."

Franklin says, "A Father's a treasure, a Brother's a comfort; a Friend is both."

I think a friend is just someone who likes you. That is enough for me.

I went to say goodbye to my bunkmates: to think the Chief Boatswain for the popcorn, the cake, the name on the door, and for his unlimited, unqualified hospitality. They were both there—in the cubicle the size of a two-man prison cell on Alcatraz—in the "Dungeon." After being ashore, the place seemed dowdier than before. Ed was working on class lists. He would be going directly to another ship: that is how he made his living; he has been on 29 or so. Bob sat at his desk strewn with papers and motorcycle magazines. They said that they were made despondent by my leaving, but admitted that they would have traded me for *any* corpulent, unsightly hag from the beach at the drop of a hat. Ed was thrown off his feed by my departure, cutting down his eating to only four meals today. Bob's eyes glistened, so did mine. Must have been something in the air: *that damn ventilation system!* I shook Ed's hand. I started to shake Bob's, then thought, *Aw Fuck it!* I hugged him, turned . . . and left.

Take care shipmate!

On the outside of the hatch, I had posted a sign for my students that read, "Professor Gunn will not be available until 8 AM tomorrow." Ed and Bob had crossed out the *available* substituting "SOBER." As Wilai, my Thai significant other would say, "They jealous me too much!" Resentful because I am leaving this tub and they have to stay. My friends . . . Ha! I probably will never see those bums again.

I will miss my friends. *Someone who likes you.*

*****

Eric Klinker, the ersatz civilian admiral, who roamed the fleet solving computer problems, and Indiana Jim stayed a few days at the Chateau Sydney on the hill above King's Cross

As I said, Eric chose the room for the balcony overlooking the entrance to Sydney harbor. We could not see the *Indy* at dockside from the room, but we knew when she was sailing and she had to come right around the point of land we were on. Eric received a phone call and not half an hour later we were sitting on the patio with a cool drink at hand when suddenly the bow came into view as the ship slid by the point less than half-a-mile away. Like a sliding screen, the ship came into view from around the point. Proceeded by two Navy submarine-hunting Sikorsky SH-3D Sea King helicopters and surrounded by a flotilla of power boats, sail boats and three hovering news helicopters, the mighty carrier passed the point dwarfing the boats, houses, and hotels around it. It was a silent, giant among clamorous pigmies. Eric and I stood wordlessly at the same instance and watched quietly as the carrier, with elephant-like dignity, squeezed through the harbor entrance, and churning a wake fifty yards wide, quickly left its entourage behind.

Watching the *Independence* leave Sydney harbor, its big, boxy shape dominating the land, making even the distinguished city of Sydney with its modernistic opera house, the world's longest arched bridge, and its 4,000,000 people seem small by comparison, I wondered at modern technology. Wondered that *that* floating weapon, that city of over five thousand men and women, that mighty ship could have brought me from Japan across the immense Pacific Ocean to this continent. We left Japan February 14 just forty days ago—it seems much longer. We saw mostly ocean—"Join the Navy and See the World"—Guam for a few days, then Australia. Australia is the forty-fourth country in my beat-up, wrinkled, coffee-stained expired passports I keep in a wooden chest at home. By the time this book was put to bed, the total came to sixty-eight. Sixty-eight countries out of an ever-changing total—Africa is always adding a country now and then—a total of 308 countries in this world. I doubt I will see them all. Do not want to see them all—not really. Russia does not tempt me. Why? I do not really know. It seems grim, a gray country.

Germany I have never been to. Flown over it. Everybody says it is a neat country, a friendly country, a country that has beer. I remember the Nazi's, the concentration camps from newsreels as a ten-year old. I remember a Norwegian couple I met on the ferry from Hull, England going to Rotterdam in 1984; an old couple who say they will never go to Germany; they were young when the German army invaded their country. They have too many memories, too many unforgiving memories, too many friends and relatives gone. Visit Germany—I do not think so; I am not partial to beer.

Japan is a country I do not like though I have been there many times. Too expensive . . . and a country of regimented craziness. That is what Japan is: a land of rigidly organized, crazy people. You do not believe me, then just watch some of their games on television.

I like the East. Especially Thailand. Thai's like everybody except the Russians and Arabs. The Russians do not spend money and the Arabs evidently do not used deodorants. Thai's like Americans, Chinese, and Japanese. They like Americans the most. They take English in high school and they all want to come to live in America. They like the Chinese because of their historical link with that country, and they like the Japanese because the Japanese are used to shelling out big yen in their own country and will overpay for anything in the tourist traps of Bangkok, Phuket, and the resort town of Pattaya where I live. However, even if the tourist overpays in Thailand, he is still getting a good deal when compared to Europe. Hong Kong: do not waste your time and money. Hong Kong is crowded, noisy, and overly expensive—you say you like the shopping there; shopping is better in Bangkok. I have visited four communist countries. All four charges you to get in, overcharges when you are there, think you are trying to steal secrets, and charges you to leave. Suspicious and humorless, they are not a fortunate people.

Two days after the *Indy* departed Sydney, Eric and I rented a little red car and took off for a two-week tour of southeast Australia. We were sure that we had seen the last of the *Indy*. She was on her way to Perth on the other side of the Australian continent, then to Thailand, then Hong Kong, then home to be decommissioned. We knew she was scheduled to be decommissioned the following year—decommissioning meant, eventually, the scrap yard. South of Sydney, in Port Campbell National Park, we pulled off the road at Cape Patton to look at a staggered line of eroded sandstone pillars called the Twelve Apostles, a popular tourist stop. It was chillingly cold, quite the opposite of what we had just left up north. Standing on the cliff with the wind buffeting me about, I was ready to seek the warmth of the car when suddenly Eric exclaimed, "LOOK!"

I searched in the direction he was pointing seeing only sea, sky, and the horizon. Zippered in my safari jacket was a monocular folding glass my daughter and son-in-law bought me. Taking it out, hunched up against the cold, I followed his point again, gazing out to sea toward the horizon. I saw a light gray sea and an equally gray sky, nothing else.

"It's the *Indy*!" Said Eric.

Again I put the small monocular eyeglass to my eye and adjusted the range finder. *There she was*! A smudge on the horizon that appeared sharply, then blurred, and came into focus again. Eric's young, sharp eyes found the indistinct shape that blended so well with the wispy cold, colorless clouds on the horizon. The *USS Independence* CV-62, "Freedom's Flagship", the United States Navy's only forward deployed aircraft carrier was just entering the northern edge of the Tasman Sea, pushing the ocean swell before her. Like us, the *Indy* was still on the move, heading steadily south, to new lands, and to new adventures.

Jim Gunn
Pattaya, Thailand.
January 2003

Sidewalk Café, Sydney

Me at Bahrain souk.

Me and one of my Thai students, Miss padchareeporn sangkla.
Thais use no capitals in their names.

They let me dress up, but wouldn't let me fly it!

USS Independence
Follow Up

My trip aboard the *Indy* in 1997 was a four-month "SOUTHERN SWING" deployment, covering several major military exercises and seven ports of call. Included in these ports of call were two historic port visits. The first was on 28 February to the island territory of Guam. *Indy* was the first aircraft carrier to pull into Guam in 36 years. The second historic port visit two months later was Port Klang, Malaysia. The *Indy* became the first aircraft carrier in the world to make a port visit to Malaysia.

Before sailing back to her home port in Yokosuka, Japan, the *Indy* made her last port of call of the deployment in May to Hong Kong. *Indy's* port visit was the last U.S. Naval port visit to the territory before it revision to China in July 1, 1997.

On January 21, 1998, the Secretary of Defense, William Cohen spoke to the crew of the *USS Independence* (CV 62) aboard the flight deck officially announcing the *Independence's* deployment to the Arabian Gulf. Secretary Cohen said the *Independence* would relieve the *USS Nimitz (CVN 68)* to keep the presence of America in the Gulf as a reminder to Saddam Hussein that he needs to comply with the United Nations resolution. On January 23, 1998, the 39-year old aircraft carrier got under way for the Arabian Gulf.

After a long and prestigious career, *the USS Independence* was decommissioned September 30, 1998. The might ship, old and tired, but still a warrior, rest in Bremerton Naval shipyard, Washington,

USS Independence
"By the numbers"

Builder.................................New York Naval Shipyard, Brooklyn.
Length..1,070 feet.
Flight deck area...4.1 acres.
Height from keel to mast top..229 feet.
Displacement...80,000 tons.
Propellers....................................Four, 21 feet in diameter.
Anchors..Two, 30 tons each.
Anchor chain length..............................88 fathoms (528 feet).
Chain weight..122 tons each.
Chain links..........................an average link weighs 260 pounds.
Top speed...............................30+ knots (35+ miles per hour).
Boilers..eight.
Fuel...oil.
Average daily fuel comsumption.........................120,000 gallons.
Main engines...four.
Shaft horsepower...300,000.
Laundry.......................................200,000 pounds per month.
Fresh water produced daily...............................380,000 gallons.
Meals served daily..15,000+.
Telephones...2,300.
Hospital beds, operating room, full medical lab, x-ray suite.

Indy Order Form

Use this convenient order form to order additional copies of
Indy

Please Print:

Name____

Address______________________________________

City______________________ **State**______________

Zip________________

Phone(**)**_______________________

_____ copies of book @ $16.00 each $ ________

Postage and handling @ $2.70 per book $ ________

CA residents add $1.30 tax $ ________

Total amount enclosed $ ________

Make checks payable to James Gunn

Send to James Gunn
1731 Howe Ave. Suite 122 • Sacramento, CA 95825